Mary Magdalene

Mary Magdalene: Panel from a Triptych
(tempera on panel), by Paolo Veneziano (1300–1362).
Photo: Worcester Art Museum, Worcester, Massachusetts
(Museum Purchase, 1927.19)

Mary Magdalene: The Woman whom Jesus Loved

Robin Griffith-Jones

CANTERBURY
PRESS

Norwich

This edition published in 2008 by the Canterbury Press Norwich
Editorial office
13–17 Long Lane,
London, EC1A 9PN, UK

Canterbury Press is an imprint of Hymns Ancient and Modern Ltd
(a registered charity)
St Mary's Works, St Mary's Plain,
Norwich, NR3 3BH, UK

Published in the United States in 2008 by HarperCollins

www.scm-canterburypress.co.uk

British Library Cataloguing in Publication data

A catalogue record for this book is available
from the British Library

978 1 85311 818 0

Printed and bound in Great Britain by
CPI William Clowes Ltd, Beccles, Suffolk

For two brothers:

HENRY
(who will, I hope, enjoy reading this book)

and

LOUIS
(who is for the moment more likely to colour it in)

CONTENTS

LIST OF ILLUSTRATIONS

PREFACE

Mary Magdalene: From Individual to Icon

> *Simon Peter, the leader of Jesus's disciples, calls upon Mary Magdalene to address them:*
> Peter said to Mary Magdalene, "Sister, we know that the Saviour loved you more than the rest of women. Tell us the words of the Saviour which you remember—which you know, but we do not, nor have we heard them."
> *Mary Magdalene does so. Now Peter, resentful, changes his tune:*
> Peter answered concerning these things. He questioned them about the Saviour: "Did he really speak without our knowledge with a woman and not openly? Are we to turn about and all listen to her? Did he prefer her to us?"
> Then Mary wept and said to Peter, "My brother Peter, what do you think? Do you think that I have thought this up myself in my heart, or that I am lying about the Saviour?"
> *Levi, another man among Jesus's disciples, breaks in:*
> Levi answered and said to Peter, "Peter, you have always been hot-tempered. Now I see you contending against the woman like the adversaries. But if the Saviour made her worthy, who are *you* to reject her? The Saviour certainly knows her without faltering. That is why he loved her more than us."[1]
>
> From Gospel of Mary *10.1–8;17.7–18.20*

According to the *Gospel of Mary,* a fusion of two Gnostic Christian texts from the second century, Jesus the Saviour loved Mary Magdalene more than he loved the men known ever since as his disciples. No wonder Jesus entrusted secrets to Mary that, as Simon Peter admits, he did not entrust to those men. No wonder it is for Mary to teach the men, for she knows what the men do not know and has an authority that Peter has no right to resist.

Most of us who read about the past have our eye on the present. Mary Magdalene is not just interesting in herself; she may be important for us. We wonder if Jesus himself did invest her with an authority resented by the men around her and denied by men to the churches' women ever since. Why would she have been given that authority? Mary surely won

Jesus's love thanks to her wisdom, and thanks to that love won greater wisdom still. "Are we," asked Peter, "to turn about and all listen to *her*? Did the Saviour prefer her to us?" Such questions are still heard from some of the men who run the churches today: "Are we to turn about and all listen to *women*?"

Another question is not far away. Was that illuminating, life-transforming love of Jesus for Mary Magdalene the love of a husband for his wife? If so, we would be facing an intimacy between Jesus and Mary Magdalene that the churches, dominated by celibate men, have refused even to consider possible. If a sexual love between Jesus and Mary was the setting for the deepest, most personal revelations he ever made, who are most likely now, two thousand years later, to be attuned to such revelations and able to interpret and impart them to others? Nobody can stand now in the physical relation to Jesus in which Mary Magdalene stood, but we are bound to wonder who is most likely able to occupy its spiritual equivalent. Celibate men? Hardly. Women in general? Well, not necessarily. There is clearly something special about Mary Magdalene that sets her apart from other women as well as from men. But it may be vital that she *was* a woman. Perhaps there is something in the nature of a woman that, when she is intimately linked with a man, gives her at least a capacity for understanding the depths of that man beyond the capacity that any other man is likely to possess. It is then among the churches' women that the churches should find their teachers. Even suggest such a thing to the churches' present—male—leaders, and Simon Peter's sharp question in the *Gospel of Mary* becomes shriller still, "Does the Saviour prefer women to us?"

In the first chapters of this book we shall hear how much (or, to be honest, how little) we learn about Mary Magdalene from the four gospels of the Bible's New Testament. About her portrayal by later churches, on the other hand, we know a great deal. Much of it may make us angry. Mary Magdalene was for centuries maligned by the Roman Catholic Church as a prostitute; she became the archetypal sinner, and her sin—sexual sin—became the icon of human sinfulness. Let all women be aware: in their sexual energies they epitomize all human sinfulness. Let all men be warned: the women around them—in the streets, at home, and in their own bed—have just the allure that Eve once had and will by their very nature stir their men to share, as Adam had, in sin.

But there is no evidence that Mary Magdalene had ever been a prostitute. In the 1960s the Roman Catholic Church—four hundred years after the mistake became clear—at last admitted its calumny against Mary's memory. Mary was vindicated; and she has become an icon of women's gradual vindication from the abuse to which men have subjected them and from the silence men have imposed on them.

In the same decades of the twentieth century a new vision of Mary Magdalene came into focus, the Mary of the Christian Gnostics, groups on the fringes of the churches between the second and fourth centuries. A cache of Gnostic documents, discovered in Egypt in the 1940s, was being published. Other Gnostic texts, long known and long ignored—such as the *Gospel of Mary* itself—were being brought into the spotlight too. Text after text spoke of Mary Magdalene as a woman who understood completely, a being of pure spirit, whose heart was utterly directed to the kingdom of heaven, who was blessed beyond all women upon earth. These Gnostics remembered Mary Magdalene as a woman of *authority*. And what was the source of her authority? The hints heard in the *Gospel of Mary* were heard again, more loudly; she was, according to the *Gospel of Philip,* "the Saviour's companion" whom he "often kissed." John's gospel, within the Bible, had spoken of a particular *disciple whom Jesus loved*—this is now Mary's role, she is the truly Beloved Disciple.

And what do we read in these texts of her sinfulness, described with such horrified prurience by the later churches? Not a word. On the contrary, Mary Magdalene is now so wise that she is nearly divine. A good many modern readers find here at least a hint of the goddess that the churches have never dared acknowledge. Such readers hope to find here too a Jesus who at last is human, a Jesus, married to Mary, who is far more credible—and more attractive—than the celibate miracle worker of whom the churches speak.

It is no surprise that our generation has relished the rediscovery of the Gnostics. These sects wrote freely in erotic terms; they promoted self-knowledge; they were attacked by the male leaders of powerful churches. From 312 CE, when the emperor Constantine declared his allegiance to Christ, the mainstream churches were deeply compromised by the patronage of the worldly powers-that-be; the churches' hierarchy could impose—on all of Europe, northern Africa, and half the Middle East—doctrine, rituals, and ways of life. The Gnostics, opposed by those churches, did not stand a chance. Mary Magdalene can seem to represent everything in the Gnostic groups that was resented and feared by the churches, and some of us may feel we have more in common with these Gnostics than with the heirs of the churches that attacked and defeated them. For centuries the Gnostics had been vilified as self-obsessed, heretical—and, in the face of persecution, cowardly—fantasists; in our age they have become heroes of individualism, independence, and self-discovery.

These Gnostic sects were brought to prominence by the success of Dan Brown's novel *The Da Vinci Code*. Its characters describe the love of Jesus and Mary Magdalene; its plot revolves around their descendants; the Catholic Church, we read, has sought throughout its history to suppress any evidence of those descendants. Might any or all of this be based on fact? Cardinal Bertone of Genoa, Italy, is riled by the book's influence. The book, he says, "aims to discredit the Church and its history through gross and absurd manipulations. I think I have the responsibility to clear things up: to unmask the cheap lies contained in books like that."[2]

Of course, if we trust the cardinal, the issue is closed; but *The Da Vinci Code,* if it aims to discredit anything, aims to discredit cardinals. The cardinal may be right in everything he says, but his interests are obviously served in saying it. The cardinal has urged Catholic bookshops not to sell this book and Catholic readers not to read it, and this *sounds* like the Catholic Church trying to suppress a book that is so popular because it tells us how readily the Catholic Church suppresses books.

Dan Brown drew on the bestselling *The Holy Blood and the Holy Grail*. This tells how the love of Jesus and Mary Magdalene led to a daughter and to a dynasty of kings; their descendants are alive in Europe to this day. One of the book's authors, Henry Lincoln, was challenged about its incredible claims. Lincoln replied: "Is it more plausible that a man should be married and have children, or that he should be born of a virgin, attended by choirs of angels, walk on water and rise from the grave?"[3] It is a good question. The churches ask us to believe in a very strange Jesus.

And what if Jesus *was* married? Among today's church leaders—almost all of them still men, many of them celibates—the celibates are hardly the best people to face dispassionately a challenge that would threaten the rationale and dignity of their own lives and the lives of all those who have preceded them. The Roman Catholic Church finds in consecrated celibacy a "brilliant jewel" that husband and wife cannot enjoy; such celibacy "reaches and transforms man's being and imbues it with a mysterious likeness to Christ's in its most hidden depths."[4] The Catholic Church claims to be "an expert in humanity"; but faced even with the overall likelihood that Jesus was married, many believers would be confronted by the dire possibility that the church has, for centuries, got humanity profoundly *wrong*.

The churches may well respond angrily: If we want to know about Jesus, we should go to the Bible and the churches' teaching; we have no reason to invent the Jesus we want, and we gain nothing except a fantasy if we do. This is disingenuous. Every generation—and that has generally meant every generation of the churches' leaders—has refined the image of Jesus inherited from the past, for each generation has hoped for a Jesus in its own image, as an ideal for that generation to aspire to. In 1906 Albert Schweitzer published a brilliant survey of the lives of Jesus attempted in the eighteenth and nineteenth centuries. Here are some of his opening and closing comments (lightly adapted to create a summary). If you have followed, in recent years, the debates over the historical Jesus, you will wonder if anything has changed since Schweitzer wrote. In rationalist and liberal schools from the 1770s, claimed Schweitzer,

> the historical investigation of the life of Jesus did not take its rise from a purely historical interest; it turned to the Jesus of history as an ally in the struggle against the tyranny of dogma. . . . Each successive epoch of theology found its own thoughts in Jesus; that was, indeed, the only way in which they could make him live. But it was not only each epoch that found its reflection in Jesus; each individual created him in accordance with his own character. . . . Hate as well as love can write a Life of Jesus, . . . not so much hate of the person of Jesus as of the supernatural nimbus with which he had been surrounded.[5]

The Jesus predominant within the scholarship of Schweitzer's own day was "a figure designed by rationalism, endowed with life by liberalism, and clothed by modern theology in an historical garb." But the historical study that had envisioned this figure was destroying it. "The study of the Life of Jesus believed that when it had found the historical Jesus it could bring him straight into our time as a Teacher and Saviour. But he does not stay; he passes by our time and returns to his own."[6]

The search for the historical Jesus is still pursued as energetically as ever, both inside and outside the churches. Within the world of scholarship, ever more research and teaching posts in theology (and so, ever more salaries that make possible a lifetime of scholarly writing) have been freed from the churches' control. And outside the academy, standards of decorum have changed. In our day, Jesus can be profitably depicted, free from almost all restraint, in print or on screen. It is no surprise that some popular writers have made him into the ideal the present secular world is looking for—a man who made and honored the greatest commitment any human can make to any other, a man who was *married*. The more fragile marriage becomes in our culture, the more highly we may value the example of married life offered to ourselves, our children, and grandchildren in the marriage of Jesus and Mary Magdalene.

So Mary Magdalene *matters*. The last few paragraphs will, nonetheless, leave us feeling uneasy—there has been a lot of "maybe," "perhaps," and "what if." We have good reason to ask whether Jesus and Mary were in fact married, whether he did in fact entrust deep secrets to her alone, whether she did in fact teach the male disciples. Once we see how radically she has been manipulated through the ages, we want to avoid such manipulation ourselves; we want to do her simple and honest justice.

I will start, then, with Mary Magdalene as she is portrayed in the biblical gospels. There is history to be done. We will survey all four gospels, and John's gospel—home to the greatest and fullest story about Mary—will occupy most of our attention. We will be looking for all the facts we can find about Mary Magdalene. We will be panning for gold in the gospels. We are ready with our sieve in hand and our eyes peeled. There may be pebbles and mud to discard, but John's story of Easter is clearly the place in the river, above all others, at which our search will be richly rewarded.

But there is far more than history to be undertaken here. John's gospel is vital to any understanding of Mary, and the gospel is a wonderfully rich, poetic text in which Mary appears, right at the end, as the climactic figure paired with Jesus on Easter Day. To pick through that one scene in isolation from the gospel as a whole is to lose all chance of understanding either the gospel or the scene. But to survey the gospel as a whole is to discover—perhaps with surprise, and (I hope) with real excitement—that John was trying with his gospel and with Mary Magdalene to achieve something quite extraordinary. We started out with our eyes on history; now we are attuning our ears to literature.

It is not just Jesus who, as Schweitzer described it, walks past us back into his own time; John's gospel does too. If we limit ourselves to the history of Jesus, we risk missing the point of John's gospel completely. As prospectors in the gospel's river, we are simply failing to see what sort of river it is that we are splashing through; bent low over the water, we have eyes only for our own particular interest. We think we are prospecting in a narrow, pebbly stream. We are in fact on the edge of an Amazon. We must straighten up, look around, and take in the awesomely beautiful landscape in which we are standing. It is fed by the vast depths and richness of John's gospel, a text that has, I think, been systematically misread for centuries. Why does this matter to us, our fingers itching to get back to our own shallows, to scrabble around for our precious gold? Because Mary Magdalene is far more than the woman who meets Jesus on Easter Day. *Mary Magdalene stands for the reader of John's gospel, who must go through the whole drama of the gospel in order finally to see what Mary sees in the garden on Easter Day.*

The Bible's gospels reached their present state some fifty years after Jesus's death. Scroll down several more decades, into the second or even third century, and the Gnostic gospels such as the *Gospel of Mary* (quoted in this chapter's epigraph) were being edited into their present forms. These will occupy our central chapters. The portrayals of Mary Magdalene in the various texts differ widely, but can nonetheless be recognized as the branches of a single tree, all of them springing from one trunk: John's gospel. The Gnostics inherited more from John than just the relationship between Jesus and Mary. Their authors saw what John was trying to *achieve* with his gospel, and several of them set out to achieve the same. The Gnostics may in the last resort have read John's gospel wrongly (as will become clear, I think they did), but they read it with extraordinary depth and care.

The Gnostics pursued, with relentless honesty, deep questions about God, creation, and humanity. They inherited those questions—and the ways in which to answer them—from Greek and Jewish thought, and in both they found one structure that, they came to believe, underlies and shapes all reality: the ubiquitous, dynamic relationship between male and female. So we open our minds as well to some ancient philosophy. With a particular accent, of course; the Gnostics sought the truths of the sexed universe within their own sexed psyches and the truths of their own psyches writ large in the structure of the universe. In all this, are we leaving Mary Magdalene behind? Far from it. One man above all mattered for the Gnostics, and one woman: Jesus and *Mary Magdalene*.

Towards the end of this book we will do justice to the famous—or infamous—charge to which Mary Magdalene was subjected in western Europe, that she had been a prostitute. The claim was groundless and its propagation is enough to make us angry. But there is, even in the Western understanding of Mary, much of beauty, which mere anger, however well-justified, will never see. Mary—fallen, penitent, forgiven, and restored—was an icon not just of women, but of all humanity.

We shall uncover the questions about men and women that drove our forebears to tell Mary's story, over and over, in ever more intense and poignant ways. I should warn you in advance that no modern-day faction will find in those questions or their answers any ammunition, ready made for its own artillery, with which to bombard its present-day opponents inside or outside the churches. We will find something far wiser and far deeper. The story of Mary Magdalene was deployed for centuries in the fundamental inquiry that should shape the thought and life of every generation: what is it to be *human*? Each generation can look back on the answers of its ancestors and deride their—obvious!—flaws. Far better to let the efforts of the past (partial and prejudiced as they were) throw light on our own (partial and prejudiced as they are in their turn). We have as much to learn about humanity as our forebears had. We can evoke the figure of Mary Magdalene as they did, learn from and avoid their mistakes, and wonder at and value their insights. This book about a woman of the ancient past is as well a book about *ourselves*.

Part One

MARY OF MAGDALA
IN THE NEW TESTAMENT

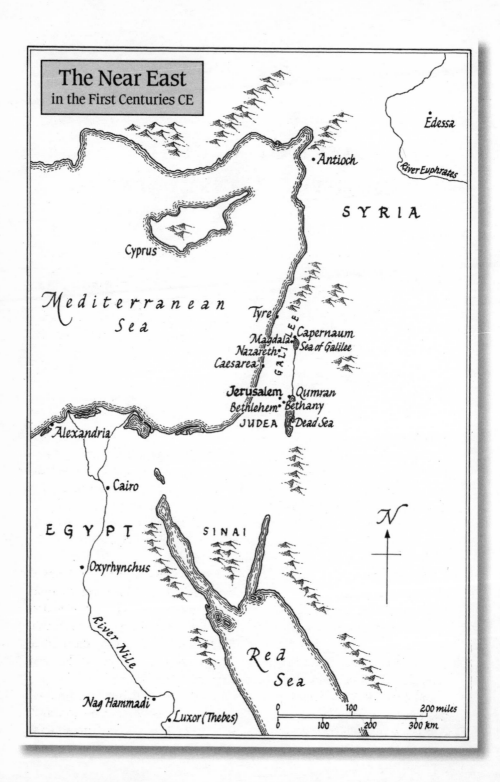

The Near East
in the First Centuries CE

Edessa

Antioch

River Euphrates

SYRIA

Cyprus

Mediterranean
Sea

Tyre

GALILEE

Magdala   Capernaum
Nazareth   Sea of Galilee
Caesarea

Jerusalem   Qumran
Bethlehem   Bethany
JUDEA   Dead Sea

Alexandria

Cairo

EGYPT

SINAI

Oxyrhynchus

River Nile

Red
Sea

Nag Hammadi

Luxor (Thebes)

N

0   100   200 miles
0   100   200   300 km

WITH JESUS IN GALILEE
Mary of Magdala

> *Jesus went on through cities and villages, preaching and bring-ing the good news of the kingdom of God, Jesus and the Twelve with him, and some women who had been healed from evil spirits and sicknesses: Mary who was called Magdalene, from whom seven devils had gone out; and Joanna, wife of Chusa, Herod's steward; and Susanna; and many others—who used to provide for them out of their means.*
>
> *Luke 8.1–3*

Imagine any painting you may have seen of Jesus and his entourage. There is Jesus in the middle, dark-haired and bearded. Around him are twelve men, some of them distinctive: probably Peter, with grey beard, on one side of Jesus; John, young and still beardless, on the other side; Judas Iscariot, swarthy and sinister, on the edge of the group. And not a woman in sight. We might well ask what has become of the women who, according to the Bible itself, travelled with him around Galilee and to Jerusalem—among them Mary Magdalene.

Magdala (its name derived from the Hebrew *migdāl*, "tower") was a village on the western shore of the Lake of Galilee, so Mary was at home in Galilee, as Jesus was. She and Susanna are mentioned without reference to a husband or son; it is likely that they were unmarried. (Or Susanna may simply have been well enough known in the churches that she needed no other designation. Mary was an immensely common name, so that any Mary needed to be further specified; Susanna was not.)

And Joanna? We might well wonder if she was a widow. It is hard to imagine her having her husband's permission—or defying him—to travel with Jesus and his strange band of misfits. Her retainers were presumably looking after her property and bringing funds and supplies to Jesus's group as necessary. Chuza may have been the manager of a royal estate (and so a powerful and wealthy man) or the finance minister (far more powerful and wealthy) of Herod Antipas's whole Galilean kingdom. Joanna, then, was a member of the Galilean elite in her husband's right and probably, to have secured such a husband, in her own. Chuza is known as a Nabatean name. Nabatea bordered Herod Antipas's kingdom to the east, and Herod married the daughter of the Nabatean king. Herod may well have taken on a Nabatean dignitary as his steward, who would—in a similar spirit of political solidarity—have married a woman from the Galilean aristocracy, Joanna. Joanna appears again in Luke's story as one of the women who come to Jesus's tomb on Easter morning; she may be, as well, the woman Junia who is described by Paul in his Letter to the Romans as an apostle.[1]

Luke tells of other women who could afford to be benefactors of the early churches: Martha and Mary of Bethany offered Jesus hospitality; Tabitha was generous to those in need in Jaffa; a group of believers met in the house of Mary, the mother of John Mark; Lydia, who traded in (high-value) purple dye, provided hospitality for Paul in Philippi; and Priscilla, with her husband Aquila, was among Paul's most stalwart allies and put him up in Corinth.[2] Joanna and Susanna and the other patrons of Luke 8.3, however, were startlingly different from these: they travelled around with Jesus.

We are used to thinking of Mary Magdalene as one of the women who supported Jesus, but it is at least worth wondering if, on the contrary, Luke is naming among the women in Jesus's entourage just a few from widely differing social and economic backgrounds. Here, on the one hand, is Joanna, the wife of Herod's steward, and there, on the other, is Mary Magdalene, a woman who had been beset by seven devils. Mary would likely have been an outcast before her healing and dependent on Jesus's protection after it; we cannot be sure, then, that she was herself one of those who helped pay for Jesus and his disciples.

With the three names—Mary Magdalene, Joanna, and Susanna—we are still in danger of imagining just a handful of women in a large group of men. But Luke mentions *many other women* travelling round Galilee. They will be important later. From elsewhere in the gospels we hear some of their names: Mary, the mother of James the Small and of Joses; Salome; the wife of Zebedee and mother of James and John, two disciples called in Galilee; the sister of Jesus's mother; and Mary, the wife(?) of Clopas.[3] There may well be overlap here, with the different gospels describing the same woman in different ways.

Imagine the scene. Jesus and his male disciples are walking from village to village around Galilee. Galilee was an area about fifty miles from north to south, thirty from east to west. Upper Galilee, its northern area, was thinly populated. Jesus and his followers, travelling the towns and villages of Lower Galilee, would never have been more than two days' walk from home. Along the lakeside the fishermen (Peter and Andrew, James and John) and in a good many villages Jesus *the son of the builder* would have been recognized and in principle welcome. Simon Peter, we know, was married,[4] and we have no reason to assume that the rest of the disciples were too young or too poor to have found wives yet. So where were their wives? At home? Who was managing—and paying for—any children's upkeep?

Jesus warns his followers how much they must renounce. Here is the warning in Luke's version, the most extreme of all. His Jesus says, *"If anyone comes to me and does not hate his own father and mother and wife and children and brothers and sisters, yes, and even his own life, he cannot be my disciple."* But the disciples did not, in the long run, leave their families. In the mission around the eastern Mediterranean after Jesus's death, Peter travelled with his wife *like the other apostles*, Paul tells us, *and the brothers of the Lord.*[5] Perhaps the wives travelled in the group during Jesus's lifetime too or just brought provisions to Jesus and the disciples when the group was within easy distance of their homes at Capernaum or Nazareth. In the absence of more evidence, we can only envisage some plausible scenarios.

We might, of course, ask how much time Jesus and his disciples were actually on the road. John's gospel tells of Jesus making up to six visits to Jerusalem over the course of three years at the time of festivals there; the journey each way would have taken a week, and the group would have stayed for at least a week for each festival. Matthew, Mark, and Luke all tell how Jesus in Galilee sent out his followers to preach without him. Mark tells of the twelve disciples, sent out in pairs. Matthew's Jesus instructs the same Twelve to keep to the towns of Israel and not to work outside the Holy Land; Matthew may even think of Jesus as about to visit the disciples' own hometowns. Luke's Jesus also issues preaching instructions to seventy (or seventy-two) followers who were to go ahead in pairs to the places he would himself be visiting on his way to Jerusalem. Mark and Luke make clear that the missionaries reported back to Jesus; Matthew's story has the disciples back with Jesus in the very next chapter. These all sound like short, focused missions, and Matthew and Mark at least do not envision any women among the missionaries. It is no surprise that after Jesus's death Simon Peter, the sons of Zebedee, Thomas, and Nathanael went back to their old livelihood, fishing on the Lake of Galilee, but they might in fact have been fishing for several months of the year even during Jesus's lifetime, in between trips away of a few days or weeks each.[6]

Travelling with Jesus himself, according to Luke, there were women, among them both Mary Magdalene, formerly bedeviled, and Joanna, the well-heeled wife of a grandee. We could do with more details. Some of the women, as we have seen, were from the generation of Jesus's mother: his own aunt and the mother of two disciples. We readily imagine Mary Magdalene as a beautiful young woman, but we have no reason to do so; she could have been of any age. Let's for the moment envision a group with women of all ages. What did the disciples, their wives, and the villagers of Galilee make of this? In summer the travelling group could sleep outside, but in winter they would need shelter at night; both settings would lend themselves among the younger men and women to troubling intimacy. It is hard not to imagine some social and sexual tension between the disciples, their wives, and these unattached women with whom the disciples were sharing times of intense excitement and triumphant success. Things would have got more difficult still if the wives were left at home when Jesus was in Jerusalem with, according to Luke, *all his acquaintances and the women who had accompanied him from Galilee*. It may be no surprise that the second-century theologian Tatian emended Luke's text to speak of "the wives of those who followed with him from Galilee." Tatian was fiercely ascetic and no friend of marriage, but he would rather have the disciples' wives on the scene than the independent women of Luke's gospel.[7]

We have a good many questions and really no answers. Let's acknowledge the gaps in our evidence rather than fill them with speculative solutions. We must leave Jesus and his entourage walking together through Galilee; around him are the male disciples—and the women with them.

* * *

This first mention of Mary Magdalene in Luke 8.2 teases us with fascinating questions. She appears in just two more scenes within the New Testament itself: at the death of Jesus and on Easter Day. This may strike you as odd. Surely she appears in a far more tantalizing story, as the prostitute who washed Jesus's feet with her tears, dried them with her hair, and anointed them with perfume? It is a story told by Luke about Jesus's time in Galilee.[8] The greater the detail in which we imagine the scene, the more revealing the story becomes. It was a gesture of wild extravagance to anoint a person's feet with perfume, and surely a gesture with erotic overtones for a woman with long, loose hair to caress a man's feet and rub them with ointment. Even as she renounces her trade, she uses the most suggestive tricks she has learned from it. Never has sexual degradation been admitted and regretted with a more potent sexual charge.

There is much to be said about this story, but not yet. Luke never mentions the woman's name and describes her as *a sinner in the city,* not as a prostitute. We will see (in Chapter 10) how readily the later churches identified this woman with a Mary who lived in Bethany (just south of Jerusalem) and hence with a second Mary, Mary Magdalene. But everything suggests the confusion of three women here, not the discovery of one. The story of the sinful woman itself, then, really belongs in any book about Mary Magdalene as an appendix, and that is where we will attend to it, at the end of this book. I hope that you will eventually turn to Appendix A; the story is told in Luke's most effective style.

Was Jesus Married? First Considerations

It is not surprising that the names of Jesus and Mary Magdalene have been linked, and we have not even heard yet the most suggestive stories about Jesus and Mary: of her loyalty at Jesus's crucifixion and of her meeting him on Easter Day. We are about to immerse ourselves in these. But we do well, from the outset, to ask a more general question. Which is more plausible in the setting of his time, a single or a married Jesus? (I ask this as a historical question, without reference to Christian dogma. I am already, therefore, declaring an independent attitude towards dogma, which some churches would resist.)

"Be fruitful and multiply" was God's first command in Genesis to the humans he had made,[9] and it was almost unheard of for a mature Jewish man of Jesus's day to be unmarried. We readily think of Jesus, therefore, as a married man. His wife is never mentioned, but this hardly affects the argument at all. Wives, as we have already seen, were all too easily omitted from the narratives of the early church. (It is only from a couple of passing comments that we know Simon Peter was married; we certainly cannot assume from the Bible's silence that all the other disciples were single.)

So far, so good. Yet we must not be blind to the possibility of unknown but simple circumstances. Elsewhere in the Roman Empire wealthy men, with the means to support a wife and children, were the youngest to be married; it may simply be that Jesus, with limited resources, had not yet found a family to accept his suit. Or he might already have been widowed, perhaps by his wife's death in childbirth. Or—a possibility rarely spoken of—his orientation may not have drawn him towards women at all.[10]

Miriam the Hairdresser

There was confusion within the Christian tradition, which identified Mary Magdalene with various other women mentioned in the
New Testament. There was confusion in the non-Christian Jewish
tradition too. Here is a short passage from the Babylonian Talmud;
the Talmud amplifies and comments on the Mishnah, the collection of cultic and other regulations compiled in the third century
CE. Here the Talmud assembles various views on the legality of
cutting letters into the flesh (tattoos?) on the Sabbath. I have put
in italics the words from the Talmud itself and glossed them in
roman type.

*Rabbi Eliezer said to them, "Isn't it the case that Ben Stada
brought magic marks from Egypt in the scratches on his flesh?"* Ben
Stada, "Son of Stada," was a code name used for Jesus in Talmudic
literature.[11] So the topic shifts. *They said to Eliezer, "He was a mad-
man and you cannot base laws on the actions of madmen."* But the
issue is not so easily settled. The text's compilers knew of another,
more famous, designation for Jesus: Ben Pantera, "Son of Pantera."
How then could he be the son of Stada? *"Surely he was the son of
Pandira?"* The text records a first reconciliation of these two traditions: *"Rabbi Hisda said, "The husband was Stada, the lover* [that
is, the father of the illegitimate Jesus] *was Pandira."* But the compilers knew this might not do. *"Was not the husband Pappos ben
Judah? It was his mother who was Stada."* This solution created its
own problem. *"But wasn't his mother Miriam the hairdresser* [hair-
dresser in Aramaic is *megaddlela'*]*? Yes, but she was nicknamed
Stada, that is* s'tat da *or 'From-her-husband'"*—that is, "She has
turned away in adultery from her husband."

Here is Miriam, another version of the name Mary. She had
been unfaithful to her husband, so she could be called *s'tat da,*
and Jesus was indeed Ben Stada, son of *s'tat da.* Her lover—and
Jesus's father—had been Pandira or Pantera, so Jesus was also
Ben Pantera.

Miriam was *megaddlela',* a hairdresser. We are bound to wonder whether the Talmudic tradition has distorted a memory of one
Miriam of Magdala in the story of Jesus. The hairdresser was an
adulteress, a sinner (as was the anonymous woman who used her
hair to dry Jesus's feet). But this Talmudic Miriam was Jesus's
mother, as the Virgin Mary was in Christian tradition, not his
lover. Unexpected connections, imperfectly made, flicker between
the Christian and Talmudic stories of Jesus.

But there are additional considerations. To be chaste was central to some special tasks in Judaism and some special ways of life. First, soldiers fighting God's wars had to be chaste on active service. Second, priests had to be chaste during their periods of service in the Temple in Jerusalem, in part because the Temple was the presence on earth of heaven itself, the court of God. To be in the Temple, then, was to be in heaven. The angels of heaven—immortal creatures who needed no children—were celibate; it is no wonder, then, that the priests on duty, as temporary creatures of heaven, were chaste. And, finally, later Jewish tradition tells how Moses, once he had been commissioned to be God's prophet, was (although still married) chaste by contrast with the prophetic figures around him, his brother Aaron and sister Miriam.[12]

As in Jerusalem, so at the other "Temple" of which Jesus would have known: Qumran, site of the Dead Sea Scrolls and their sectarians, who saw themselves as priests. Out in the desert, far from the Temple in Jerusalem, their community *was* the Temple, true to God's law, which the priests in Jerusalem had betrayed. The Qumranites were, then, priests living *as* their Temple and on permanent duty within it. So they were living some part of the life of heaven, and—as we would expect—they were celibate. They saw themselves too as soldiers in the vanguard of God's battle against his people's enemies; here was a second calling that demanded chastity, even if only until the campaign ended in God's final victory.[13]

The Qumranites had a clear influence on John the Baptist, the prophet who lived in the desert and proclaimed the coming of God's dominion. We hear of the Baptist both from the biblical gospels and from the Jewish historian Josephus, active towards the end of the first century CE. The Baptist seems likely—living as he did—to have been celibate. The Baptist was the teacher (and according to Luke, the cousin) of Jesus, so it would at least be no surprise if Jesus had been celibate too. Jesus himself, according to Matthew, spoke of the service that some people offered to the dominion of God; Jesus only describes and does not recommend such service, but it is not perverse to suggest that he lived it out himself:

> *There are eunuchs who were born that way from their mother's womb, and there are eunuchs who have been made eunuchs by men, and there are eunuchs who have made themselves eunuchs on account of the kingdom of heaven.*
>
> Matthew 19.12

Angels, priests on duty, and the Qumranites were chaste. So was John the Baptist. And we are still not quite at the end of this thread, for one more famous figure in the early church was celibate: St. Paul, who by his celibacy was living out the most drastic implications of his own teaching. Paul told his converts they were members of the new Adam, with Adam's glory restored at this end time to the glory of creation's first days. He quoted to his Galatian converts a formula they had heard at their baptism:

> *There exists no Jew nor Greek,*
> *There exists no slave nor free,*
> *There exists no male and female,*
> *For you are all one person in Christ Jesus.*
>
> Galatians 3.28

There exists no male and female. Really? So much, in practice, was intractable. The order of the fallen world still dominated the lives of the converts and the different roles they had to play, men and women, in society. The laws, heavily patriarchal, did not change; patterns of employment and civic power, all of them overwhelmingly in the hands of men, did not change. But at home? Some members of Paul's churches in Corinth—even some married members—were clear (almost certainly thanks to Paul's own preaching) that they were called to chastity. And no wonder; for this was the most vivid way in which (if only symbolically) they could nullify the deepest biological distinction between men and women.[14]

Paul's churches looked both backward to the first times and forward to the last. It was widely (but not universally) believed in the Judaism of Jesus's time that the righteous were destined, either straight after their death or at God's final intervention in history, to see the glory of God himself. The righteous dead would be heavenly beings, as angels were, and would live such a life as angels lived. Jesus himself had spoken of it with a distinctive slant: *"In the resurrection they neither marry nor are given in marriage, but are like angels in heaven."*[15] Now resurrection, in the Jewish thought of Jesus's day, involved the body, and the bodies of the dead were still in their graves. Jesus, then, had surely been holding out hope for the final future. But in the churches the distinction between the present and that future was becoming blurred. Jesus spoke of the future, when God's purpose would finally be fulfilled; Jesus's followers believed that Jesus himself, by his death and reembodied life, had inaugurated that future. Jesus himself had been the disclosure of the glory of God on earth, and his resurrection had been the first movement in the final, bodily resurrection of the dead; so his followers were offered, straightaway in their lives on earth, some part of the resurrection and thereby of the angelic life that many Jews hoped for in heaven, and angels were celibate. Had Jesus himself consciously lived out such a quasi-angelic life? We cannot know, but it would not be surprising.

None of this is conclusive, and there are moments of tantalizing silence. On the one hand, Paul urges his unmarried Corinthian converts to remain unmarried, as he is, and, on the other, he acknowledges that most of the missionaries have their wives with them; but in neither direction does he cite the precedent of Jesus himself. Mark tells us how Jesus's family came to take charge of him because they thought he was mad, but there is no mention of his wife among them. Does this show he was at that time single, or that his wife (unlike some at least of his family) had confidence in his mission? Jesus speaks of eunuchs for the kingdom of heaven, but does not speak of himself as such a "eunuch." If he was celibate, why not? He may have been simply acknowledging a way of life, not praising it. He certainly did not give intense attention to the kind of ascetic and ritually pure life that we find among the celibates at Qumran, and his own contemporaries contrasted his apparently self-indulgent lifestyle with the rigorism of the Baptist. Celibacy was odd in Judaism and was linked with other rigors, and Jesus—said to be a *glutton and drinker, friend of tax farmers and wrongdoers*—would have been a very odd celibate.[16]

Was Jesus married? The question so far remains open. So much the better. It is helpful to loosen old knots of historical and dogmatic certitude and look at their constituents afresh. We have the great story about Jesus and Mary Magdalene still to read, perhaps the most intimate and sensuous story in the Bible. Mary, who watched Jesus die on the cross, comes with ointment as the sun rises over a springtime garden to mourn his death and to tend his body.

She is in for a surprise.

2

AT JESUS'S DEATH
AND RESURRECTION

"Why are you looking for the living among the dead? He is not here, but has been raised."

Luke 24:5

We will devote most of our attention here to the story of the resurrection. But let's first locate Mary Magdalene at Jesus's death. We have four gospels before us; the relationships between them are still the subject of dispute. I will be adopting a widespread scholarly view that Mark's gospel was the first to be finished (65–75 CE); Matthew and Luke had Mark's gospel among the principal sources on which they drew for theirs (75–85 CE); and John (finishing his gospel 85–95 CE) stands apart in style and content, but at some moments his wording, uncannily close to the wording of another gospel, suggests that he knew the other gospel or that the other evangelist knew his or at least that they were drawing here on a single tradition available in written form.

Four stories, one series of events. We may well be inclined to iron out every difference between the gospels' accounts and to create one composite narrative. But in that way we fail to see how much the gospels differ—and *why*. We need to recapture the distinctive drama of each narrative and the particular aims of each evangelist. It is widely and fruitfully recognized that the evangelists were countering what they saw as errors or dangers threatening the churches, and different evangelists saw different perils. But in this book we will be casting light on a quite different concern that (I will argue) has radically affected our gospels: how was the revelation from God in Jesus to be made *accessible*?

The New Testament is now so easily available and so often heard that we fail to register how very strange its Jesus is. At least two, however, of the evangelists (Mark and John) did not proclaim our domesticated Jesus, but an awe-inspiring figure from heaven—a figure whose true nature and standing were in principle *incomprehensible* to normal human thought. The gospels were, of course, concerned with what their readers needed to know, but just as important was the question of how those readers were to be enabled truly to know it. Mark and John designed their entire gospels to bring their readers to a capacity for understanding, and in this process the pivotal figure in Mark's story and the climactic figure in John's are one and the same—Mary Magdalene.

Mary Magdalene at the Death of Jesus

Mark and Matthew tell how Jesus's disciples had run away when Jesus was betrayed; there is no sign of them at the crucifixion; there are only the courageous women, loyal to the end.

> *And there were women too looking on from a distance, among whom were both Mary Magdalene and Mary the mother of James the Small and of Joses, and Salome, who—when he was in Galilee—were his followers and attended to him, and many other women who had come up to Jerusalem with him.*
>
> Mark 15.40–41

> *And there were many women there looking on from a distance, who had followed Jesus from Galilee to attend to him, among whom were Mary Magdalene and Mary the mother of James and of Joses, and the mother of the sons of Zebedee.*
>
> Matthew 27.55–56

We may expect Luke, who is following Mark's account closely, to record the part played by Mary Magdalene in this climax to Jesus's story. But he doesn't. He avoids any mention of the disciples' flight and, right after Jesus's death, tells us that *all his acquaintances were standing there, at a distance; and the women who had followed him as well, who saw it.*[1] Luke had named three of them way back in his gospel, Mary Magdalene, Joanna, and Susanna, and does not name any at the crucixion. Once again at Jesus's burial, Mark and Matthew name the women who look on, but Luke speaks only of *the women who came up from Galilee with him.*[2] We are bound to wonder why Luke does nothing to remind his readers who they were.

It is John who pares down the scene to the concentrated form in which artists have preferred to portray it for centuries:

> *There stood by the cross of Jesus his mother and the sister of*
> *his mother, Mary [the wife] of Clopas and Mary Magdalene. So*
> *Jesus, seeing his mother and the disciple standing by, whom he*
> *loved, says to his mother, "Woman, look, your son"; then he*
> *says to the disciple, "Look, your mother." And from that hour*
> *the disciple took her into his own home.*
>
> John 19.25–27

Jesus's mother had appeared at the start of John's story, when Jesus turned water into wine; she is present again, as blood and water flow from his wounded side. With this closure, her role in the narrative is complete. It will be Mary Magdalene who is left to reappear on Easter Day.

Mary Magdalene at the Resurrection

Here at last Mary comes into her own. She is one of the first to be told that Jesus has been raised from the dead, and, according to Matthew, she is one of the first to see him risen. What should be a grand moment in the gospels, however, turns out on closer inspection to be, well, *odd*. At issue here is not the mysterious grandeur of resurrection, but the quirky, uneven ways in which the different gospels tell the story. It is worth doing justice to these oddities, for we need to get clear what these stories were *not* designed to tell or to achieve in their readers—and so to free ourselves up to recognize what they really had to offer. By the end of this chapter we shall see the Mary Magdalene of Mark, Matthew, and Luke in a quite new light; and in the next chapter we shall rediscover the whole purpose of John's gospel and within it the vital role, as it has hardly been seen in centuries, of Mary Magdalene. An extended survey of Mark and John shows that these two gospels, so unlike each other at first reading, share a startling, long-forgotten strategy and goal.

Many of us, when we think about Easter, try to reconstruct the exact order of events. Now, the gospels themselves provide the fullest but not the only—and not the first—account we have of Jesus's appearances after his death. We have a list of such appearances within a ringing statement of faith that Paul quotes to the churches in Corinth, around 54 CE; he had already invoked this formula when he had been in Corinth in 50–51 CE. To our eyes, there is a striking omission—Mary Magdalene does not feature in this list at all.

> *I handed over to you, first and foremost, what I also received*
> [and now Paul quotes]:

*that Christ died on account of our sins according to the
   scriptures,
and that he was buried,
and that he was risen* [roused, but as an established state,
   not an action] *on the third day according to the scriptures,
and that he appeared to Cephas* [Simon Peter],
*then to the Twelve.
Afterwards he appeared to over five hundred brothers at once
   (of whom the majority remain right up until now,
   although some have gone to sleep);
afterwards he appeared to James,
then to all the apostles;
and last of all, as if to a child prematurely born,
   he appeared to me too.*

1 Corinthians 15.3–8

The formula had probably been crafted within a few years of Jesus's death. (It reads now like an expanded version of a list that had once lacked any reference to the *five hundred, James,* and *all the apostles;* it is likely then to have evolved outside Jerusalem, where James was prominent. Paul himself has clearly added slightly to the formula, not least in the remark that some of the five hundred were still alive.) Did those who crafted and used the formula know about Mary Magdalene at all? Probably not. But even if they did, she would in the eyes of the churches' patriarchs have added nothing to the list. She was not (as far as we know) a leader of any churches in her own lifetime, so no church needed her to enjoy the authority of a witness. And she would not as a woman—and a woman once liable to demonic possession!—add luster to the list as a whole. Would Paul, then, have learned about her perhaps on his visit to Jerusalem some six years after Jesus's death? It is possible, but he too would have seen no advantage in her mention.

As we can tell from the formula as quoted by Paul himself, such formulas were open to expansion—and also, we may expect, to abbreviation—to meet the needs of the moment. It is not clear which, if any, of those appearances to the five hundred, James, and all the apostles are actually referred to anywhere else in the New Testament itself. We may find it startling that different Easter traditions were circulating and evolving in different directions in different churches. It was one task of the evangelists to bring these divergent and partial stories, as far as they knew them, back together into a manageable whole. Let's watch them do so, with our eye on that one woman above all, Mary Magdalene.

Mary Magdalene at the Tomb: The Gospel of Mark

And when the Sabbath was past, Mary Magdalene, and Mary of James, and Salome bought aromatics so that they could go and anoint Jesus. And early, very early, on Day One of the week they come to the tomb, when the sun had risen. And they were saying to each other, "Who will roll away the stone for us, from the doorway of the tomb?"—and looking up they see that the stone has been rolled away—for it was very large.

And coming up to the tomb they saw a young man sitting on the right, clothed in a white robe, and they were utterly amazed. But he said to them, "Don't be amazed; you are looking for Jesus the Nazarene, the crucified one. He has been roused, he is not here. Look, there is the place where they laid him. But go and tell his disciples and Peter, 'He is going ahead of you, to Galilee. There you will see him, just as he told you.'"

And the women went out and fled from the tomb, for trembling and bewilderment had hold of them. They said nothing to anyone, because they were afraid.

Mark 16.1–8

And there, as Mark's text now stands, the gospel ends. Some modern Bibles print the fuller endings added in the second and third centuries. We cannot now know whether the editor whom we name "Mark," who brought the rest of the gospel to its present state, did in fact write a fuller ending himself that had been lost within a few decades of his writing it. As will become clear, I am among those who believe that our editor Mark actually intended the gospel to end where it does,[3] but I am the first to admit that it is the most baffling end to any book from the ancient world. It is abrupt and bleak and contains no suggestion—quite the opposite!—that the women relayed the angel's message and got the disciples to Galilee to see the risen Jesus. A "gospel" (Gk, *euangelion*) is "good news" (*eu*, "well"; *angelia*, "message"). Mark's gospel, as it now ends, crumples to an end in the women's terrified silence.

But we have so far read the story in isolation from the rest of the gospel, to which it is the climax. This is not the way to read anything. Here, then, to help us make sense of this strange conclusion, is an admittedly slanted summary of the gospel as a whole, picking out just those moments and motifs that matter when we reach Easter. Mary Magdalene will seem to fade from view over the next couple of pages. But when she reenters the scene, right at the story's end, she will be accompanied by all the motifs we are about to hear.

To read any of the gospels well, we need a couple of preliminaries. First, you may wonder why I will be paying so much attention to patterns of allusion and imagery—surely these are just charming extras to the real business of the gospel. On the contrary, these patterns are not mere adornments, like the decoration on the façades of art deco skyscrapers; they are the girders at the core of the text, shaping and supporting its whole structure. The allusions are of two kinds: to the Jewish Scriptures and to other passages within Mark's text. Thanks to the Jewish Scriptures (and only to them), the story of Jesus made sense in the first century CE. It may seem disingenuous to declare the results of long analysis in the form of a simple summary glinting with references to the Old Testament, but we will do no justice to the gospels until, with some part of our minds, we accept their authors' invitation to see our world as a dramatic world in which the prophecies, dreams, and stories of the Old Testament have *come alive*. I am not trying to persuade you that the gospels' writers were right, but a summary of allusions allows us to sense for ourselves just something of the stories' character and the awe they were designed to engender.

Now when we add to the mix Mark's references to other parts of his own gospel, the text becomes a sea of allusions shimmering through the story. We will be discovering in the following pages that all the biblical gospels are as richly textured as this; most modern readings of them are by contrast impoverished and thin. We are, in this book, going to be utterly true to the gospels by hearing these texts, pregnant with poetry, as they were written to be heard.

And as the second preliminary, we will be trying as well to imagine something of the setting in which the gospels were heard. Churches are deeply concerned, in our own day, to demonstrate against skeptics that the story told in the gospels is at least probably and perhaps demonstrably true. Insiders want to convince outsiders (and doubters among the insiders) that Christian belief is reasonable, and the gospels are deployed as evidence in this persuasion. The evangelists themselves—and particularly Luke—did at some crucial moments aim directly at such persuasion, but it was not, I suggest, the primary function of Mark, Matthew, or John at all. Imagine the settings in which the gospels were heard or read. Christians in the first century were generally under suspicion, sometimes in dire danger. Mark himself is said to have been the amanuensis of Peter, who was martyred in the first great persecution of Christians, after the fire in Rome in 64 CE. Most of those who encountered Mark's gospel would have heard it in a church meeting, and only those who were known to be no danger to the community would be invited to such meetings. The text itself circulated in handwritten form, from person to person; it would have been given or lent only to those known to be sympathetic.

The gospel's story, as we shall see, evokes the Old Testament in almost every line, but hardly ever makes an overt reference; and it makes no effort to introduce the notion, strange to most pagans in the ancient world, of a single God demanding exclusive worship and threatening dire punishment on his people's idolatrous enemies. The gospels were best suited to listeners and readers who already knew about and had been attracted to a Christianity firmly and frankly rooted in the Jewish Scriptures. These Scriptures—the Christian Bible's Old Testament— were coming to fruition: the Messiah or Christ, who was to rescue God's people, was *Jesus;* the kingdom of God was inaugurated *by Jesus.* The gospel had to show that its Jesus *fitted*—despite all appearances and every reasonable calculation—the hopes and expectations laid out in the Jewish Scriptures.[4]

Those, then, who heard or read the gospel upon its completion almost certainly knew the story of Jesus in outline before they encountered its sophisticated retelling here; and church members were likely to hear or read (sequential sections of) the text itself regularly at the church's gatherings. The ancient world valued the retelling of thoroughly familiar narratives, and the gospel's audience or readers would gladly have been taken through their church's gospel, over and over, in mind and heart. There is a feigned innocence in readers who know a story well and hear it (perhaps in exactly the same version) again, but this innocence is only partial. From their prior knowledge of the story and from the literary allusions engineered by the gospel's wording, the gospel's audience and readers came over time to know far more than any of Jesus's entourage had known during the events described, and they were to make full use of that knowledge.

As we survey these stories, we must not be misled by our own focus on the single figure of Mary Magdalene herself. Early readers would have been concerned for the other characters too who were evoked, together and in sequence, within the cumulative effect of the gospel. But particular characters can still have a particular role, steering readers to a successful grasp of the story and its significance. There is a vital group of figures through whom Mark finally opens his readers' eyes to the nature of the story he tells: the women who come to Jesus's tomb on Easter Day—and, first among them, Mary Magdalene.

* * *

Here, then, is a summary of Mark's gospel, with all and only those themes in mind that will reverberate at its end, when Jesus encounters Mary Magdalene on Easter Day. At the gospel's start Jesus is baptized in the river Jordan, and as he comes up out of the water the heavens are torn open and a voice declares him to be God's beloved son. Readers are being introduced to a story that will reveal the secrets of heaven itself, beyond the reach of normal human apprehension. Jesus comes into Galilee and preaches the dominion of God. He speaks over and over of *the Son of the Human One,* always, it seems, with reference to himself, but always as "he," never as "I." To readers of Mark who knew only Greek, the phrase had no significance except as an allusion to the figure *like a son of a human one* whom the visionary prophet Daniel had seen in a dream of heaven; this figure, invested by God with everlasting power, represented the *saints of the people of the Most High* who were suffering terribly on earth.[5] Daniel was told he could rest assured that as God invested the figure *like a son of a human one* with all sovereignty, so God would rescue and reward his saints. Daniel has been granted an apocalypse, an unveiling in heaven of God's indefeasible purposes for his people on earth.

In his teaching Jesus warns that *those outside,* for all their determined attention, will fail to understand his parables, *"so that they might not turn and be forgiven."* This is in fulfilment of a prophecy by Isaiah; those "outside" are blind and deaf by God's own design.[6] The gospel is meant to be obscure; even those closest to Jesus fail over and over to understand Jesus, and most readers will too. This is, to our ears, a dark warning. Jesus's message was (so Mark believed) going to be understood and accepted only by an inner circle, and even there with difficulty; it was not intended to be openly accessible to all.

In a succession of miracles, Mark's Jesus overcomes the powers of chaos and death and amazes or terrifies those who look on. He stills a storm on the Lake of Galilee, controlling the sea's wild, primeval power as only God controls it, and (no wonder!) he strikes deep fear into his disciples. He heals a demoniac who, beyond the restraint of any chains, has lived among tombs in a place of death. He raises a girl from death, and those who see it are out of their minds with awe. He walks on the surface of the sea as only God can walk, seems about to pass by his disciples' boat as God had passed by Moses and Elijah on the sacred mountain, and in the words of God's own name he declares himself, *"It is I!"*—leaving his disciples utterly out of their minds. At the midpoint of the gospel he predicts his own death and rising. And then on a mountain, before his three closest followers, he is transformed, his clothes shining with a brilliant whiteness as the disciples see him talking with Moses and

Elijah; they are utterly afraid. When he comes down from the mountain the crowd sees him and is utterly amazed. He sets out for Jerusalem: *and they were on the road, going up to Jerusalem, and there was Jesus going ahead of them, and they were frightened, and those who followed were in amazement.*[7]

The story draws to its climax when Jesus reaches Jerusalem. Just days before his death a woman comes into a house where he is dining, breaks open a jar of precious ointment, and pours it over his head. Some of those present disapprove of the extravagance, but Jesus corrects them: *"What she could do she has done: she has undertaken in advance to anoint my body for burial. Truly I tell you, wherever the gospel is proclaimed through all the world, what she has done will also be spoken of, as a memorial to her."* Jesus's comment was apposite in more ways than we readily recognize now. At a dinner in the ancient world, guests reclined on a couch; among pagans, the position and posture could all too readily bring a funeral pyre to mind.[8]

After the Last Supper with his disciples Jesus warns that they will all be made to stumble, *"but after I have been roused I will go ahead of you, to Galilee."* Simon Peter insists that even if everyone else is made to stumble, he will not. Mark has clearly inserted, for reasons of his own, the mention of resurrection and Galilee into the dialogue about stumbling. Within hours, Jesus is betrayed and arrested in Gethsemane. The disciples, *abandoning him, fled, all of them; and a young man was following with him, wearing a linen cloth and otherwise naked; and they* [the posse] *get hold of him, and leaving the linen behind, he ran away naked.* Jesus is brought before the Jewish council for a sinister, nighttime trial. *The high priest went on asking him, "Are you the Christ, the son of the Blessed One?" And Jesus said, "It is I, and you will see the Son of the Human One seated at the right hand of the Power and coming with the clouds of heaven."* At last the allusion to Daniel's figure is unambiguously clear, but the prediction of his triumph is followed immediately, as it seems, by Jesus's final defeat.[9]

My God, my God, the psalmist had pleaded, *why have you forsaken me?* Jesus cries out with the same words as he nears his death. As Jesus dies, the great veil of Jerusalem's Temple, as blue as the sky and embroidered with sun and stars, is torn from top to bottom.[10] The view is open through this imagined sky into the most sacred place on earth, the Holy of Holies at the heart of the Temple. This was the place of God's throne and was imagined as his home and thereby as heaven itself.

It is not enough to say just that the Holy of Holies represented heaven; our imagination must be asked to go further, to recognize an intersection there between our human world and the realm of God. The story of

Daniel (whose visions we have encountered already) drew on the practices, already current in the first century CE, of privileged visionaries who were given a sight of heaven and of God's glory there, a sight—and so knowledge—way beyond an unaided human mind. The seers' heaven resembled the Holy of Holies in the Temple, for the Holy of Holies *was* heaven, the home of God on earth. We will hear more of the apocalyptic texts (Gk, *apo-kalypsis,* "away-veil-ing") in which these seers described their journeys and their visions. When Jesus died and the veil of the Temple was torn, the deepest secrets of heaven were unveiled. And where were these secrets to be seen? On the cross of Jesus. The death of Jesus *was* the ultimate self-disclosure of God.

Jesus is removed from the cross, wrapped in linen cloth, and buried in a tomb chamber cut into natural rock. A stone is rolled in front of the entrance. Mary Magdalene and Mary of Joses see where the body is put.[11]

* * *

With these elements of Mark's story in mind, we are ready to hear his story of Easter itself. Mark, writing some forty years after Jesus's death, has left his fingerprints all over this narrative. Let's discover, as best we can, what Mark had learned about Mary Magdalene and what he added or changed for his own profound and stirring purposes. Such analysis is not an exact science. We are hammering lightly on an ancient and complicated structure and interpreting the sounds of hollows or cracks beneath the surface of its walls. We are tapping where others have tapped before; we hear the same sounds and must interpret them in our turn. In the end I will be coming, as it happens, to some unfamiliar conclusions; but, as I know only too well, none of us can ever be *sure* that our own interpretation is correct.

Two things about this story might well strike us straightaway. First, the women expect the stone still to be in place over the mouth of the tomb. How odd, that they bring for Jesus's body aromatics that (as far as they know) they will not be able to use. Second, even if they do get into the tomb, they will (so they expect) have to unwrap the corpse from its linen shroud, by now stained with sweat and blood; Jesus had died over thirty-six hours before, and his body would have begun to decompose. The women's action is strange, irrational, surely destined to be fruitless. That's the point. These women who stayed by Jesus as he died are doing after his death the—slightly manic, pointless—best they can, and they will, against all the odds, be vindicated.

(Matthew, seeing the story's oddness, skirts it, and John orders events differently. Neither makes any mention of the aromatics. John emphasizes that spices were applied to Jesus's body at his burial—the appropriate time for washing and anointing—together with long linen burial bandages, more elaborate than a simple shroud. Luke does not specify that the women planned to anoint Jesus. We know of royal burials at which spices were burned to fill the tomb with a sweet smell, and Luke may have envisioned the women coming to light spices outside the tomb as the highest honor they could offer to Jesus, entombed within.)[12]

Mark wants us to notice the time. He had alluded over and over to Psalm 22 in his story of Jesus's death. Then followed Jesus's burial and the stillness of the Sabbath. Psalm 23 comes readily to mind, *"Though I walk through the valley of the shadow of death, I will fear no evil; for you are with me."* And now Mary Magdalene and the other women are approaching the tomb, as Mark tells us in elaborate detail, *very early on Day One of the week, when the sun had risen.* Mark is surely evoking Psalm 24, set *For Day One of the Week,* a triumphant hymn for the morning, to be sung as the Temple's gates were flung open at sunrise: *Lift up the gates, those who rule you; and you ancient gates, be lifted up; and the king of glory shall come in.*[13] The women are approaching a place of death, but at a time of new creation and new life and solemn celebration.

A place of death and a time of new life—every expectation is about to be overturned. Mary Magdalene and the other women come up to the cave; there they see *a young man, seated on the right.* Surely he is an angel, and it is already a shock to encounter a power of purity and life in a cave of putrefaction and death. But he is more than just an ordinary *angelos* (Gk, "messenger"). He is seated on the right, as Jesus foretold that the Son of the Human One would be seen seated on the right hand of the Power and so of God's throne in the Holy of Holies: *"You will see the Son of the Human One seated at the right hand of the Power."* For readers who hear the allusion, the young man represents Jesus in his glory; and this tomb, a place of death, has become as sacred as the Holy of Holies in the Temple, the place of God's own presence. The power of God in Jesus, encroaching on death's dominion throughout the gospel, has now occupied death's last redoubt, the tomb itself. Who is the young man? He is not Jesus, but he reveals what is true about Jesus by taking the position that belongs to Jesus. The glory of this Son of the Human One is revealed, not by the opening of heavenly clouds or a seer's passage through a door into the splendours beyond as in Revelation, but by the women's passage through the door of a tomb.[14]

The young man speaks in a solemn, liturgical form: *"You are looking for Jesus the Nazarene, the crucified one."*[15] Such an elaborate formula is not used for the benefit of Mary Magdalene (she gains nothing from this grand reminder of Jesus's identity), but for the benefit of *readers*, who have heard such formulas in their church liturgy. The young man is reminding readers of the Jesus they would assemble each week to worship, in the very meetings in which they heard the gospel read out loud. Readers have heard as well what Jesus promised after the Last Supper, *"but after I have been roused I will go ahead of you, to Galilee."* Now Mark picks up the thread: *"Tell the disciples and Peter,"* says the young man in the tomb, *"that he is going ahead of you, to Galilee; there you will see him, as he said."*[16] The first statement of the promise interrupted the dialogue after the Last Supper, and its renewal here interrupts the Easter scene. It matters to Mark to have Galilee so strongly emphasized, and in a moment we shall see why. (One important—if maverick—manuscript, Codex Bezae, recognizes the role of the young man, who is made to speak there in the first-person singular: *"Tell the disciples and Peter that I am going ahead of you, to Galilee; there you will see me, as I said."*)

Mark ends his gospel with one of his favourite motifs: Mary Magdalene and the women are amazed, beside themselves, and afraid. It has been asked over and over in recent decades whether the women are, in Mark's eyes, right or wrong to be frightened into silence.[17] The question is too crude. To begin with, the women are not simply seeing something amazing; they are effectively within the throne room of God and have every reason to be scared witless. Paul himself, a visionary within the Jewish mystical tradition, would be taken up to the third heaven, to paradise, and there would hear *unspeakable speech which it is not permitted a person to say.*[18] At any hint of God's self-revelation, the prophets urge silence. Zephaniah says, *Silence before the Lord, for the Day of the Lord is near! The Lord has prepared a sacrifice, he has made his guests holy.* And Zechariah: *Be silent, all flesh, before the Lord; for he is raised up from his holy dwelling.*[19] But Mark's setting is not the Holy of Holies as it should be. On the contrary, the Holy of Holies had been revealed in the person of the dying Jesus, when the veil of the Temple was torn in two; and now the women enter the home of God—by entering a grave. As the setting for God's self-unveiling this is inconceivable, too terrible for human thought.

We are following the actions and responses of Mary and the other women, but time after time Mark is offering a clue specifically to his readers: the young man *seated on the right* who recalls Jesus's prediction (at his trial), which the women did not hear; the liturgical grandeur with which the young man describes Jesus; the reference to the walk after the Last Supper at which there is no mention of any women.[20] All the stories of Jesus that had told of his power over the sea and death had hinted at the power of God himself. Everything is now falling into place for readers who had wondered, as the disciples had, *"Who is this, that even the wind and the sea obey him?"*[21] The women at the tomb have reason to be both frightened and confused; and readers, who see more than the women can see, have reason to be more frightened still.

Mark forever has his eye upon his readers. In Jesus's disciples Mark has offered ambiguous exemplars. They answer Jesus's call; they follow him and head out, at Jesus's command, as his missionaries in his own lifetime. But nonetheless the disciples remain blind, their hearts hardened. Three times Jesus predicts his own death and three times—in the immediately following lines—the disciples show how little they understand him. Peter is appalled, the disciples vie for leadership, and James and John ask to flank Jesus himself in his glory.[22] These leaders are a foil, at once prestigious but fallible, to the readers, but they do not represent the readers, for they are, precisely, leaders in the way that most of those who were to read or hear the gospel were not. And, at one vital moment, these leaders let the readers down. Most of the disciples run away when Jesus is arrested; Peter (who does not run away) then denies all knowledge of him. The disciples do not see Jesus die.

But Mary Magdalene does. She appears, with the other women, at the crucifixion. They are strangers to the readers and bring with them no freight from scenes prior to the crucifixion—no apostolic grandeur, no expectations to be lived up to or disappointed. And so they are more nearly *like* the readers. More clearly than ever, readers are addressed from within the story itself. *"You"*—the readers, used to the formality and formulas of the liturgy—*"are looking for Jesus the Nazarene, the crucified one."*

What, then, does Mark expect—or want—his readers, when they reach the end of the gospel, to *do*? I have argued at length elsewhere[23] that readers themselves are to go back to Galilee, *to the start of the gospel;* there readers will find the Nazarene they seek. We may balk at this. Surely any such reader will learn again, from the gospel's start right through to the crucifixion, about the Jesus who had not yet been killed and had not yet risen; and this is *not* the risen and exalted Jesus whom the reader needs to encounter after Easter. But precisely here is Mark's deepest claim. The members of his churches, restarting his gospel in the liturgy when they had reached its end, would come gradually to realize what they had been offered in the gospel throughout. Hidden in the story of the earthly Jesus *is* the story of the heavenly Son of the Human One, seated at the right hand of the Power; Jesus was waging here on earth the battle that the visionary Daniel saw in his dreams of heaven. Everything is out of kilter. What should be disclosed only to privileged seers in heaven has been enacted on earth. The battle at which God will finally defeat his people's enemies has—unbeknownst to everyone who depends for their knowledge on ordinary human comprehension—been fought and won already. The whole gospel has been a giant parable. Only those in Jesus's inner circle can see its dazzling truth and understand it; all the rest, *those outside,* will fail to understand, *so that they might not turn and be forgiven.*

The moment of Jesus's terrible defeat is the moment of ultimate disclosure—all God's secrets, hidden from human view in the heaven of the Holy of Holies, are revealed in the death of Jesus. And the place at which that defeat is to be made most brutally clear, where Jesus's corpse should surely be rotting, is the place at which the Son of the Human One is seen to be enthroned at the right hand of the Power. The women who see this terrifying sight are well named: Mary Magdalene; Mary, the mother of James (Gk, Jacob); and Salome. The patriarch Jacob, forefather of all Israel, had wrestled with an angel all through one night: *"I have seen God,"* he said, *"face to face."*[24] Salome is the equivalent, for women, of "Solomon," the name of the king who built the first Temple in Jerusalem and its Holy of Holies as the home of God on earth. And Mary herself bears the name of Miriam, sister of Moses and a prophet in her own right.

Mark, I have argued, has engineered an end to his gospel that was frightening to the women and would be awe-inspiring to his readers; he had inherited the story of the women at the empty tomb and decided to stop his story there. And how significant was it, for Mark, that those who came to the tomb were *women?* Perhaps Mary Magdalene is one of the gospel's pivotal figures because Mark wanted to invoke something specific to a woman's understanding and sensibilities that equipped these women for the sight—the dazzling *insight*—they were given at the tomb. Or perhaps Mark is emphasizing yet again that the ways of the world are not the ways whereby the truths of his gospel will ever be seen. It was startling even to suggest that men should rely on the claims of women; women's testimony, in Jewish law, was of little value. And to make women testify to the empty tomb was to risk incredulity in readers.[25] But in the new world of the gospel it is precisely women who will relay the young man's news and will trigger the return of Jesus's disciples to one Galilee and the return of the readers to another.

The women as witnesses have been moving centre stage as the gospel comes to its climax. A woman's action, anointing Jesus, is the first acknowledgment among Jesus's followers that Jesus must die; the men grumble at her extravagance. Women are the only friends who watch Jesus die, when the men have run away. Women bring aromatics for his body, with no men to help them move the stone. Mary Magdalene and the other women are not right about Jesus's body, but they are unremittingly resolute, and they are the window through which readers watch the drama unfold. Mark has, at the very least, invited his readers to see the story's climax through women's eyes.

The women's prominence does not last. The readers go back to Galilee, to Jesus's entourage of men and to the viewpoint they offer. But Mark has allowed into the Galilean narrative just a few flashes of a different light to shine. Jesus had said as his group made its way to Jerusalem, *"The Son of the Human One has not come to be served but to serve, and to give up his life as a ransom for many."* We reread the start of Mark's story and hear afresh of Peter's mother-in-law, ill with a fever: *Jesus roused her . . . and the fever left her, and she began to serve them.* Again, Mary Magdalene and her companions at the tomb had been *frightened* and seized with *a tremble.* We reread the Galilean story and hear how a woman touches Jesus's garment and is healed: *with fright and trembling* she comes forward to admit what she has done. Again, Jesus had foretold he must die and then *arise*, and had indeed been *roused* from death. We reread that in Galilee he came to a house where a girl had died. He takes her by the hand, *"Rouse yourself,"* he says—and *she arose.* Time and again, in the Galilean story, Mark hints at the resurrection to come. And occasionally he reminds us, in those hints, that the first to be affected at the story's end by the roused and risen Jesus will be women.[26]

Mark has carefully and purposefully been introducing women during the story's course, but with no hint of any sensibility specific to women; he is unlikely, then, to be evoking any such sensibility here at Easter. He is, rather, correcting an imbalance. It was three men who saw Jesus transfigured into glory, just before he set out towards Jerusalem and his death; and the young man's instruction to the women seems to promise a sight of Jesus only to the disciples and Peter. Fine, but Mark insists that *women* are vital to the story too.

We had been looking just for the Mary Magdalene of history, but already, in this earliest of our biblical gospels, we are being offered far more than just history. Mary Magdalene is recruited by Mark to help create a new form of literature, an apocalypse or unveiling in which God's heavenly plan for his people is, against all expectation, revealed in the person and life of a single man on earth. The Son of the Human One has stepped out of heaven and onto earth; Mark finds in Mary Magdalene and the other women the pivotal figures he needs to turn his readers, overawed, back to the start of his gospel, this time to open their eyes and *see* what they are offered there. Mark himself does not diagnose anything specific to women that equipped them for the sight and insight they were given at the tomb. But Mark, already bold and imaginative in his deployment of the women, stands right at the start of a tradition. There would be others, in the decades to follow, who would find more—far more—in the story of Mary Magdalene.

Mary Magdalene Sees Jesus on Easter Day: The Gospel of Matthew

It is in John's gospel that Mary Magdalene will come once more into the foreground. Let's look, then, just briefly at the Easter stories of Matthew and Luke, and then move on to John.

Did Mary Magdalene actually *see* the risen Jesus? According to Matthew, yes. His story of Easter is fuller than Mark's. He omits mention of the aromatics (to avoid the oddity of the women's action) and has the stone moved by an angel with terrifying grandeur. Mary Magdalene and the other Mary make their way to the tomb:

> *And look, there was a great earthquake; for an angel of the Lord came down from heaven, approached and rolled away the stone and sat on top of it, and his face was like lightning and his clothing white as snow; and the guards* [posted by Pilate at the tomb] *shook from fear of him and were like dead men.*
>
> Matthew 28.2–4

The angel is a grandly apocalyptic figure, written up to impress Matthew's chiefly Jewish readership. Pilate and the Jewish authorities had sealed the tomb to ensure it could not be covertly opened, just as King Darius, when Daniel was thrown into the pit of lions, had sealed the stone on the mouth of the pit; and all their plans were brought to nothing by an angel who could have walked out of Daniel's visions.[27] The Marys see the angel and get their instructions: they are to tell Jesus's disciples that he has been roused and is going ahead of them to Galilee, where they will see him:

> *And leaving the tomb quickly with fear and great joy they* [Mary Magdalene and the other Mary] *ran to tell his disciples. And look, Jesus met them, saying, "Greetings." And they drew near and laid hold of his feet* [in an act of homage] *and prostrated themselves before him. Then Jesus says to them, "Do not be afraid. Go and tell my brothers to go away to Galilee, and there they will see me."*
>
> Matthew 28.8–10

The foreign Magi, the first people to acknowledge the infant Jesus, had *fallen to the ground and prostrated themselves* before him;[28] the Marys are the first to see the risen Jesus, and they in turn fall down before him. (Matthew's intended audience was largely Jewish and, whether men or women, thoroughly used to men's preeminence; the expectations of this audience are being picked to pieces by the insights first of the foreigners and then of the women.) Matthew will next tell how the guards and Jewish authorities, their plans foiled by the empty tomb, conspired to spread the story that Jesus's body had been stolen by his disciples (*and to this day,* says Matthew, *that is the story among the Jews*).[29] Then the gospel comes to its climax on the mountain in Galilee where the eleven disciples meet Jesus and are commissioned to preach to the whole world.

This is a welcome addition to our stories of Easter morning and of Mary Magdalene, but it is also, on reflection, rather strange. The angel is introduced with immense brio and tells the Marys what to do. Jesus then makes a modest appearance, only to reiterate what the angel had said. We might well wonder if Matthew had heard of such an encounter between Jesus and Mary in a bare list, such as the list that Paul quoted to the Corinthians, and put together some conventional motifs to create a small scene. But why would Matthew have bothered? I suspect he had in mind, throughout this last chapter of his gospel, the story that Jesus's disciples had stolen the body. He confronts the rumour overtly in his account of the guards and local authorities and is quietly undermining the rumour throughout. Matthew will end his gospel's narrative in Galilee, but that is a hundred miles and a week's journey north of Jerusalem, and the gaps in time and place leave room for those who hear the story to doubt the real identity of the figure eventually met by the disciples on the Galilean mountaintop. So Matthew builds into Easter morning itself an encounter with two women who saw Jesus die and, immediately after his burial, sat outside his tomb.[30] There can be no doubt that the Jesus whom they themselves saw die and buried in that tomb was the Jesus they saw risen from that same tomb, which was opened only as they approached.[31]

Mark had ended his gospel at the women's flight from the tomb in fear and so made Mary Magdalene a critical figure in the reception and understanding of his gospel. Matthew's two Marys are being nudged away from the centre of the stage. Matthew has not seen (or has not chosen to replicate) Mark's disguised apocalypse. Matthew's Marys are messengers and are the first to see the risen Jesus, but the gospel is building up to a quite different climax, on the mountain in Galilee, in which only Jesus and the eleven male disciples have parts to play.

Mary Magdalene Is Sidelined: The Gospel of Luke

We have been watching just two or three named women at Jesus's tomb. Luke does not home in on such a particular group. *All Jesus's acquaintances,* Luke tells us, *and the women who had accompanied him* had seen Jesus die; *the women who had come from Galilee together with him* had seen him buried; and these women (not specified further) come to the tomb on Easter morning. This matches the impression Luke gives throughout his gospel that Jesus was surrounded by a sizeable group: a *great crowd of his disciples* hear him teach, he sends out seventy followers to preach and heal and proclaim the kingdom in advance of his own arrival, and *the whole crowd of disciples* celebrate his entry into Jerusalem. At Easter itself we hear of *the Eleven and all the others, the Eleven and those with them.* The *brethren* in Jerusalem after Jesus's ascension will number about 120.[32]

The women *who had come from Galilee together with him* make their way to the cave tomb. Luke declares clearly that *they did not find the body of the Lord Jesus.*[33] Unlike Mark, he presents them as unambiguously going right into the cave:

> And it happened, while they were at a loss about this, look, two men stood by them in dazzling clothes. The women were afraid and bowed their faces to the ground, and the men said,
>
> "Why are you looking for the living among the dead? He is not here, but has been raised. You remember how he spoke to you when he was still in Galilee, talking of the Son of the Human One, that he must be handed over into the hands of wrongdoers and be crucified and on the third day rise again." And they remembered his words.

> *Luke 24.4–8*

These angelic figures (unlike the angel in Mark and Matthew) do not tell the women to relay the news to the disciples. Nothing is formally entrusted to the women; they simply pass on the news, unbidden, *to the Eleven and all the others.* Three of the women had been named, way back in Galilee (chap. 8); only now does Luke specify, with an overlap of two, *Magdalene Mary and Joanna and Mary of James,* and then *the others with them.*[34]

You may well find it unnerving (you would not be the first) that Luke seems to be consistently playing down the women's role. He has a reputation, after all, for being the evangelist most alert to the women in Jesus's story. Jesus's mother, Mary, dominates Luke's narrative of Jesus's conception and birth (Joseph is hardly mentioned); and where the source Luke shares with Matthew had given one illustrative story about a man, Luke has more than once added a second and parallel story about a woman. (The kingdom is like a mustard seed planted by a man and like yeast mixed by a woman; a shepherd seeks out a lost sheep in the wilderness, and a woman looks for a lost coin at home.) But here, at the story's end, Luke's concern for such balance is overtaken by a higher priority: to elevate Simon Peter in Jesus's estimation and so in the readers'. Luke consistently adapts the stories he has inherited about Peter to minimize Peter's failings and show off Peter's importance. Peter alone, for example, makes an early confession of Jesus's divinity and is commissioned to fish for people. Peter does not criticize Jesus for predicting Jesus's own death, nor therefore does Jesus criticize Peter for his almost demonic failure, stressed by Mark, to understand Jesus's mission. Peter is singled out as the one to strengthen the other disciples after Jesus's death. Who then, in Luke's story, is the first person to see the risen Jesus on Easter Day? Not Mary Magdalene—but Simon Peter. Luke's mention of this encounter is the one clumsy moment in Luke's whole story of Easter, and it is easy to conclude that Luke is juggling his narrative to give precedence to Peter, his favourite disciple.[35]

The women do, as it happens, relay the news of the empty tomb, but they are not believed. Surely the women in Jesus's life are already being airbrushed out of his story. Yes, but we have not yet done justice to Luke's Easter narrative nor, then, to the role that Mary Magdalene does have in it. Let's pick out just the themes in Luke's story that reach their climax at Easter.

As ever, we do justice to the text if we have some sense of Luke's intended readers, for readers come to a text with their own background and expectations. What likely presuppositions or needs in those readers did Luke take into account as he brought his gospel to its present state? I suspect (but only on the evidence of the gospel itself, not least the stories we are about to survey) that Luke was reassuring his readers that the men and women in Jerusalem who had believed the story of Jesus had not been gullible or over-impressionable. For Luke's readers might themselves be sceptical—and with good reason!—about Jesus's resurrection, the most dramatic Christian claim of all. He records a mixture of awe-inspiring encounters and moments for the disciples—and readers—to take stock; and he presents, in the disciples' reactions, the range and sequence of reactions that readers in their turn might well have undergone when they first warmed to the Christian message and that, being sceptical and thoughtful people, they might be undergoing still.

We have seen, in Mark, how important is the recurrence of motifs over the course of the gospel. Luke too plays a long game, threading through his gospel the themes he values most highly. At the gospel's start, Jesus's parents take him to Jerusalem for Passover. They fail to notice, when they set out for home, that he is not in the crowd with them; they return to Jerusalem and for three days look for him. They find him in the Temple. *"Why,"* he says, *"were you looking for me? Did you not know that I must be about my Father's business?" And they did not understand the saying he spoke to them.* At the gospel's end Jesus commends his spirit, as he dies outside Jerusalem, into his Father's hands, and the angelic men in his tomb, on the third day, ask Mary Magdalene and her companions, *"Why are you looking for the living among the dead?"*[36] The gospel is coming full circle.

Three times, in the Galilean ministry, Jesus foretells the death of the Son of the Human One; Luke had inherited the sequence from Mark, but reworks all three predictions. (Mark had juxtaposed the predictions with drastic failures by the disciples to understand the need for Jesus's death; Luke makes no mention of those failures.) Luke's Jesus tees up the second prediction (*"Get these words into your ears"*), and Luke follows it with an elaborate note: *They did not understand this saying and its meaning was quite veiled from them, so that they should not acknowledge it; and they were afraid to ask him about this saying.* And then again after the third, *they understood nothing of this and the word was hidden from them and they did not know the things being said.*[37] There is still much to be done at Easter, to get the disciples—and the readers—to credit and to understand what had been happening all through Jesus's ministry.

At Easter Luke details events, reports of events, and the participants' responses to both. First we hear of Mary Magdalene and her companions at the tomb, in an encounter with patently heavenly creatures who remind the women of Jesus's own prediction that the Son of the Human One must die and rise again. And the women now *remembered his sayings,* so the empty tomb actually vindicates the prophet Jesus. Next, from encounter to report: the women tell their news to *the Eleven and all the rest,* and at last Luke mentions three of the women's names, two of them familiar from the early days in Galilee. Surely these women should be trusted; there is no credit, here, to the incredulous apostles who think the women are talking nonsense.[38] Peter, according to most of our manuscripts, *got up* despite his incredulity *and ran to the tomb and, peering in, sees the grave clothes by themselves, and he went home, amazed at what had happened.*[39] Readers have now been given two clear statements that the tomb was empty.

Readers can respect, even so, Peter's amazement. In the following scenes Luke portrays the disciples' extreme responses both to further news and to Jesus's own appearances. Twice Luke allows the information, as it reaches the readers, to be strikingly indirect. He tells, through a character's speech, of events he has not narrated; as in real life, what we see for ourselves is only a small part of the action, and we must assess the testimony of others (not least, of Luke himself!).[40] In one story instruction and encounter are combined: two followers, on the road to Emmaus, fail to recognize Jesus; they are offered a firsthand encounter, but see only instruction. These two followers on the road become models of self-reflection; they will remember how their hearts had burned when Jesus explained the Scriptures about himself and how they recognized him in the breaking of the bread. Luke's self-reflective readers too may well have found—and may still be finding—themselves surprised by their own progress towards belief.

Now Jesus himself appears to the whole group, *the Eleven and those with them.* Despite all they have heard, they are badly flustered and frightened; far from finding confirmation here, they think he is a *spirit.*[41] Reassured by Jesus, they next disbelieve for joy. So finally comes the third lesson: Jesus reminds them both of his words and of the Scriptures relating to his necessary death, and *opens their minds* to understanding—for they still cannot believe without the gift of revelation.[42]

Who is being drawn through this long, circuitous progress towards belief? *The readers,* who will never have Jesus to see, but will be offered the weekly, ritualized breaking of bread; who have heard the predictions of the prophets and of Jesus himself, but who wonder nonetheless what stories they can trust; who need to be brought in their imagination—and perhaps in the credit they actually give to the gospel's climactic claims—from mere memory and despair through incredulity, a burning heart, fear and mad joy, at last to belief. Luke acknowledges within his story the turmoil through which readers might expect to go and so guides them to belief.

And in all this, Mary Magdalene and her companions are just the first to be incredulous and the first to be reminded of Scripture. They relay (without being ordered) what they have seen and then they disappear. For Mark they had been pivotal, securing the success of his story in the readers' awe and fear and return to Galilee and to the gospel's start. For Luke they typify just one stage in a reader's reasonable doubt; they are then left behind. It is a sad diminution of their role.

* * *

Mark has two questions forever before him: what do his readers need to learn and *how can those readers be enabled to learn it?* Luke confronts the same challenge at the end of his gospel. His readers had in the body of the story encountered not the apocalypse of a heavenly drama here on earth, but the biography of a righteous and faithful martyr. There were things to puzzle the readers here, but those readers really needed help— and got it—only when confronted with the resurrection.

Mark's Mary Magdalene opens the eyes of readers at last to the upside-down apocalypse they have been reading all along. Matthew needs her to guarantee the identity of the figure whom the Eleven, in Matthew's climactic final scene, will see in Galilee. Luke, like Matthew, has his eyes firmly fixed on the male disciples and on the precedence of Simon Peter. The Mary Magdalene of Matthew and Luke is a minor figure, but what Mark saw in the story of Jesus and in Mary Magdalene will be seen again—by John. It is time to encounter our fourth gospel and the most beautiful, famous, and sensuous of all the stories about Jesus and Mary Magdalene.

3

IN PARADISE
The Gospel of John

> *Mary stood outside the tomb, weeping. As she wept, she stooped down, facing the tomb. And she sees two angels, in white, sitting where the body of Jesus had lain, one where his head had been and one where his feet.*
>
> *And they say to her, "Woman, why are you weeping?" She says to them, "Because they have taken my lord, and I do not know where they have put him."*
>
> *Mary turns around and sees Jesus standing there, and does not know that it is Jesus. "Woman," says Jesus, "why are you weeping? Who are you looking for?" She thinks he is the gardener and says, "Sir, if you have taken him away, tell me where you have put him and I will take him away."*
>
> *Jesus says to her, "Mary." She turns and says to him, in Hebrew, "Rabbouni" (which means "Teacher").*
>
> John 20.11–16

We expect nowadays to go to John's gospel for a biography of Jesus, and within that biography to find further details about Mary Magdalene, but I will be suggesting that John has designed his gospel to become the spiritual biography of its readers. Bear with me, as I take you on a short tour through the most extraordinary text in Christian history. By the time we reach its climax, we will see Mary Magdalene as she has hardly ever been seen before.[1] It may be as well to outline my portrait of John's gospel at the outset, before filling in the details bit by bit. Here at the start, then, I must declare what I will in the coming pages hope to demonstrate. I will then survey some of John's details—as I surveyed Mark's in the last chapter—in a (distinctively weighted) summary, for we need once more to hear the music of the text as one sweeping, symphonic whole.

The Gospel of John famously "functions for its readers in precisely the same way that the epiphany of its hero functions within its narratives and dialogues."[2] But the true depth of this symmetry has, I think, been long since forgotten. Within the story Jesus riddles, teases, warns, and promises; he also heals, gives sight, and brings to new life. And what Jesus does among the actors in the gospel, the gospel does among its readers. How? By taking the individual readers through the riddles and warnings and healings of Jesus that the gospel records—and thereby *bringing readers to that new life of which John speaks.*

We are inclined to think that we should assess the gospels as we might assess any other text. The gospels make claims to historical truth, and we have to decide if we believe those claims. But we should beware. Rightly or wrongly, John thought that his Jesus confounded all our normal ways of thought; John, as he himself saw it, was not just showing his readers what to know and think, but was enabling them to know and think it.

A drama is played out within the readers. They are to see and define themselves as the successive characters who, one by one, encounter Jesus: the first disciples, Nicodemus, the Samaritan woman, the cripple, the blind man, and Lazarus. Readers themselves, as they read, are to be brought from incomprehension to healing and through to new birth from above. How was this transformation to be effected? Readers were not intended to be observers appraising the miracles, but protagonists undergoing them. John was stirring—and steering—the readers in their imagination, not to acknowledge the symbolism of various past healings, but to experience present healing themselves. And the outcome of this cumulative healing is depicted at the climax to the gospel—*in the character of Mary Magdalene, united with Jesus on Easter Day.* All that readers undergo in the course of the gospel enables them to "be" Mary Magdalene at its end. Here, then, are just some of the critical moments in the execution of John's design.

In the beginning, writes John to open his gospel's poetic prologue, *was the Word; and the Word was with God, and the Word was God.* John's gospel is steeped in the Old Testament. In the beginning, we read in Genesis, God created the heavens and the earth. And the earth was invisible and unformed, and darkness was over the deep. God launched creation with a word, *"Let there be light,"* and the work of Day One was under way.[3] God spoke his command on each of the days of creation, and it was done; his word both expressed and realized his plan.

According to Genesis, God made, as the climax and perfection of his plan, the Human. God planted a garden in Eden and put the Human in the garden to work it and keep it; the Human was the gardener of Eden.

But the Human was alone, so God decided to make a helper for him. God formed every beast and every bird and brought them to Adam to see what he would call them. And whatever Adam called every living creature, that was its name—and so the creation of each creature was complete at last. But there was no creature suitable as a mate for Adam, so God created Woman. Adam and the Woman were in Eden, but not for long; the serpent deceived them, and they were expelled.

But God's plan for humanity would not be foiled. John declares that the Word of God itself—his plan and its perfect, unalloyed expression—*became flesh* and so, as a human being, made its *home among us*. It is an extraordinary claim, and the gospel itself will give its readers the means to grasp this claim, to accept the Word himself and so themselves to become *children of God,* begotten from God. The gospel is written by an initiate working in the name of initiates, for the benefit of those who are imagined to be outsiders at the gospel's start. John and his fellow leaders can say at the beginning, as such readers cannot, *We have seen his glory; what we know, we speak, and what we have seen, we bear witness to.*[4]

The prologue to John's gospel ends, and the story gets under way. On the advice of the Baptist, Andrew and his companion follow Jesus. *"What,"* says Jesus, *"are you looking for?" "To see where you are staying." "Come and see."* The invitation is an invitation to the readers too; they will discover over the course of the gospel where they themselves should "stay" and how.[5] Readers are encouraged to follow the lead offered by those first disciples who acknowledged Jesus from the start to be the Christ, the one foretold by Moses and the prophets, the son of God and king of Israel.[6]

Jesus goes to Jerusalem, enters the Temple's outermost area, and disrupts its trade, the sale of sacrificial animals and of the coinage acceptable for the payment of tribute to the Temple itself.[7] Towering above him, up three flights of steps, past walls and balustrades, is the heart of the Temple, the court of the priests and the sanctuary itself. This area was seen as a model of all creation: the courtyard represented land and sea; the great veil, which kept the innermost sanctuary from view—dark blue, embroidered with stars—represented (as we saw when discussing Mark) the skies above us; and the innermost sanctuary, the Holy of Holies, entered only once a year by the high priest on the Day of Atonement, *was* the court of heaven, the home of God. The Holy of Holies was a perfect cube. In the old Temple, built by King Solomon, the Holy of Holies held the throne of God, flanked by two winged figures, one on each side; its walls were decorated with pilasters and friezes showing the trees and plants of paradise.[8] The garden of paradise was the home of God and had been offered to Adam and Eve as their home too.

Why was Jesus making trouble down among the traders in the outer-most courtyard? The authorities had good reason to ask, *"What sign have you got to show us, that you can act like this?"* Jesus replies, *"Destroy this temple, and in three days I will raise it up."*[9] John is advancing, over the course of his gospel, a vast schema of replacement and renewal. The Word has dwelt among us. Sacred places have been displaced by the sacred person, the Temple itself by Jesus, its worship by worship *in spirit and truth,* its symbolic water by Jesus as water, its light by Jesus as light, its Passover by Jesus as the sacrificial lamb. As the Holy of Holies had been the place of God's dwelling on earth, so now was Jesus the intersec-tion between our human world and the realm of God.[10]

Next, Nicodemus comes to Jesus by night. His mind is on Jesus's signs; he concludes that God must be present in them. Readers, then, have as much reason as Nicodemus to be unnerved when Jesus insists that no-body can see the kingdom of God without being born again from above. Nicodemus is baffled: *"How can it be?"* He asks questions that readers too, baffled in their turn, have good reason to ask. Jesus answers in terms of *eternal life* or (perhaps a better translation) *life of the new aeon.* Jesus will speak of this life over and over through the first half of the gospel. It is no accident that in this episode Nicodemus fades from view; John's Jesus is addressing the readers.[11]

The Samaritan woman, by contrast with Nicodemus, shows some—but incomplete—growth within a single encounter with Jesus. She comes first to see Jesus as a prophet. She knows that the promised Christ, when he comes, will announce all truths. Jesus tells her unambiguously that he himself is that Christ. She returns to her town, acknowledging all the truths he knows about her, and asking her townspeople, *"This couldn't the Christ, could it?"* She urges the people, *"Come and see,"* and after Jesus has been with them for two days, they recognize him as the saviour of the world.[12]

With the healing of the lame man, John's readers witness Jesus's power in action. They still have good reason, nonetheless, to be bemused by his greater promise, that *"the hour is coming and now is when the dead shall hear the voice of the son of God, and those who hear shall live."*[13] With the next healing, sight and insight come programmatically to the fore. The man born blind, now given his sight, acknowledges Jesus first as a prophet, then as one who has come from God; this involves little more than common sense, bravely applied by a man who has just been healed. But Jesus then asks the man born blind whether he believes in the Son of the Human One. Readers know of this cryptic figure; over the course of the story, Jesus has come gradually to identify him as Jesus himself.[14] But the healed man has no reason ever to have heard of this mysterious Son. *"Who,"* he asks, *"is the Son of the Human One?"* It is a good question, and Jesus declares openly—for the man's benefit and for the readers'— that he, Jesus, is this Son. The man has been brought to sight; readers are brought to insight. The man worships Jesus as this Son of the Human One; so can readers. But the authorities do not, so the blind see and those with sight become blind.[15] From sight back to hearing: Jesus next warns against false shepherds. He himself is the true shepherd who calls his sheep by name; they know his voice when they hear it and follow him.[16]

Demands and promises have assailed John's readers. They must be born again, but how? The dead shall live, but when? In the gospel's climactic miracle, the raising of Lazarus, the demands are met and the promises fulfilled—within the readers and within their reading of the story. Lazarus of Bethany is ill; his sisters Martha and Mary send to Jesus for help; Jesus arrives only after Lazarus has died. Now, Jesus *loved Martha and Mary her sister and Lazarus;* the three figures form, for John's purposes, a unit. (There is no hint that this Mary is Mary Magdalene.) Together they represent the readers. Martha declares her trust in Jesus, while Mary in despair admits only what might have been; here are the voices of Lazarus, who cannot speak for himself. So John draws together the threads of his gospel's first half. Jesus has insisted that only those shall see the kingdom of God who are *born again from above* and has promised that *"the hour is coming and now is when the dead shall hear the voice of the son of God, and those who hear shall live."* Now Jesus cries with a loud voice, and the dead man emerges from the tomb;[17] Lazarus is born again from above. So is the reader of John's gospel, whom Lazarus represents.

The Insight and Faith of the Women Around Jesus

Characters step forward into the spotlight, have their scene with Jesus, and leave; the darkness swallows them up forever. (Nicodemus, with three poignant appearances, is an exception.) Four scenes, nonetheless—one near the gospel's start, two right at its centre, and one at its end—are linked by the various women who star in them: first, the Samaritan woman at the well; then Martha and Mary in Bethany; then Mary again, with the ointment; and finally Mary Magdalene.

The Samaritan woman has had bad press from (male) scholars. She typifies, we are told, the aberrant life of those who reel from desire to pleasure. We are asked to recognize her sinful way of life and her guilt; she is "mincing and coy, with a certain light grace."[18] None of this is justified by the story John tells. The woman has been married five times and is now with a sixth man, but neither John nor his Jesus says she was immoral. Scholars have sensed an air of intimacy between Jesus and the woman and do not like it. (They cannot have a woman flirt with Jesus; still less, Jesus flirt with a woman.) So they ignore the story's palpably evocative setting. Jesus and the woman meet at a well, and such meetings in the Old Testament *portend marriage*. Abraham sent his servant to find a wife for Isaac; the servant came to the city of Nahor and waited at a well. Rebekah approached. *"Please give me,"* he said, *"a little water to drink from your jar."* She did so, and he was assured by this sign that she was the woman he was looking for. Isaac's own son Jacob first met Rachel, who would be his wife, at a well. And Moses met Zipporah and her sisters at a well in Midian.[19]

Marriages are made at wells. *A garden locked is my sister, my bride,* sings the bridegroom in the Song of Songs, the Old Testament's love song ascribed to King Solomon, *she is a fountain sealed, . . . an orchard with trees of myrrh and aloes, . . . a well of living water.*[20] Is John suggesting that the woman and Jesus had an affair, that he entered her own well out there in the countryside, away from prying eyes? Of course not. So why does John value this setting and its associations? Because the woman is more receptive than Jesus's own disciples, and there is something (however elusive) in the spark between Jesus and herself that enables her to be so. What are John's readers to learn from this woman? How to relate to Jesus, with a frisson of attraction and intimacy. As we shall see, readers shall be encouraged to allow themselves such a sensation again. The Samaritan woman is perceptive; and then she returns to her town, and spreads the news of this Jesus who knew everything she had done.[21]

Jesus encounters the Samaritan woman near the start of John's gospel. He meets Martha and her sister Mary right at its centre. Martha believes that Jesus can still help her dead brother; she makes the gospel's great declaration of faith. *"I am,"* says Jesus to Martha, *"the rising and the life. . . . Do you believe this?"* *"Yes, sir. I have come to believe that you are the Christ, the son of God, the one coming into the world."* What the Samaritan woman saw as a (surely unlikely!) possibility (*"This couldn't be the Christ, could it?"*), Martha confirms; the development of the readers' own insight is marked in the movement from one woman to the next. Martha fetches Mary, who remains in angry despair. Martha in her faith speaks for Lazarus and for the reader, and so does Mary in her hopelessness. Between them the sisters represent the tumult of faith faced with irremediable loss. This fractured faith and their devotion are together enough—the sisters win their brother back from the tomb. And once more a woman brings Jesus to the attention of others: the Jews who had come to the house follow Mary to the tomb, see what Jesus did, and come to believe in him.[22]

Women of Authority in Ephesus

It has been noticed that in Ephesus—probably the city in which John's gospel evolved and was completed—an exceptional number of women held important civic offices. The temple of the goddess Artemis, the city's principal and world-famous shrine, was served by priestesses, high priestesses, and "adorners" who were responsible for the temple's treasures (not least the adornments for Artemis's statue). Several women served as the city's *prytanis,* or chief magistrate; one of them, serving for the year 92–93 CE, was a poetess, two of whose hymns in praise of the divine fire, which the *prytanis* had to keep forever burning on the civic hearth, have survived. Various women ran a civic gymnasium (a vital centre of the city's life) or helped fund public projects (an aqueduct, theatre, and temple); one was given the rank of a Roman senator. It may be no coincidence that John, in Ephesus, can and does give such prominence to the women of his story.[23]

John 12–20: Reading as a Reader Reborn

The lame man is healed; the reader is "healed." The blind man gains sight; the reader gains insight. Lazarus is summoned to life, the reader to "life." The gospel has taken its readers through rebirth from above; it is the midwife of the eternal life of which it so insistently speaks.

The second half of the gospel is duly cast as a story to be read by those who have been reborn and are equipped to see the kingdom of God. Such readers are ready to join the innermost circle of Jesus's disciples for the private discourses of John 13–17 and to stay in him as he will stay in them. We might well ask who is the unnamed "Beloved Disciple" who plays such an important role in this second half of the gospel. On Jesus's last evening with his disciples before the crucifixion, the Beloved Disciple reclines on the breast of Jesus; at the crucifixion Jesus commends his own mother and the Beloved Disciple to each other's care; and there is a clear hint at Jesus's death that the Beloved Disciple is the eyewitness who vouches for the truth of the gospel itself. During Jesus's life on earth the Beloved Disciple was Jesus's closest friend; during the reception of the gospel he is also the reader, beloved by Jesus. Such a disciple will recline on the breast of Jesus as Jesus himself is at his Father's breast.[24] The disciple beloved by Jesus, and Mary Magdalene who loved Jesus: these two figures, a man and a woman, are together deployed by John in his gospel's second half to portray the readers themselves, already reborn by the text from above and so ready to hear of the events that made possible that rebirth.

Jesus washes the feet of his disciples; Simon Peter objects. Jesus will do for his disciples with water what Mary of Bethany had done for him with precious ointment. Judas the traitor could not see the value of Mary's action; Simon Peter, leader of the disciples, cannot see the value of Jesus's. Readers are ready to hear Jesus's private instruction to his disciples. Jesus addresses the disciples' confused questions. They want to see the Father, but *"anyone who has seen me,"* says Jesus, *"has seen the Father."* By the end of this dialogue, Jesus's position is ambiguous: is he on earth or already in heaven? *"I am no longer in the world,"* he says, *"and I am coming, Father, to you. . . . When I was with them . . ."* And then, by contrast: *"Now I am coming to you, and I am saying this in the world."* This Jesus is already on his way to heaven. Those around Jesus listen in on his movement to the Father. And their position is ambiguous too. John's Jesus insists he does not want the disciples taken out of the world, but he wants them where he is. Readers are invited, while still in the world, to share something of Christ's ascent even as they read the prayer that represents it.[25]

Within their reading of the narrative, John's readers experience the effect of Jesus's life (their own rebirth and elevation) before reading of the events (at Good Friday and Easter) that completed that life. They are ready to read about Jesus's new life only after they have been born into their own and to recognize Jesus's elevation only after they themselves have shared it. To understand Jesus's death, readers must first undergo the transformation that only this death has made possible.

The reader is ready at last to read of the crucifixion and then of Easter, to take the role of the last person to be introduced by John for an encounter with Jesus: *Mary Magdalene.* Mary Magdalene is the reader who has undergone the whole of this baffling, teasing, cajoling gospel and is now ready to watch—and to understand—Jesus's death.

In the scenes of Jesus's trial and death John evokes the story of creation, cruelly distorted. The devil had entered the Garden of Eden; Judas Iscariot, possessed by Satan, betrays Jesus and enters the garden as the guide to Jesus's enemies. Genesis had told how God created the Human; now as Jesus is displayed in mockery Pilate tells the priests and guards, *"Look, the human one!"* On Day Six of creation, *the heaven and the earth . . . were completed, and God completed his work;* now on the sixth day of the week Jesus speaks his last words before he dies: *"It is completed."*[26] God rested on Day Seven, as Jesus will rest through the Sabbath, the seventh day, in the tomb. The parody is grotesque, but the achievement is real. Jesus is dying at Passover, a festival linked not with atonement, but with liberation, with the re-creation of God's people when they left slavery in Egypt, and with creation itself. Far more than just Lazarus—and far more than just the reader—is being reborn from above; all creation is being made new.

It is completed at Jesus's death. Nothing is left undone, and readers should not expect—and *do not get*—in the Easter story an account of any further change or achievement. And yet Jesus still has a woman to meet one-to-one: Mary Magdalene.

What then is the function of John's Easter story? For John, readers could grasp what is being revealed in his Easter story only if they had themselves gone through the rebirth from death that Lazarus goes through in the story. At Easter John describes, in the form of a poetic, dreamlike story, the outcome of the transformation through which the rest of the gospel has already brought the readers, and he offers those readers a rich, allusive language in which to envision that outcome and the standing it gives to those readers themselves. At the crucifixion the world saw the death of Jesus, but John's readers saw creation completed, and those readers are now shown how and where in this newborn world they belong—in the figure of Mary Magdalene. The story stands uncannily between worlds, on the threshold of day and night, love and death, the garden and the grave. So too readers stand between one world and another.

After God completed his work, the next story in Genesis tells of the Garden of Eden. John's Jesus completes his work and is buried in a garden. The garden, symbol of life, has become the place of death. The garden is as well, in the Old Testament, a symbol of love. A man and woman have met in a garden in Solomon's Song of Songs and have sung of their love: *"My bride is an orchard with trees of myrrh and aloes."* But the woman loses her beloved:

> *On my bed at night I sought the man that my soul loves, . . .*
> *I sought but could not find him. . . .*
> *When I found him whom my soul loves,*
> *I clasped him and would not let him go,*
> *Not till I had brought him to my mother's house,*
> *To the room where she conceived me!*
>
> Song of Songs 3.1–4

After Jesus's death a night passes, then the Sabbath day, then another night. On Day One of the new week, very early, while it is still dark, Mary Magdalene comes to the garden with myrrh and aloes to anoint the body of Jesus; the bride, herself described as trees of myrrh and aloes in

Women Coming to the Tomb
of Jesus: Dura Europos

Dura-Europos was a garrison town of six thousand people in the Syrian desert on the Roman Empire's eastern frontier, about 250 miles from Israel. A house there was converted into a church complex in the third century. Two rooms were knocked into one for the main assembly hall, and the courtyard was paved and embellished with benches and a portico. A capital cost was involved: the latrine was covered over and the house could no longer be used as a family home. That must have been a serious decision for a church whose membership (to judge from the size of the new assembly hall) numbered few more than sixty-five. If this building was the city's only church, those sixty-five formed the city's whole Christian presence.

One room, in the northwest corner, was converted into a baptistery; at its west end was a font set under columns and a canopy. The room's two doors were on the long south side. A narrow door at the far end from the font led from the central courtyard of the house and gave almost the only natural light in the room; a wider door, next to the font, led into a second room and from there one could pass into the main assembly hall. The floor of the baptistery was lower than the floors elsewhere and required a step down at the doors; when the baptistery was converted from its previous use, its ceiling was lowered. The baptistery was being made to resemble, as best it could, a cave.

The walls were decorated with painted scenes and figures, only fragments of which survive. Along the east end five women are shown walking towards the north; these figures are immediately to the right of anyone entering from the daylight of the courtyard and walking in the same direction. Around the corner on the north wall, opposite the courtyard door, a door was painted half open. And along the rest of the north wall are five women, holding torches and walking westward towards a large sarcophagus. The sarcophagus itself was painted next to the font and opposite the doorway leading to the assembly hall. One of the accompanying illustrations is the surviving fragment of the women and the sarcophagus on the north wall, and the other is a reconstruction to make the composition clear.

How should we "read" these paintings? Here is one possibility. The five women on the east wall are approaching the door of Jesus's tomb. Its door (painted on the north wall) is open. The same women are shown again along the north wall; now they have entered the tomb and are carrying torches. They are approaching Jesus's sarcophagus. Two stars are shining at its top; they represent the angels at the tomb of Jesus, and their brilliance makes dim the light from the women's torches (whose flames are painted in black). The sarcophagus itself is seen from one end; it is still closed, for the Christ who had come from a virgin's womb could emerge as well from an unopened coffin.

As the women came to the cave tomb of Jesus, found its door open, descended into the cave, and saw two angels there, so did the candidates for baptism at Dura-Europos. Down into the cavelike baptistery they went, surrounded by torches, to see for themselves the empty tomb and to hear for themselves the angels' Easter message.[27]

The Women at the Tomb (fresco fragment, third century, and reconstruction), Christian Building, Dura-Europos. Photos: Dura-Europos Collection, Yale University Art Gallery (Y2242, Z84).

the Song of Song's garden of love, now brings the same spices to care for the corpse of the one she loves.

Mary finds the tomb empty and runs to tell Peter and the Beloved Disciple, who come to the tomb and see the graveclothes. John has inserted this story of Peter and the Beloved Disciple into a narrative about Mary Magdalene. He wants to give the men the first entrance into the tomb itself and the first assessment of the evidence there; he wants too to keep a careful balance between Peter (the first to go in) and the Beloved Disciple (the only one said to *come to belief*).[28] Scholars generally see church politics behind this carefully weighted story. But far more important is the role the men play in the enlightenment of the readers. Here, from the men, is assessment of the evidence, and from the Beloved Disciple, conviction. It is an important preliminary to the next scene, given over to Mary Magdalene and her encounter with Jesus.

> *Mary stood outside the tomb, weeping. As she wept, she stooped down, facing the tomb. And she sees two angels, in white, sitting where the body of Jesus had lain, one where his head had been and one where his feet.*
>
> John 20.11–12

Two angels with an empty space between. Just so, two angels had once flanked the empty throne of God in the Holy of Holies of Jerusalem's first Temple, built by Solomon. In this awe-inspiring conversion of a grave into the Holy of Holies, the dead body of Jesus had been lying where God himself should be enthroned.

> *And they say to her, "Woman, why are you weeping?" She says to them, "Because they have taken my lord, and I do not know where they have put him."*
>
> John 20.13

Mary is at the tomb of the man she revered and loved; she loved him so much that she wants only to care for his broken body. But the body has been taken away. Has it been stolen? Or removed from this grand tomb and discarded?

> *Mary turns around and sees Jesus standing there, and does not know that it is Jesus. "Woman," says Jesus, "why are you weeping? Who are you looking for?" She thinks he is the gardener and says, "Sir, if you have taken him away, tell me where you have put him and I will take him away."*

> *Jesus says to her, "Mary." She turns and says to him, in He-*
> *brew, "Rabbouni" (which means "Teacher").*
>
> *Jesus says to her, "Do not go on touching me, for I am not*
> *yet ascended to the Father. But go to my brothers and tell them:*
> *I am going to my Father and your Father, to my God and your*
> *God."*
>
> *John 20.14–17*

Mary turns. She sees Jesus. She thinks he is the gardener, set to work this garden and keep it. The light is rising. Jesus says, *"Mary."* He has called her by her name, and her creation is complete. She turns again, now in true recognition; the good shepherd knows his sheep, and now at last she knows him. Mary longs to have Jesus as the human presence she loves and misses; she reaches out for him. Like the lover in the Song of Songs she has found the one she loves with all her soul; she takes hold of him and will not let him go. The scene is deeply erotic; the garden of death has become the garden of love. But this is not the love that Mary must have for Jesus. He refuses her touch: *"Do not go on touching me."* She must go to tell the others that Jesus is ascending to his Father and theirs; for a third time in John's gospel a woman spreads the news about Jesus.

Who are these two, this man and this woman, in a springtime garden as the light rises on Day One? They are Adam and Eve, together again and at one; they are the lover and the beloved in the Song of Songs, re-united in their garden of love. Mary Magdalene is in paradise, *and so are John's readers.* John's reborn readers see the Holy of Holies, Jesus's body, in the Holy of Holies that is paradise. God once walked in Eden in the cool of the day, but Adam and Eve hid themselves in shame. Now at dawn the Redeemer and the redeemed, the Lord and the soul, are together again in Eden, and all creation is made new.

* * *

Jesus's closest disciples have seen the empty tomb, "believed," and gone home. How very sensible, rational, orderly, and male. Left behind and disregarded is a woman, weeping. She gets everything wrong. She has misunderstood the empty tomb, she looks still for Jesus's body, she fails to know him when he stands before her, she longs for an earthly love and a human touch. But it is not to those knowing disciples that Jesus first appears. It is to Mary.

By Jesus's tomb, in the grey half-light, Mary Magdalene speaks for the readers of John who have undergone his story as he hoped they would, readers who have taken the roles of the Samaritan woman in her insight, of Martha in her faith and of her sister, Mary, in despair. All that these women have seen and all they have obtained from Jesus has been born of a deep, compassionate intimacy between Jesus and themselves. Mary Magdalene is the last of this series. She has nothing to offer but tears of inconsolable love, and this will win her more than her despair could dream of, for nothing—not knowledge, cleverness, understanding, or even faith—is as important as love.

Mary's tears are the readers' tears. When Jesus calls Mary by her name, he calls the readers as well by theirs. The Song of Songs sings:

> Set me as a seal upon your heart,
> as a seal upon your arm.
> For love is strong as death. . . .
> Many waters cannot quench love,
> neither can the floods drown it.
>
> Song of Songs 8.6–7

Mary Magdalene has found her beloved. So have John's readers. The light is rising in paradise.

Part Two

TOWARDS THE
GNOSTIC MAGDALENE

4

MAKING MARY MALE
The *Gospel of Thomas*

No one has seen God, ever;
God the only son,
he who belongs at the Father's breast,
he has shown the way.[1]

John 1.18

The historical Mary Magdalene is proving hard to grasp; so is her intimate relationship with Jesus. In her place emerges a rich, poetic figure
who belonged in the gardens of Eden and King Solomon's Song of Songs;
she is the second Eve to the second Adam, the new Beloved of the new
King's Song. John explored—as did no other author in the New Testament—the power of sensuous love and longing. His journey was steered
by texts and traditions already ancient when he wrote. He sought, as they
had, to marshal every human faculty and instinct to help his readers recognize and realize human life as it was meant to be.

When John's Mary Magdalene saw Jesus, she saw the perfect image—
humanly perfect and perfectly human—of God. Mary Magdalene recognized this humanity, yearned for it, and in some measure attained it. She
herself was now the new Eve in Eden, at one with the new Adam and at
home with God. She represents all those who recognize the new creation
and who alone are part of it.

To visit heaven, as we have seen, was to visit paradise. It became known
as the place of rest for the blessed dead. *"Today,"* said Jesus to the penitent thief just before they both died, *"you shall be with me in paradise."*[2]
There the privileged seers, during their lifetime, would be given the sight
of God's glory normally offered only to the dead. And visionaries themselves were transformed—as they rose towards heaven—into the glory
of the creatures of heaven. So grew the claims, which we have heard in

outline in Chapter 1, for Christian life here and now: all Christians were given a foretaste of heaven here on earth.

Jesus had been the ultimate disclosure of God's plan; he had been an unveiling or "apocalypse" in person. And John insisted that Jesus had been such a revelation *on earth*. The readers needed no privileged intermediary to tell them about heaven; they only needed to open their eyes and *see* what Jesus in his person and works had revealed. John writes in his way what Mark had written in his—an upside-down apocalypse. What should be seen in heaven on the throne of God is being revealed on earth, on Jesus's cross and in his empty tomb.

And who was to represent the believers, reborn from above and thereby transformed within the confines of a life on earth? For the first part of their new life, the Beloved Disciple, intimate friend of Jesus, given at Jesus's death the standing of Jesus's brother, and first on Easter Day to come to belief on the basis of evidence coolly assessed. But who was the first to *see* the risen Jesus and to represent the believer who encountered Jesus and shared his life of the new creation? A woman, ignored and in tears: Mary Magdalene.

The *Gospel of Thomas* and the Mystical Ascent—of Men

John crafted a powerful text. He needed to. He evoked Mary Magdalene to represent the believers in their new paradise, but quite different claims were being heard: that true believers would aspire to visionary journeys to heaven and that the image of God to be restored in such believers was utterly and exclusively male. These antagonists denied that a woman, for as long as she had the character of a woman, could be worthy of the kingdom of heaven at all. John's churches had a fight on their hands. It is time to meet their opponents. Welcome to the world of the Coptic *Gospel of Thomas*.

The *Gospel of Thomas* has become the most famous of the texts discovered in the 1940s at Nag Hammadi in Egypt. We will be hearing far more of this Gnostic library, but I introduce *Thomas* here quite deliberately before we encounter the Gnostic Christians themselves. (If you have not heard of these Gnostics before, do not worry; I will be doing them justice in the following chapters.) There is an important reason for this order. The gospel was highly valued by some Gnostics, but in itself it is hardly a "Gnostic" text at all. Its origins and character lie elsewhere—in a mystical Christianity towards the end of the first century CE. It was almost certainly written in Syriac, the language of Syria, to the north of Palestine. It was translated into Greek, taken along the trade routes south to Egypt, and translated again, into Coptic, the language of almost all our Gnostic texts. There we shall revisit *Thomas,* in its final home, for the influence of its ideas; but at the moment we need to turn our eyes not to the Egyptian-Coptic Gnosticism of the late second century, but to the Syrian mysticism of the first.

Let's speak of the text's final editor as "Thomas." He left us 114 short dialogues between Jesus and his disciples. We can start by glancing at just three of the most startling sections. Here is the first. So far is the gospel's world from our own that we are hard pressed to recognize the aggressive questioners who are, we hear, likely to challenge Jesus's disciples. But Thomas's readers would have known exactly who these adversaries were: the guards who defend a visionary's route upward to the heavenly realms and repel any unauthorized intruder from our world.

> Jesus said, "If they say to you, 'Where did you come from?' say to them, 'We came from the light'—the place where the light came into being on its own accord and established itself and became manifest through their image. If they say to you, 'Is it you?' say, 'We are its children, and we are the chosen people of the living Father.' If they ask you, 'What is the sign of your Father in you?' say to them, 'It is movement and repose.'"
>
> Gospel of Thomas 50

Here are Thomas's instructions to the readers for safe passage, past successive guards and their challenge, to the heaven awaiting the children of the kingdom.[3]

When will the readers confront such danger? After death, we might assume. But that is far too crude an answer. Rare, privileged Jewish visionaries ascended to heaven before death and were transformed on their journey into creatures suited to their destination. Thomas did not just offer such ascent before death; he demanded it. Here is the second of the three sayings with which we will introduce his gospel:

> Jesus said, "Look for the Living One while you are alive, lest you die and then seek to see him and you will be unable to see him."
>
> Gospel of Thomas 59

Those who wait until death for their sight of God will have waited too long; they will never see him. Seek to see him, Thomas exhorts his readers, *now.* But this brings us back to John's gospel. Such visionary ascent is just what John's communities refused to value and perhaps even to credit. John was adamant that such visions were redundant. Jesus himself was the new Temple, and the sights and knowledge that had seemed to belong exclusively in heaven were offered to John's readers, on earth and as they read, in their growing insight into Jesus himself. John offered all the knowledge his readers needed, and this knowledge would bring them from death to new birth from above.

Thomas offered an ascent to heaven and so a transformation into the brilliance of the creatures of heaven. We may wonder why John so vehemently opposed him. The issue was far more important than we can readily see now. John almost certainly saw the danger that such visionaries would drift away from commitments to this earth, its inhabitants, and the community of earthbound Christian believers. The glory of God, John insists, was made dazzlingly visible on earth at the death of Jesus, and the darkest of all moments was the moment of greatest splendour. John insists that the place of God's total, undistorted self-disclosure was the person of Jesus *on earth*. Humankind had been made in the image of God; to become more perfectly human was to bear that image more clearly, to polish away the damage and tarnish that obscured it. *This* was the transformation that his readers needed on earth and that his own gospel, as it took them through rebirth, made possible.

John wrote his gospel to bring his readers to paradise within the reading of his gospel, and his readers as they reached the gospel's end were represented in his gospel by and as Mary Magdalene. In their gospel— and no doubt in their daily teaching—John's communities had made a startling move. It was, they insisted, women who best understood Jesus over the course of his life and who won from him the greatest privileges. But Thomas will have none of it. And so we come to the last saying in this survey of Thomas and the last saying in his gospel. In every way, it is Thomas's last word:

> Simon Peter said to them, "Let Mary go out from among us, because women are not worthy of life." Jesus said, "See, I myself shall lead her, so that I will make her male, so that she too may become a living spirit, resembling you males. For every woman who makes herself male will enter the kingdom of heaven."
>
> Gospel of Thomas *114*

What a thing for Peter to say. There is nothing quite like it in any other text from early Christianity. We shall encounter some stark beliefs held by various groups: that women were secondary in the order of human creation; that men called to a spiritual life should keep clear of women;

and that childbirth itself—and with it the role for which women were indispensable—would one day come to an end. But none of this is as uncompromising as Peter's claim. *And Jesus does not disagree with him or correct him.*

What can and should be known by whom and how? The communities of John and Thomas each faced these questions and came to very different answers, and nothing divided them more sharply than the role and standing to be given to Mary Magdalene.

Mary Magdalene: Thomas and John in Opposition

The *Gospel of Thomas* has become immensely popular. Its discovery in the desert at Nag Hammadi has a romantic air. Texts came to light that had been hidden fifteen hundred years ago. Why had they been hidden? By whom? From what danger? We are invited back into a world that had been buried in oblivion for centuries. Among these texts, the *Gospel of Thomas* is conveniently short and complete. Its sayings seem accessible to modern readers; they do not obviously require any knowledge of the strange myths expounded in most of the Nag Hammadi texts. We are spared as well a lot that our generation finds awkward in the biblical accounts of Jesus—there are no miracles to be believed in and no talk of Jesus's resurrection.

There is, instead, just a voice of Jesus that we have not heard before. It is mysterious, yes, but it is fresh and bracing and does not reach us through the filter of official doctrine or through the solemn voice of a priest or minister browbeating us in church. The Jesus of the *Gospel of Thomas* speaks, it seems, in his own voice and through no intermediary in this slim volume of strangely attractive sayings. "Recognize what is in your sight, and what is hidden from you will become plain to you"; "Split a piece of wood, and I am there; lift up the stone, and you will find me there."[4] Wherever we look, there is Jesus, if only we would open our eyes and see. His kingdom is here and now, around and within his believers. The discovery of Jesus is the discovery of our own world and of ourselves.

But can we trust this gospel to show us Jesus as he really was? There is certainly an irony in any supposition that Thomas's Jesus is a straightforwardly human figure unencumbered by the churches' doctrine. "The living Jesus" of the text is almost certainly the risen, post-Easter Jesus who will star in all the Gnostic stories. Thomas does not ignore the resurrection, but presumes it.

We will still want to assess the connection—in a good many cases quite manifest—between the sayings of this Jesus and those of the pre-Easter

Jesus in our biblical gospels. It was easy to assume, when Thomas was first published, that any saying there that resembled a biblical saying was dependent on that biblical version.[5] But it has famously been argued by some American scholars that Thomas's versions of a good many sayings have not been derived from the Bible's versions at all. On the contrary, the biblical versions (according to these scholars) show evidence of drastic editing over several decades after Jesus's own death, and Thomas's versions have been subjected to far less revision. In some parts of the *Gospel of Thomas*, then, we are reading words far closer to the words of Jesus himself than the words we read in the Bible. Here is an enthralling prospect; no wonder it has attracted so many readers to the gospel.

And are such scholars right? The argument will continue, and I am certainly not going to try settling it here.[6] (We shall be looking at several sections that are, I believe, carefully and wittily constructed responses to sayings of Jesus that Thomas inherited in more or less the form recorded in our biblical gospels.) My chief concern here is not with the origins of the gospel's various sayings, but with the character of the gospel as a whole as a deliberately teasing, riddling text. The gospel begins,

> These are the secret words which the living Jesus spoke and Didymus Judas Thomas wrote. And he [either Jesus or Thomas] said, "Whoever finds the explanation of these words will not taste death." Jesus said,
>
>> "Let him who seeks, not cease seeking until he finds,
>> and when he finds, he will be troubled,
>> and when he has been troubled, he will marvel
>>   and he will reign over the All."
>
> <div align="right">Gospel of Thomas, <i>Preface, 1–2</i></div>

And where should such seekers look?

> Jesus said, "If those who lead you say to you, 'Look, the kingdom is in heaven,' then the birds of the air will precede you. If they say to you, 'It is in the sea,' then the fish will precede you. But the kingdom is inside you and it is outside you. If you know yourselves, then you will be known and you will know that you are the sons of the living Father."
>
> Gospel of Thomas 3

We may well find the gospel mysterious, and so we should. Thomas wants his readers to *work* for the understanding he offers them; he has relayed—and perhaps constructed—cryptic sayings that tease readers into seeing themselves and their world as they never have before. Jesus said, "I shall give you what no eye has seen and what no ear has heard and what no hand has touched and what has never occurred to the human heart."[7]

"Whoever has ears to hear, let him hear" is a well-known saying of the biblical Jesus, and for Thomas it is a mantra, warning readers over and again to understand the riddles of his text. Thomas has no doubt that the sayings of Jesus are hard to grasp and that at least some of the people who encounter them will be obtuse to their real meaning. We may find Thomas perverse, turning the good news of Jesus into an esoteric puzzle. On the contrary, Thomas saw in this slogan—and in the sayings of Jesus overall—what the biblical authors saw too, that Jesus was all too easily misunderstood. No readers should assume that the obvious sense of Jesus's sayings was the sense Jesus wanted his audience to see there. Thomas has acute ears; he has heard in the traditions about Jesus a tendency and a warning to which most modern readers of the Bible, trained to find there an open and accessible Jesus, are deaf.[8]

And this riddling text ends with Jesus's promise that he will make Mary Magdalene male. At last the door swings open to reveal clearly to Thomas's readers one of the fundamental "truths" about Jesus and themselves that Thomas has been teasing them into seeing. It involves a claim about human perfection that in isolation may seem simply bizarre (and frankly offensive). But this claim coheres with hints dropped throughout the gospel. Let's hear, in outline, the understanding of humanity of which it forms an integral part.

Every one of us, as either man or woman, represents the division of humanity into male and female, and this division makes space for the most coarsely physical, irrational, and tumultuous instincts in human life, the urges of sex. But God is beyond all sexual differentiation; and then in turn the First Human, created by God in God's own image, contained in that one figure who first dwelt in paradise everything that would become male and female; and we ourselves are called to recover the image within ourselves of that First Human and so the image of God. So we were not made for our present sexual division or for the inner tumult to which it leads. We will in the fullness of eternity overcome them both, and in our social roles and self-understanding we can in good measure overcome them in this life. We can make our way back to the primordial unity of the First Human and will do so through a journey to the heavenly paradise, the home of God. And how should we envision this reconstituted androgyne? As the beautiful fusion of all that is characteristic of men and all that is characteristic of women in human nature and culture? No, for

Thomas, certainly not. Thomas shares with almost all the (male) thinkers of the ancient world a clear view that men are well suited to rational and spiritual life and endeavor, and women to the irrational turbulence of our bodily life and to its febrile appetites. So, says Thomas's Jesus, "I myself shall lead Mary Magdalene, so that I will make her male, so that she too may become a living spirit, resembling you males. For every woman who makes herself male will enter the kingdom of heaven."

And so the communities of Thomas and of John found a gulf opening between them. Both Thomas and John wrote to transform their readers during the course of their gospel's reception; in each case, readers had to "become" individuals ready to reenter the realm for which humanity was made. For both, it was vital to clarify what changes such readers had to undergo in their journey towards and finally into the new creation. Thomasine Christians were setting out on a trajectory whose destination the Johannines saw and fiercely resisted—the gradual abandonment of this world and its difficult physicality.

In John's gospel, Jesus and three of his disciples—Peter, Thomas, and Philip—have a strange conversation on the evening before Jesus's death about his departure. Jesus promises that he is going to prepare a place for them, *"and where I am going to—you know the way."* Thomas is baffled. *"Lord, we do not know where you are going. How can we know the way?"* Jesus replies, *"I am the way and the truth and the life. No one comes to the Father except through me."* Thomas does not need to travel along a heavenly way to find the truth at its end and thereby attain the life of the First Human. The person of Jesus, revealed to the disciples in his life and to the readers in John's gospel, *is* the disclosure of God that makes all such journeys redundant. Jesus continues,

> *"If you have known me, you will know my Father too. And from now on you do know him and have seen him."*
>
> *Philip says to him, "Lord, show us the Father, and that is enough for us." Jesus says to him, "Have I been with you for so long, Philip, and you still do not know me? He who has seen me has seen the Father."*
>
> John 14.3–9

It has long been argued that John presents the disciple Thomas as a man repeatedly in error. This may not be quite fair; it is Philip, after all, who gets the most brusque response from Jesus in this conversation. (It may be telling that Philip will also be linked, in Gnostic circles, with such visionary aspirations.) But Thomas at his climactic appearance after Easter is indeed made to represent just the aspirations of the Thomasine communities that John knew and resisted:

> *Thomas, one of the Twelve, called Didymus, was not with them when Jesus came. The other disciples began telling him, "We have seen the Lord." But he said to them, "Unless I see in his hands the mark of the nails and put my finger in his side [where Jesus was speared], I will not believe."*
>
> John 20.24–25

A week later Jesus appears again and invites Thomas to touch him:

> *And Thomas answered and said to him, "My Lord and my God." Jesus says to him, "Because you have seen me, are you therefore a believer? Blessed are those who have not seen and who have come to belief."*
>
> John 20.28–29

"My Lord and my God": Thomas has seen the God whom no human has ever seen—and not by a glimpse of God's glory in heaven, but by his sight of Jesus on earth. At last he sees what it is he has been seeing all along.[9]

Thomas's believers will rise to heaven, will see Jesus there, and will be transformed. Thomas's icon of these privileged, insightful believers is the ideal "male androgyne" stripped of all earthly passions, constraints, and delusions, stripped of everything linked in the ancient world with *women*. John's believers will encounter Jesus in a paradise that is the Holy of Holies and the home of God and is still anchored in this world. To attain this new paradise is to be in relationship, human to human. John takes his readers from the intimacy between Jesus and the Beloved Disciple through to the climactic encounter between Jesus and John's readers—*whose part is now played by a woman, Mary Magdalene.*

Mary Magdalene, the Disciples, and the Kingdom

Mary Magdalene features in two sayings in the *Gospel of Thomas*. Here is the first. The disciples ask Jesus to reveal two secrets: "Tell us how our end will be," and "Tell us what the kingdom of heaven is like."[10] He does so. Now Mary speaks up:

> Mary said to Jesus, "Whom are your disciples like?" He said, "They are like little children who have installed themselves in a

field which is not theirs. When the owners of the field come, they will say, 'Leave our field.' They take off their clothes before them to abandon it, giving back their field to them."

Gospel of Thomas 21

Yes, the owners of this coarse material world can have their field back. When the Woman was created out of Adam, the two were naked in Eden and unashamed. But after eating the forbidden fruit they were ashamed of their own nakedness, and at God's approach they covered themselves with leaves; God gave them skins to wear.[11] What were these "skins"? Some rabbis argued that they were the skins of the physical flesh with which Adam and Eve, previously clothed in light, were only now invested. The disciples, at present dressed in clothes of flesh as Adam and Eve had been, will remove these clothes as children who in all innocence enjoy their nakedness; and so the disciples will return to innocence and to a spiritual life free from sexual shame and the urges of the flesh.[12] The disciples do not belong in this world and must be ready, on demand, to leave its conditions behind. Or perhaps there is more to be shed than just flesh. Thomas decries the soul (since the disciples' true life is in their spirit), and we shall later be hearing of Gnostics who saw in the skins of Adam and Eve *the soul* that Gnostics must discard so that their spirit, freed from its worldly burden, can ascend as pure and naked spirit to the highest realms.[13]

Jesus has answered Mary's question by reference to children, and Thomas stays on the subject of children. Jesus, in the biblical gospels, famously welcomes the young; Thomas's Jesus explains why, in a strikingly formal saying. We may be hearing language familiar in Thomas's communities from their rituals of initiation; how we would love to know what different *stages* of such initiation are represented here.[14]

Jesus saw babies who were being suckled. He said to his disciples, "These babies who are being suckled are like those who enter the kingdom." They said to him, "Shall we, then, as babies, enter the kingdom?" Jesus said to them,

"When you make the two one,
and when you make the inner as the outer
    and the outer as the inner
and the above as the below,
and when you make the male and the female into
    a single one,
so that the male will not be male and the female
    not be female,

when you make eyes in place of an eye and a hand in
    the place of a hand
and a foot in place of a foot and an image in the place
    of an image,

then shall you enter the kingdom."

Gospel of Thomas 22

Thomas has framed, with an introductory dialogue and pithy conclusion, a series of three sayings. (The first gives a clue to Thomas's proce-
dure. The saying is recorded in several other texts, independent of the
setting Thomas gives it here. For one of these texts, see the box on page
62.) Thomas enjoys the possibilities offered by shifting the context of sayings well known to his readers. The setting, mothers suckling their children, is vital. Mother and unweaned child belong in the outer, material
realm and represented (to the ancient world) all that was most inescapably
physical; but Thomas insists they represent an inner union. An infant has
been separated from its mother's womb, but at her breast is reunited with
her. So Thomas engineers a riddle. What can his readers see in this physical reunion, part of the outer and lower world and easily despised? Seen
aright, this physical bond shows how the inner and higher should be; the
outer and lower union can lead the readers to see and realize their inner
and higher calling.

A child is newly made with eyes and hands and feet; Thomas's readers
are to imagine the new creation they must undergo with the new limbs of
presexual infants. A child is an image of its parents and grows to become
more like them, but there is an additional image into which readers must
grow: the "image" of God, which the readers bore before being born
as mortals at all and which they will rediscover—and recover—at the
climax to their visionary ascent.

"The images are manifest to man, but the light in them remains
concealed in the image of the light of the Father. . . . When you see
your likeness, you rejoice. But when you see your images which
came into being before you, and which neither die nor become
manifest, how much will you have to bear."

Gospel of Thomas 83–84

The disciples want to know how their end will be, but Jesus turns their
minds to the *start* of things and to their own origin as, each of them, a preexistent, presexual heavenly image of the preexistent, presexual heavenly

When Two Become One

Those who called for true Christians to renounce all sexual activity appealed to the *Gospel of the Egyptians*. The theologian Clement of Alexandria (Egypt, 150–215 CE) opposed such rigorism, but clearly had some respect for this text and tried to show that the radical ascetics had misinterpreted its starkest sections. Clement quotes or paraphrases a few of these sayings, and his citations are almost all that now survives of the gospel. They appear to have formed parts of a dialogue between Salome and the Lord. Salome was one of the women at the foot of the cross and at the tomb,[15] and a fourth-century tradition named a sister of Jesus as Salome. The dialogue in the *Gospel of the Egyptians* ran something like this:

SALOME: How long shall death have power?
THE SAVIOUR: So long as you women bear children.

THE SAVIOUR: I am come to undo the works of the female.
SALOME: Then I have done well in not bearing children.
THE SAVIOUR: Eat every plant, but that which is bitter, do not eat.

SALOME: What I have asked about—when shall it be known?
THE SAVIOUR: When you have trampled on the garments of shame and when the two become one and the male with the female is neither male nor female.

From Clement, Patchworks (Strōmateis)
3.6.45; 9.63; 9.66; 13.91–93

The ascetics wanted the cycle of birth and death to be brought to an end. They claimed that by "the female" the Saviour had meant lust and by "the works of the female," birth and decay. The second part of the exchange teased readers, in the cryptic style we are used to in Thomas, to see the point of God's prohibition in Eden, *"Of every tree you may eat, but of the tree of knowing good and evil you shall not eat."*[16] Beware of the bitter tree, warned the ascetics, that would give sexual knowledge and lead once more to the works of the female.

In Chapter 8 we shall hear another echo of Salome's dialogue. In the Gnostic *Dialogue of the Savior* Matthew interprets a saying of Jesus by appeal to that stark slogan "to undo the works of womanhood."

First Human, himself the image of God. "Have you discovered the beginning, that you look for the end? For where the beginning is, there will the end be. Blessed is he who takes his place in the beginning; he will know the end and will not experience death." The biblical Jesus, the Son of the Human One, had offered to people of faith the power to move mountains. Thomas, reworking the promise, offers the standing of the Son of the Human One to those who find their own beginning: "When you make the two one, you will become the sons of the Human One, and when you say, 'Mountain, move away,' it will move away."[17]

* * *

Individuals were to overcome within themselves the distinction between male and female and so to inhabit the realm of the First, androgynous, Human. The disciples themselves could anticipate the removal of their garments of flesh, by their literal or symbolic nakedness in the baths of baptism and by mystical access to the sight of heaven, for both were a foretaste of the life, free from flesh, that would follow death.

> His disciples said, "When will you become revealed to us and when shall we see you?"
> Jesus said, "When you disrobe without being ashamed [unlike Adam and Eve after their Fall] and take up your garments and place them under your feet like little children and tread on them, then you will see the son of the Living One, and you will not be afraid."
>
> Gospel of Thomas 37[18]

This is not a voyage of new discoveries, but our return to the pristine nature we were made to have. It is a nature that, in the realms of the spirit, was never lost; there still exists our real self, spiritual and pure, awaiting rediscovery. How shall we find and reoccupy it? Thomas evokes the ritualized experience of the mystics in their journeys to heaven itself past the dangerous, tempting powers of the physical world, which must be renounced. The journey may be described as a journey *upward*, past the sky to the realm of God beyond, but this is inseparable from a journey *inward* to our truest selves, long hidden from ourselves by our division into male and female and by the consequent storms of passion and worldly cares that dominate our lives. At the greatest height of heaven we shall discover the living Father and his living Son; in the innermost depths of our own being we shall discover ourselves. And in reaching the one we reach the other; in finding the Son we find ourselves, and in finding ourselves we find the Son. Jesus said, "He who will drink from my mouth will become like me. I myself shall become he, and the things that are hidden will be revealed to him."[19]

"When you make the male and the female into a single one, so that the male will not be male and the female not be female . . . then shall you enter." But we do not yet know what this change would mean for men and for women psychologically, socially, and politically; what converts were required to *do,* in the communities that valued Thomas, to be regarded as disciples; or where the gospel would leave its readers in relation to their families and the world at large. One general answer is clear: such converts would inhabit the margins of any normal social life and network. They would be celibate, denying to themselves the roles of parents and to their family, clan, and city the vital progeny without which family, clan, and city would not survive. They would be the self-conscious recipients of a knowledge to which (so they would claim) almost all their families and neighbors were blinding themselves. They would be ascetic, out on a limb, and in every sense *solitary* and so would vividly represent the reintegrated, self-contained, tumult-free singleness of the human being who has transcended the divisions and urgencies of sex and gender.

> Jesus said, "Blessed are the celibates and elect, for you will find the kingdom. For you are from it, and to it you will return."

> Gospel of Thomas 49

The gospels and letters of the New Testament speak of God's kingdom in terms of marriage. Thomas knows of the theme and startles his readers into seeing it afresh. Jesus said, "Many people are standing at the door, but the celibates are those who will enter the bridal bedroom." The celibates are the last people we would expect to be going into a bride's bedroom, but these are the blessed in the kingdom envisioned by Thomas.[20]

Salome and the Place of Women

John gave to the women in his story places of great privilege: the Samaritan woman understood Jesus better than his own disciples did; Martha and Mary in Bethany secured the new life of their dead brother; Mary in Bethany anointed Jesus's feet; and Mary Magdalene was the first to whom Jesus revealed himself on Easter morning. We have seen that this might reflect the standing given to (at least some) women in John's communities. Thomas offers to women no such prestige. He treats Mary Magdalene more as an onlooker than as a disciple herself. "Whom," she asks, "are your disciples like?"[21]

What role, then, does Thomas see for women in his communities? It is another woman, Salome, who, right at the centre of the gospel, feels herself challenged.

> Jesus said, "Two people will rest on a couch. One will die, one will live."
>
> Gospel of Thomas *61.1*

This is a variant of a saying familiar in the biblical gospels: *"I tell you," said Jesus, "on that night two shall be on one couch, and one will be taken and the other will be left."*[22] Salome pursues its implications and poses a question that Jesus will be asked three times in all: "Who are you?" Couches were used for both lying on (to sleep) and reclining on (to dine).

> Salome said, "Who are you, sir? That is, from whom? You have reclined on my couch and eaten at my table."
>
> Gospel of Thomas *61.2*

It is hardly a coincidence that Salome speaks; her name is the feminine form of Solomon, the king of the Song of Songs. The Song's bride brings to mind their times of love and of Solomon's arrival for their marriage: *"Our couch is the deep shade. . . . On my bed at night I sought the man that I love with all my soul. . . . Look, here is the couch of Solomon!"*[23] Thomas's Jesus will clearly live. Will Salome herself, who surely has a claim on Jesus's loyalty, be among those who live—or will she be the second person on the couch, the one destined to die?

> Jesus said to her, "I am he who comes from the one who is an equal. I was given some who belong to my Father."
>
> Gospel of Thomas *61.3*

This is a riddling reply and may have been as cryptic to Thomas's first readers as it is to us. Let's try a tentative explanation. The Jesus who had been in some form of equality with God came from God without unsettling the internal balance or "equality" of God; and there are those, given him by the Father, with whom and within whom he will himself form an equality or balance—for only one of those given to him, Judas Iscariot, will be lost.[24] Here is hope for Salome, but in the face of Jesus's riddle she can only insist that she herself is among those given to Jesus to keep:

Salome said, "I am your disciple."

Jesus said, "Therefore I say, when a person becomes equal, he will be filled with light. But if he becomes separated, he will be filled with darkness."[25]

Gospel of Thomas 61.4–5

Now Jesus gives her more guidance: that perfect balance internal to the Father both before and after Jesus's descent can be—and must be—repeated in Jesus's own disciples. The disciples must become the single person in whom the male is no longer male and the female no longer female; and the symbol of this union, in a deft paradox, is Jesus and Salome, man and woman, together on a couch. Such singleness of being is symbolized in the union of bodies, which a truly single being will forever transcend. To describe how the distinction between male and female shall be overcome, Thomas evokes the sexual union that makes that distinction most vivid. (Thomas is not of course claiming that Jesus and Salome were lovers!) Thomas hints at the union of Jesus and disciple, which will evolve into one vast imaginative schema among the Gnostics; and Salome plays the part here that Mary Magdalene will play in those highly developed Gnostic stories.

Jesus said, "I tell my mysteries to those people who are worthy of my mysteries."

Gospel of Thomas 62

This dialogue has grown over time.[26] Thomas, with a note of warning, is making his readers ask carefully, who *could* attain an inner equality of male and female and so become equal to Jesus and worthy of his mysteries. A woman such as Salome might be eligible, but en route she has much to undertake and undergo. Jesus does not confirm her standing among those worthy of his mysteries—perhaps because, at this stage in the gospel, Thomas does not want to.

Thomas's Last Word: Making Mary Male

From Mary Magdalene to Salome and then back to Mary. At the gospel's end a cluster of sayings recalls passages earlier in the text. In particular, right at the beginning of the gospel Jesus had said, "If those who lead you say to you, 'Look, the kingdom is in heaven,' then the birds of the air will precede you. . . . The kingdom is inside you and it is outside you" (Saying 3). Now at the end we come full circle:

His disciples said to him, "When will be kingdom come?" Jesus said, "It will not come by expectation. They will not say, 'Look, here!' or 'Look, there!' But the kingdom of the Father is spread upon the earth and people do not see it."

Gospel of Thomas 113[27]

We seem to be reading a climactic closure to the gospel; the reader who has been troubled by the gospel and has marveled at it will come at last—as Thomas had promised at its start—to reign over the All in the kingdom of the Father. Did the gospel once end here? It would make a tidy conclusion. But as the text now stands, one more saying remains—that infamous comment about women:

> Simon Peter said to them, "Let Mary go out from among us, because women are not worthy of life." Jesus said, "See, I myself shall lead her, so that I will make her male, so that she too may become a living spirit, resembling you males. For every woman who makes herself male will enter the kingdom of heaven."

Gospel of Thomas 114

How startling it is that our generation is captivated by the *Gospel of Thomas,* a text whose climax so drastically devalues women. No wonder there are readers who seek to excuse Thomas by ignoring that last, noxious saying; perhaps, after all, we can read Saying 114 as an appendix we may properly disregard. Thomas has insisted that male and female must become one, within an individual and in social life; all sexual urgency within the individual will be neutralized, and that between individuals will be transcended. As it stood, this suggested that women and men were to meet, as it were, in the middle, in an androgyny of women made manly and men made womanly. "When you make the male and the female into a single one," said Jesus, "so that the male will not be male and the female not be female, then shall you enter the kingdom." But there may well have been rigorists among those who had control over the text, who looked instead for a one-way transformation: the believer must be stable, rational, and spiritually inclined, that is, must display all the traits linked in ancient thought with *men.* Such rigorists might have been able (even if only within their local communities) to add Saying 114 to make the position clear. It was for women to change, not men; the ideal was not a halfway house between the two; to be worthy of the kingdom, a woman must become male. The rigorists may well have inherited a short saying about Jesus's making Mary male and then added the final generalization (with its different agency and emphasis) about women changing themselves. If this is how the gospel's end has grown, then the main body of the gospel is innocent of Saying 114.

On Earth as It Is in Heaven:
Thomas, John, and the Home of Knowledge

What can believers, living their mortal lives, come to know of God, and how? Thomas and John gave conflicting answers, but the gulf between them, though deep, was surprisingly narrow. Thomas offered ascent to heaven to believers properly trained in their imagination, intellect, and way of life. John offered the total self-disclosure of God here on earth in the person of Jesus and so, for later believers, within the reception of John's own gospel, which made "present" Jesus and his power. We nowadays still envision heaven, if at all, as a place to which one might go (upward) at a certain time (after death). So we lose sight of its function as the setting for seeing divine truth, which will transform the seer. This was not a transformation of the seer's surface, on the outside (as the images of radiance or clothing might suggest); nor was the change just an increase in factual knowledge. The ascent itself already purified would-be seers, equipping them to stand in the presence of God's own dazzling, fiery pureness without being burned to nothing. The seer, by now angelic, glimpsed the creator of the universe and the creator's plans for it. The response is not assessment, but awed worship, and seers bring back to their daily life some dim remainder of their heavenly glow. We know from a liturgical text among the Dead Sea Scrolls, the *Songs of the Sabbath Sacrifice*, that hymns performed in services could take their participants, in their imagination and self-perception, into the Holy of Holies as such angelic creatures.

Such seers were members of communities that acknowledged particular leaders (the *Gospel of Thomas* polemically gives precedence to James and above all to Thomas himself, 13) and they were likely trained for their visions. Transformed by their visions, they returned to daily life with new insight into our world: "Recognize what is in your sight, and what is hidden from you will become plain to you"; "Split a piece of wood, and I am there; lift up the stone, and you will find me there."[28] Visionaries and their techniques and experiences were familiar within the Judaism of Thomas's day, but such visionaries did not (as far as we know) form exclusive communities of presexual or male-androgyne celibates such as those to which Thomas's Jesus, the Primal Human in the image of God, seems to have inspired the Thomasines.

John evokes, for his gospel's reception, a distinctive setting—his churches' public worship. John starts his gospel with the prologue. It was (in style and perhaps in its first use) a hymn; John has deliberately set a liturgical tone. *No one has seen God, ever* ends the prologue. No, of course not. God is not accessible to human sight. But *God the only son, he who belongs at the Father's breast,* he *has shown the way.*[29]

And so to the gospel's end: on Easter morning Mary sees Jesus in the new paradise, the home of God. So the readers seem to have reached the goal of a journey to heaven. But Jesus insists to Mary that she must not hang on to him, *"for I have not yet ascended to the Father"*—this Eden is still *earthly.* John evokes a wonderfully strange limbo in which readers sense the upward momentum—*surely* this Jesus belongs unequivocally in heaven—but no, the gospel's apocalypse is still upside-down and the revelation it offers is still to be seen on earth.

The encounter with Mary is followed by Jesus's first appearance to the disciples on Easter evening. The scene is alive with the echoes of liturgy: the disciples are gathered, and the Lord is present and blesses them, *"Peace be with you."* Jesus breathes upon his disciples as God had breathed the breath of life into Adam; the spirit is among them. Jesus gives to the disciples the power of absolution. A week later Jesus will appear again and will invite Thomas to touch him. John is giving his readers a clue: by now Jesus *has* ascended to the Father. How fitting that he discloses himself to his followers in a numinous, liturgical setting. The scene could easily tilt, in readers' minds, unambiguously heavenward. But John keeps the balance: the "ascended," glorified Jesus still bears the marks of his death, and the truly blessed are those *who do not see but have come to believe.* John's apocalypse is still, right to the end, upside-down. John's readers were never removed to a heavenly sanctuary safe from this brutal, physical, intractable world of ours; whatever they could see in this lifetime as mortals, they could see on earth. The gospel they heard in the liturgy brought Jesus back "down" to earth; it did not elevate its hearers to heaven.[30]

But this is, I suspect, evasive. Saying 113 wrapped up the themes of Saying 3, and this final Saying 114 resolves (albeit less openly) the promise and challenge given in the Preface and Sayings 1–2. The gospel's closure, from its very beginning to its very end, really is complete. In Saying 2 Jesus had said, "Let him who seeks, not cease seeking until he finds, and when he finds, he will be troubled, and when he has been troubled, he will marvel and he will reign over the All." This opening warns of restlessness: of seeking and—when the search has been successful—of a troubled mind. But this will not be the end of the story. In Jesus himself "the sign of the Father" is "movement and repose," according to Saying 50, and the text as a whole invites its readers through the movement of seeking and trouble to a first experience of that repose—in the stability and steadiness that were linked in ancient thought with men. And so Saying 114 rounds it off well. It is most natural to surmise that the gospel was shaped between its present beginning (Preface, Sayings 1–2) and its present end (Saying 114) at the same time. If that was when the main body of the sayings was being compiled, then the gospel really was intended by its principal compilers to conclude with a ringing (stinging!) insistence that only men and women-made-men will enter the kingdom; theirs is the vital capacity for repose.[31]

And was the place of women so important and deeply contested an issue that its resolution was a fitting climax to the whole gospel? Yes, because John's communities, quite unlike Thomas's, were finding in Mary Magdalene the icon of discipleship. John's Mary Magdalene had seen Jesus on Easter Day in the re-created Eden on earth, into which John's readers were invited; Thomas's church claimed and offered for its presexual celibates a journey to heaven, where they would see the presexual celibate son of the Living Father, would be united to him as images to their original, and would not be afraid. John saw in Mary Magdalene an icon of all believers who gained from his gospel itself new birth from above into the life of the new aeon; Thomas saw in her an icon of all that must be overcome before a human spirit could be worthy of life.

* * *

In the reintegration, demanded and offered by Thomas, all aspects of the person cohere, the personal, the social, and the cosmically anthropological. But just imagine the Thomasine life, with its discipline, intensity, and courageous resistance to every expectation in the wider world.

"I will make Mary male." A few stories have reached us of women actually impersonating men. Such women could change their appearance

(by cutting their hair short) and deny themselves any of the sexual, ma-
ternal, and domestic roles that women were expected to fill. Most telling
is Mariamne, in a fourth-century story about the Saviour and his apostles.
The Saviour tells her, "Change your appearance and your whole womanly
form"; she is to keep a record of the apostles' missionary work; and she
herself preaches with a strongly ascetic emphasis. Her setting is important: she is among the apostles, where she has protection and the means
to live. What work, after all, would a single transvestite woman find,
and what family would house her?[32] Mariamne, thanks to her change,
can function as a preacher alongside the apostles. Most women would
need immense courage to make and sustain such a change. A woman's
denial of sexual relations would at least be manageable if her husband renounced them too or her parents (if she was unmarried) approved of her
renunciation. But the men around her would have valued their masculine
stability as a precondition of what they themselves saw as their capacity
for rational, abstract, spiritual ways of thought—a capacity (as most men
believed) well beyond most febrile, emotional women. It would not be
enough for most women, dependent on men's resources and under men's
authority, to acquire in their own eyes the virtues of a man; a woman
would need the endorsement of the men around her.

"It is said by the naturalists," wrote the Jewish philosopher Philo (20
BCE–50 CE) in relation to sacrificial animals and their symbolism, "that
the female is nothing other than an imperfect male. . . . Progress is nothing other than the giving up of the female gender [or race] by changing
into the male, since the female gender is material, passive, corporeal and
sense-perceptible, while the male is active, rational, incorporeal and more
akin to mind and thought."[33] Even such an aspiration would be suspect to
some philosophers. Women were diagnosed as imperfect men, but the condition would not be corrected by artificial manliness, which could end in
an unnatural boldness.[34] If Jesus himself acted on Mary (as he promises in
the first part of Saying 114), he would no doubt successfully transform her,
but any woman who tried to make herself male (as Jesus demands in the
second part) had a steep and difficult path to tread.

What an alien world we are entering here; we will be traversing it for
some chapters to come. The gospels of Thomas and John bore witness to
a vital and deeply contested question: how will humans recover the form
and life in which humanity began, within the primordial Human? This
question would shape the thought of generations to come; it is time for us
to meet the groups who addressed it with unsurpassed intensity, care, and
imagination. We have surveyed the *Gospel of Thomas,* written by mystics
and used by Gnostics. Now it is time to meet the Gnostics themselves.

The Androgynous Christ

In a striking tradition within late antique art, some male pagan gods—especially Apollo and Dionysus—were shown with feminine features: long ringlets, beardless cheeks, round shoulders, small but obvious breasts, and wide hips. A similar tradition informed the portrayals of Jesus on several monuments from the fourth and fifth centuries. The famous statue of Christ in the accompanying illustration was originally believed to portray a sacred poetess.

Why Christian artists adopted this imagery remains a tantalizing question. Perhaps they were making clear that Jesus—*the true vine*[35]—had appropriated the place previously filled by Dionysus, god of wine. Greek artists had often shown Alexander the Great with the long, curling hair of the youthful Dionysus, and artists of the Roman Empire gave such hair to various Roman emperors, who were associated in this way with both the gods and with the glorious Alexander. The Greek-Egyptian god Sarapis (god of heaven, healing, and the dead), accumulating the features of various gods, was sometimes shown with both breasts and a beard.

Or did the Christian artists find in these motifs a welcome device to portray in the single figure of Jesus all the characteristics of humanity, both male and female? It is unlikely now that we shall ever know for sure. "I am the one who is with you always," says the Saviour in the Nag Hammadi tractate the *Secret Book of John,* "I am the Father, I am the Mother, I am the Son." But it is (almost exclusively) in Gnostic documents that we encounter such an androgynous Saviour, and Gnostic art is generally quite unlike the art of imperial-pagan and mainstream Christian monuments among which the androgynous figures of Christ belong; it would be surprising to find Gnostic influence so prominent there.[36] Perhaps it is the gentleness of Jesus that (even then) some artists wanted to represent, at a time when gentleness was seen as a woman's trait.

The other illustrations in this book are included to point up vividly something we know; this one is here to remind us how much we do *not* know. It is not easy to imagine ourselves into a starkly androcentric world in which, nonetheless, gods could be shown as androgynous and their androgyny could be transferred (perhaps with a quite different significance) to Jesus.

Statuette of Jesus: The Androgynous Christ (fourth or fifth century),
Museo Nazionale Romano, Rome. Photo: Courtesy Saskia Ltd.,
© Dr. Ron Wiedenhoeft.

5

NOT A CHRISTIAN, BUT A CHRIST
The Gnostics

> It is not only the washing [of baptism] which frees but also knowledge: knowledge of who we were, what we have become, where we were or at what point we were inserted into the scheme of things, where we are hastening to, from what we are redeemed, what is birth and what is rebirth.
>
> *Theodotus (a second-century Valentinian), in Clement,*
> Excerpts from Theodotus 78.2[1]

> The Gnostics claim that the First Human is androgynous, and called Adam. They suppose that the knowledge of him is the originating principle of the capacity for a knowledge of God, thus: "The originating principle of perfection is the knowledge of humanity, while the knowledge of God is absolute perfection."
>
> *Hippolytus (170–236),* Refutation of All Heresies 5.6.3[2]

Ancient Gnosticism may be described, without being patronizing, as popular philosophy. It was inquiring; it absorbed, in varying proportions within its various groups, the concerns of Greek, Egyptian, Jewish, and Christian thought. It was (at least in its leaders' hands) bookish; the Gnostics tirelessly reinterpreted the thought of Plato, Genesis, and St. John. It was imaginative; to reinterpret all these texts in conjunction with each other was to read truths out of each that nobody had ever seen before. It was brave; these new readings made for the Gnostics more enemies within the churches than friends. And all this was to enable individual Gnostics to discover the truths underlying *everything*.

The Gnostics lived in a world of many gods. There were the gods of Greece, brought by Alexander's armies and settlers to every corner of the

Middle East and Egypt; to worship these was in turn to worship their Roman counterparts, proclaimed by the Roman rulers who made large parts of Alexander's empire their own. Jews insisted on the existence and supreme power of their one god, the creator of everything there is; and Christians—some of them Jewish—told of this god's son, Jesus, who had been in heaven, became a human being, was killed, came back to life again, and now ruled the world in his Father's name. This Jesus could sound like a hybrid: he was like Alexander, whose heroic power was surely the power of a god; like a combination of the Egyptian gods Isis and Osiris, the sister and brother who reigned, respectively, over the living and—having been killed and in some sense restored to life again—the dead; like the invincible sun, sinking each night but renewed in dazzling power each morning; and like a governor within an all-powerful empire, with all the armies of the Roman emperor, Rome's own "Saviour" and "Son of God," behind him.

What mattered was power: the power of nature to ensure food or famine, health or sickness, birth and death; the power of rulers to protect and to punish; the power, as it might seem, of fate or mere chance to bring prosperity or failure. Power was the sign of a god at work, and any god's resentment or caprice might wreak dreadful harm; it was both due humility and common sense to stay in the gods' good favor. "Know thyself" commanded the oracle at Delphi, and the self-knowledge that mattered was the knowledge of one's mortality under the rule of the deathless gods.

Enter the Gnostics, the "Knowers," asking in their own terms the deepest of all questions. How do we fit into the great scheme of creation? What makes us human? What power can we gain over our own lives? What can we hope for?

Knowledge was the aim and offer of philosophies and religions throughout the ancient world. So who should we designate specifically as Gnostics (the Knowers in search of *gnosis,* "knowledge")?[3] Within the New Testament itself Paul mocks the Corinthians who were too proud of their knowledge. Timothy must teach the Ephesians *not to occupy themselves with myths and endless genealogies* and must himself *avoid the profane and empty chatter and the contradictions of what is falsely called knowledge.*[4] We shall certainly hear more of myths and genealogies among the Gnostics, and we are likely hearing from Paul and Timothy of people whose ideas would, over the following decades, come to shape self-consciously distinct groups of Knowers.

"The life of the new aeon is this," says John's Jesus, *"to know you, the only true God and the one you have sent, Jesus Christ."*[5] John's gospel is dominated, as we have seen, by the conditions readers must meet in

order to attain this knowledge. The Christian Gnostics were steeped in John. One follower of the great Gnostic leader Valentinus, Ptolemy, interpreted John's prologue, and another, Heracleon (active 145–180), wrote a commentary on John that is the oldest known commentary on any book of the New Testament. The heresy hunter Hippolytus tells of two heretical groups (the Naassenes and the Peratae) that drew on John's gospel. The New Testament includes three letters attributed to John, which are clearly directed against pernicious misunderstandings of Johannine theology. These supposed errors are most convincingly interpreted as tendencies that would later evolve into full-blown Gnostic thought—the Johannine churches had to counter a trajectory that the Gospel of John, their own foundational text, was furthering. The charge against John's gospel could become more trenchant still. Gaius, an apparently "orthodox" ecclesiastic of Rome at the end of the second century, denied that John wrote either the Gospel of John or Revelation; they were, he said, actually written by Cerinthus, a notorious heretic linked with the Gnostics. The heresy hunter Irenaeus (130–200), by contrast, believed that the gospel was written specifically *against* Cerinthus. John's gospel was an important text and was being widely (and wildly) used; church leaders had either to corral it to their own cause or damn it as heretical.[6]

Christian leaders who have been seen ever since as orthodox worked tirelessly to reclaim the prized terms "knower" and "knowledge" for themselves and their churches. Clement of Alexandria in Egypt (150–215) lambasts those whom we now describe as the Gnostics. He attacks their spurious claims to knowledge and the immorality to which this knowledge leads them. Then he extols the virtues of the *true* Knower. This was a philosophical turf war, and Clement claims for his knowledge just the glorious results that his adversaries claimed for theirs. True Knowers, says Clement, are those

> who know what is fitting in both theory and life: who know how a person should live who will one day become divine and indeed is even now being made like the Divine. . . . The gnostic soul [that is, in general Greek usage, the cognitive soul, what it is in us that *knows*] is just an earthly image of the divine Power, adorned with perfect virtue by the combined action of nature, discipline and reason. The Gnostic is a truly perfect human and a friend of God. The vision of God is the crowning height attainable by the gnostic soul, when it has been perfectly purified, being now deemed worthy to behold for ever the almighty, face to face. For having been made entirely spiritual, it departs to its

kindred sphere and there, in the spiritual church, abides in the rest of God.

From Clement of Alexandria,
Patchworks (Strōmateis) *7.1.3–4; 7.11.67–68*

The false Knowers dangerous to Clement were those who, emphasizing Christ, might attract believers away from Clement's version of the faith to their own. The gulf between Clement and the Knowers was deep, but in some cases quite narrow; he had to work hard to distinguish, for his readers, his creed from theirs. Such attention to details of belief might sound unnaturally cerebral; and there were no doubt many people then, as there are now, joining churches as much for a sense of belonging as from any doctrinal decision. But the Gnostics, seeking and offering understanding, *were* self-consciously thought-ful, for in knowledge lay salvation. Were the Gnostics, then, just desiccated academics? Far from it. The knowledge they claimed and offered was knowledge of the Knowers themselves, of the whole world, of the world's malignant powers and of God; and such knowledge, to be truly known, made ferocious demands upon the Knower's self-awareness and self-discipline. Such knowledge offered hope, as well, of beginning in this life the defeat of those cosmic powers of the zodiac, the planets, and fate that would finally be vanquished in the next. The questions asked by the mainstream churches were asked by the Gnostics too. What and how much is offered to devotees before death as a foretaste of what is to follow it?

Men and Women among the Gnostic Leaders

The Nag Hammadi texts were hidden in a desert cave near a known monastery of the fourth century. It was natural in the first years after their discovery to surmise a link with the monastery, but recent research suggests that the manuscripts were neither produced nor used there. The "library"[7] comprises thirteen books containing over forty texts. Almost every writing from Nag Hammadi is the work, in its present form, of successive editors, compilers, and translators active over the course of the second and third centuries. The texts evolved, decade over decade, to meet the different needs and questions of different communities in different countries over a century or more, and they evolved from different starting points and in different directions. The texts as they have reached us do not form a well-built monument to a single creed or church, but are like a jumble of stones quarried and cut from a variety of rocks, all produced by the same geological traumas of the past, but endlessly varied in shape and texture. Some of these texts, it seems, can be described as Gnostic only if the definition of Gnostic becomes so elastic as so have no real value at all.

We have already located the *Gospel of Thomas* as a mystical text that was appropriated by the Gnostics. Its principal ideas—and perhaps a form of the text itself—were likely known to Valentinus, one of the most imaginative Christian thinkers of the second century. Valentinus became famous in mainstream churches as an arch-heretic who propounded—even invented—a vast acreage of Gnostic error, but he declared himself an indirect pupil of Paul (through a pupil of Paul called Theodas), came to Rome, and aspired to be made bishop there. The myths he developed are not so far from being translations, into story form, of Pauline teaching. The Valentinians set out to interpret Christian teaching, not to be sectarians; the gospel they proclaimed was esoteric, but not exclusive.

Valentinus knew John's ideas too and built on them as Thomas never would. John had developed his stories of successive women encountering Jesus with deeper intimacy and greater insight than the male disciples managed; John's whole gospel culminates in the unsurpassable story of Jesus and Mary Magdalene meeting on Easter Day. Valentinus developed John's scheme. He saw the women in John's gospel as icons of all discipleship; Gnostic men and women alike were to be thought of, in spiritual terms, *as women* awaiting reunion with their male angelic counterparts.

Valentinus himself seems to have diagnosed our world, despite its confusions, as a well-ordered stopping place for Gnostic spirits en route back to their true home. But Valentinus's followers lived in a threatening world. Just a translucent veil had separated John's readers from a glimpse of paradise on earth and in the right light allowed the truth that Mary saw to be seen. Valentinus's generation, however hard it looked for revelation, seemed walled in by the powers of mortality and fate, and nothing else was visible within or through the dense, dark chaos of this earth. John's Mary Magdalene, the woman at the climax of his story, had seen Jesus in a strange imaginary place, but it was on earth; the Valentinians, all as "women," had to seek their sight of Jesus in a higher world, an inner world, or both. It was fitting for the Gnostics, needing to transcend this world, that they should be represented as women, who were the starkest icons of this world's passions and priorities.[8]

The Valentinians will be occupying a fair amount of our attention, but they were one constellation of Knowers among many. There was a baffling variety of such groups. The great Greek theologian Origen (185–254) knew how easy it was to mock their bizarre diversity. In this part of his defense of Christianity against the pagan Celsus (writing around 178), I have put the likely quotations from Celsus in italics. Origen writes,

> We may admit also that *a third kind* [of Christian] *exists, and they*
> *call some natural and others spiritual;* I think Celsus means the
> Valentinians. Let us admit that *there are some too who profess*
> *to be "Knowers";* but those cannot be Christians who introduce
> strange new ideas which do not harmonize with the traditional
> doctrines received from Jesus. Celsus *knows also of Marcellians*
> *who follow Marcellina and Harpocratians who follow Salome and*
> *others who follow Mariamne and others who follow Martha.*
>
> From Origen, Against Celsus 5.61–62

That list of leaders is most intriguing: Marcellina, Salome, Mariamne,
and Martha—all of them women. We have heard of Salome already in
the *Gospel of the Egyptians;* the name of her group, the "Harpocra-
tians," reminds us of the libertine "Carpocratians," whom Irenaeus links
loosely with Marcellina. We know another sect claimed that its doctrines stemmed from James, the Lord's brother, who had taught them to
Mariamne. How interesting that there were groups appealing so strongly
to the distinctive teaching or role of the women—Salome, Mariamne, and
Martha—who knew Jesus.

Marcellina is at the front of Celsus's list, although she lived long after
the New Testament's women; she must have been a prominent figure.
Irenaeus writes of her as among the self-designated Gnostics who encouraged magic and a wildly libertine life; she came to Rome "and led multi-
tudes astray." Her particular sect, we read, set up and crowned images of
Christ, Pythagoras, Plato, and other philosophers. Initiates were branded
on the right ear, a mark known also in the rites of Dionysus and Mithras.
(This neatly evokes an attempt to fuse Christianity with Greek philosophy and the mystery cults.)[9]

We hear more from other writers of women's roles among the Gnostics.
Irenaeus claims that Marcus (who, Irenaeus admitted, did seem to be a
prophet) invested women with the power to prophesy. The biblical book
of Revelation condemns the followers of Nicolas, apparently linking them
with the false prophetess nicknamed Jezebel and with the *deep things of*
Satan,[10] reminiscent of the Gnostics' Primal Depth. In second-century
Rome the oracles of a visionary virgin, Philoumene ("Beloved Woman"),
collected by the radical theologian Apelles, helped inspire Apelles's new
Gnostic sect. A woman who was a leader of the Cainite sect seems to have
denied the value of baptism with enough authority and effect to need full-
scale rebuttal from the heresy hunter Tertullian (160–225).[11]

The Gnostics were not alone in valuing the teaching of women. Either
Paul himself or a pupil had told the Corinthians that women should not

speak in church—a clear sign that women were doing so.[12] Such strictures did not suppress them; a later follower of Paul had to write crossly,

> *I permit no woman to teach or to have authority over men; she is to keep silent. For Adam was formed first, then Eve; and Adam was not deceived, but the woman was deceived and became a transgressor. Yet woman will be saved through bearing children, if she continues in faith and love and holiness, with modesty.*
>
> 1 Timothy 2.12–15

In this same letter we hear the warning against the *myths and endless genealogies* that remind us of the Gnostics. We hear as well in the New Testament itself of the four daughters of Philip who were prophets;[13] they launched a succession of prophetic leaders in Asia Minor, among whom was the woman Ammia in Philadelphia. Out of this succession sprang, in the second century, the prophetic Montanists, founded by Montanus and two women, Priscilla and Maximilla; their prophetess Quintilla encountered Christ in female form.[14] The mainstream churches opposed the Montanists and the Gnostics (two apparently unrelated movements) with equal vehemence.

Tertullian wrote angrily about the heretics who offered special knowledge. There is much of interest in his onslaught, about meetings, their openness, and their apparent lack of hierarchy; our own eyes will be drawn to the status of the women:

> They meet together, listen to one another, pray with one another. Even if non-Christians attend, they cast the holy to the gods and pearls, though false ones, to the swine. . . . They are all conceited, they all promise "Knowledge." The catechumens are "perfect" before they have even been taught. Even the heretical women— how brazen they are!—are bold enough to teach and to discuss, to perform exorcisms, to promise healings, perhaps even to baptize.
>
> *Tertullian,* The Indictment Against the Heretics *41*

The few Gnostic texts available before the discovery at Nag Hammadi included two that star Mary Magdalene as a leading member of Jesus's group. In the long dialogue *Pistis Sophia (Faith-Wisdom)*, Mary Magdalene, as we shall see, is by far the most prominent figure after Jesus himself and is resented by Simon Peter for the frequency of her questions and answers. She speaks for the readers as Jesus leads them in the text upward in their imagination through the realms of ever more dazzling light to its ineffable source. Peter, says Mary in *Pistis Sophia,* "hates our race" of women.[15] In the *Gospel of Mary* Mary herself is the heroine. She tells of a vision she has been given of Jesus, and once more she faces the opposition of Simon Peter. This Mary, who had a vision of Jesus and was beloved of Jesus above all others, now has the roles that were linked in the New Testament with Peter himself and with the Beloved Disciple.

Then came the discovery at Nag Hammadi. For students of Mary Magdalene, it was a treasure trove. In the *Gospel of Thomas* she is again the object of Simon Peter's scorn. In the *Gospel of Philip* she is the companion of Jesus whom Jesus kissed often and loved more than he loved his male disciples. In the *Dialogue of the Savior* Jesus praises her for her complete understanding. From the shadows into the light—Mary Magdalene has been reinstated right at the centre of Jesus's entourage, the follower whom Jesus loved, as the *Gospel of Mary* maintains, more than he loved anyone else. These texts will be the topics of our next few chapters.

There may be something immensely appealing, to our ears, in this Mary Magdalene, who is a visionary, spirit-filled, given deep understanding, and opposed by the patriarchal Simon Peter. This Gnostic Mary serves our modern agenda well. She is surely portrayed by these Gnostic texts with the gifts some women in Gnostic communities actually had and exercised. These women can themselves become for us icons of women in the ancient (and modern) androcentric world; they are opposed by men but unbowed, and are gifted with insight that hierarchical, hidebound men could (and can) hardly share or understand. We readily think of visionary knowledge as the preserve of inspired individuals who are either unaffected by the institutions of religion or are more likely reacting against them. Social, economic, and religious constraints can all add to pressure within the individual to speak out, freely and even wildly, with the insights that precisely those constraints have inspired. In the ancient world (and in much of the world's history since) such constraints were imposed more drastically upon women than upon men. No wonder there were women among the Gnostics who became prophets or seers, and no wonder the men whose power restrained them resented this threat to male supremacy. The voices of Gnostic women were opposed at the time and have been silenced for centuries since. Heard again at last, they seem to be modern voices; the battles those women had to fight are the battles women are still fighting today. And the voices of women are represented in the Gnostic texts by Mary Magdalene; the voices of the institutional, patriarchal churches that resent them, by Simon Peter.

But is this portrait fair? In this simple form, no. We have pitched the visionary Gnostics against the authoritarian churches as represented by Simon Peter. But the distinction is artificial. Peter himself, in the New Testament, is one of the three men (and no women) granted a vision of

Jesus in glory at the Transfiguration, and it has been argued that Peter's followers—particularly in Corinth—highly valued their own inheritance of visionary gifts.[16] What about Easter Day itself? We do not need to decide here whether the sightings of the risen Jesus could properly be described as visions. We need to note only that Paul (probably) and Luke (certainly) regard *Peter,* not Mary, as the first to see the risen Jesus on Easter Day. Mary's great Easter privilege and the standing it gave her were in some traditions ascribed to Peter. We have already encountered Valentinus, the theologian who saw every Gnostic spirit on earth as female. He was a pupil of a pupil of Paul and set out to be Peter's successor as bishop of Rome; he did not resist hierarchical authority, but sought it.

Was the visionary Peter redefined, well after his death, by some authoritarian churches that became ever more institutional, ever less visionary, and that needed in its Peter a hero to match? It is possible, of course. But some at least of the Gnostic texts themselves, from the second or third centuries, bear witness to a quite different trajectory. Peter in the *Apocalypse of Peter* and the *Letter of Peter to Philip* (both discovered at Nag Hammadi) is an enlightened Gnostic teacher, transcending the authority of the mainstream churches and the claims made about him by those churches. Jesus, speaking before the crucifixion, warns Peter in the *Apocalypse of Peter* against various future opponents, including both some Gnostic groups and "others of those who are outside our number who name themselves bishops and deacons as if they have received their authority from God; these people are dry canals." These are likely the hierarchs of the mainstream churches. Peter, then, was a hero among some Gnostics too; they wanted to claim him, if at all possible, for their own side.[17]

Peter was not the only man to whom visions were ascribed in Gnostic texts. John, Judas Thomas, James the brother of the Lord, and Paul received them too. These are all central, apostolic figures in the New Testament, and they are all in a distinctive relation to Jesus. John, the Beloved Disciple, rested on the breast of Jesus as Jesus himself belonged on the Father's.[18] Thomas and James were both reputed to be close (biological or spiritual) relatives of Jesus. Paul was, famously, converted by a vision of the already risen Lord. The Gnostics were trying to claim all these vastly authoritative men as their own.

So much for the—male and female—recipients of rare, privileged knowledge, but we have yet to do justice to the ways in which such knowledge was attained. We have encountered the visionary journeys to heaven demanded by Thomas and will hear of them again; the Gnostics adopted the language of such journeys and probably the practices that fostered them. Such visionaries were steeped in astrological lore, knew of the dangerous powers that would resist any traveler to heaven, and even learned passwords to dull the attacks; there were schools of prophecy and heavenly insight that *trained* individuals for such journeys.[19] To have the vision was a privilege, but, in some circles at least, it was one for which would-be visionaries were well prepared. And the readers of our texts, few of them visionaries themselves, would have known about such techniques and aspired to share their benefits. Thomas had warned against the adversaries who would require passwords from the seer; the *Gospel of Mary* is itself, in part, a manual of instruction for its readers. The *Gospel of Mary,* by its story of Mary's vision, equipped readers to pass the dangers on their route to heaven that she herself had passed. No wonder it was found in a grave, in a niche among feathers, as a talisman to help the dead to navigate the final, postmortem, ascent to heaven.

We have seen the danger in wanting the Gnostic texts to advance our agenda rather than their own. We too readily draw broad, simple lines of opposition and impose this map on all the evidence from our widely varied texts and the widely varied communities they represent. We are— of course we are—most keen to know how Mary Magdalene relates to the male apostles in these texts, and we watch and interpret the evidence as historians, distant from the action but with a real interest in its outcome. The authors, however, had a more insistent aim: to immerse their readers in the drama of the text itself. When the Gnostic authors deployed Mary Magdalene, how did they intend her to stand in relation not to the other characters in the story or dialogue but *to the readers*?

I tried in Chapter 3 to evoke the excitement with which John's view of Jesus might have inspired his readers. I invite you now onto a second and similar exploration, but this time we will have in view not a single text, but an entire mind-set—a theory of God's whole creation and humanity that binds our knowledge of that creation and of ourselves inextricably together. This theory inspired the various Gnostic groups to raise the vast and varied buildings of their thought. In many of them (thanks to John's gospel) Mary Magdalene was a vital constituent. At times she is part of the keystone that holds all the interlocking elements in place, but at times, far more supple and dynamic, she is the guide who steers the readers through the whole building from its dark and sinister basements to the sunlit, panoramic beauties of the penthouse, where the readers belong.

The Gnostic Journey to Knowledge: Upward and Inward

A leading scholar of Gnosticism argues for the value of a general definition of Gnosis as those movements that express their particular interest in the rational comprehension of the state of things by insight ("knowledge") in theological systems that as a rule are characterized by ideas, including the following: the experience of a completely otherworldly, distant, supreme God; the introduction of additional divine figures, not least an ignorant and even evil creator-God; and the estimation of the world and matter as evil.[20] I will be using this as a helpful summary of the beliefs we expect to be prominent in any groups spoken of—in the ancient world or among modern scholars—as Gnostic.

But we should beware. The Gnostics sought to know God and to know themselves. It was widely believed in Hellenistic Judaism that the whole universe is informed by a divine Word (Gk, *logos*), which is both the rational thought of God himself and its expression in the orderliness of the universe—an orderliness that our own human reason can discern. But there remains more to be known than even the most sophisticated faculty, content, and expression of human rationality (which together constitute our own *logos,* or reasoning word) could ever apprehend. We need more. We need the whole intellect or mind (*nous*), which embraces, as well as the power of reasoning, a suprarational faculty of contemplation with which we can intuit the truths of God; and this intuition, we shall see, is inseparable for the Gnostics from the insights of self-knowledge. To understand the Gnostics we need to embrace two premises that made Gnostic thought possible and to which we would likely deny any part in rational comprehension. The first was almost universal in the ancient Greek world; the second was widespread and was endlessly refined and extended by the Gnostics. To give them two titles, according to the first, "Like knows like," and according to the second, "The human being is a universe in miniature." Let's meet them briefly, in turn.

First, then, like knows like. Let's apply the principle to our knowledge of God. Let God himself be defined as mind. As we get to know God, our mind (the knowing subject) and God himself (the object known) and our means of knowledge (our mind) grow ever closer to each other. Next we will recognize that God's all-active, all-creative mind is not a thing that can be a passive "object of knowledge" at all. On the contrary, as we come to know the divine mind, we are being assumed into it; and the more clearly we know it, the more transparently and self-consciously divine we become. What was hidden in us even from ourselves is coming to consciousness, so we are becoming what we were made to be; our origin within the divine intellect is ever more clearly revealed and ever more purely realized as our destination. As we gaze upon the divine nature we are gazing upon the increasing perfection of our own. One motif above all expressed and shaped the growth of such knowledge: light. Light is both the clarifying means of knowledge and the object of knowledge at which, dazzled, we gaze; and what this divine light reveals is the scintillating divinity of the knowers themselves.[21] Mary Magdalene in *Pistis Sophia* represents the reader who is raised towards the ineffable light by the Jesus of the text itself.

The Gnostics had a journey of discovery to undertake; they had to free themselves from the illusions that distracted them and from the tawdry passions that have no part in the mind of God. But how could the Gnostics, immersed as we all are in the ways of the material world, equip themselves for this journey? After all, the mind must use the capacities it already has, even if only in order to move beyond them; the Gnostics had to climb the ladder to the higher plane on which they belonged, before they could kick the ladder away. We hear of visions and of journeys towards a heavenly insight; no wonder we hear too of uncertainty among the Gnostics themselves, as they pondered which faculties were engaged in such strange experiences and how.[22] Mary Magdalene in the *Gospel of Mary* is the seer who tells, from her own experience, how the ascent is made.

A visionary (in pagan, Jewish, and Christian traditions alike) might be taken "upward" through the realms of creation from the dark muddle of our world to the luminous, spiritual purity of heaven; and whatever is seen in heaven—about the cosmos, the future, or God—is infallible. We nowadays balk at this. Where did these visionaries "go"? we ask, knowing as we do that the blue vault of heaven is not the solid floor of higher, brighter worlds than our own. The Gnostics would have answered instantly: to travel upward to the spiritual heaven was to travel inward to the depths of the seer's own spirit.[23]

And so we reach the second great premise of Gnostic thought: that a human being is the universe in miniature. The hellenized Jewish philosopher Philo (20 BCE –50 CE) had already explored the theme over and over. God made humankind in his own image. This surely refers to the mind, said Philo, not the body. As God, then, is to the universe, so the mind is to the human being; the reasoning Word of God in the universe and the rational mind in the human being, each indivisible itself, divide the world into objects and categories. As the sun shines light onto the world, so our mind shines a noonday light onto ourselves. We are made up of hot and cold and wet and dry in due proportions; so is the universe. "On this principle," writes Philo, "some have ventured to say that a human, the tiny animal, is equal to the cosmos; they see that each has been made up of a body and of a reasoning soul, so they have said that the human is a small world and the cosmos a great human." With care and eagerness the soul explores the nature of a human being. "Travel again," Philo urges the soul, "through the greatest and most perfect human: this cosmos."[24]

The idea opened the doors to a vast landscape of patterns and analogies between the inner and the outer, the lower and the upper worlds. When you understand yourself—in all your depth, complexity, and ultimate simplicity—you will understand everything there is; and when you understand God and the cosmos, you will understand yourself. Mary Magdalene in the *Gospel of Philip* is Jesus's companion in the physical world who is matched by Wisdom in heaven and by Spirit in the Spirit's own, still higher, realm. Mary in the *Gospel of Mary* describes a journey heavenward that takes her past the disruptive passions within us. Mary in *Pistis Sophia* both leads and represents the Gnostic who seeks to rise psychologically and cosmically above the apparently mechanical, mindless control of the zodiac and fate.

We are made of body, soul, and spirit; so is the great creation. Only human beings—and no other creatures—have in themselves all the constituents of creation as a whole. All physical things have a body, as we humans have. All animals have life as we humans do, and at least some animals can be motivated by loyalty, devotion, and self-sacrifice as we can. But no other animal can see and reflect on its own place in creation as we can, or regret its failings as we can, or choose to leave the cares of the body behind and to seek—and find—the higher life where we truly belong and from which those cares distract us. There we are: one simple, schematic account (among many possible accounts) of the claim that we have body, soul, and spirit. And the Gnostic is called to live this life under the pure dominion of the spirit as Mary Magdalene does in *Pistis Sophia*.

So we can watch the struggle between body, soul, and spirit in ourselves, and our eyes will be opened to see the same struggle in the universe. If we locate the sources of the evil in ourselves, we will have found where evil comes from and where it lurks in the universe as a whole. If we aspire to what is highest in ourselves, we will be heading for the heights of creation. If we glimpse the source, beyond all description, of our own being, we will glimpse the unspeakable source of all things. We are faced with a journey upward and a journey inward. Both were believed to be real; so was the correspondence between them. The Gnostics told endlessly convoluted stories about layer after layer of existence and the powers that dwell there. Gnostics who recognized those layers and defeated the evil powers within their own being were seeing the layers and defeating the powers encountered by seers on their journey through the whole universe to heaven and beyond. The Gnostics, then, would come gradually to see the truthfulness of their own stories' vast pattern of descent and ascent, of self-deceit and self-discovery, of self-betrayal and self-fulfilment. The drama of which they were part, then, was both cosmically vast and utterly intimate. So Mary Magdalene in the *Gospel of Mary* tells of the journey at once to the uppermost and innermost worlds, and in *Pistis Sophia* she follows Faith-Wisdom's glorious restoration to the realms of light.

Imagining the Spirit

We will be hearing a lot of the spirit and spiritual realms, on the one hand, and of our densely material world, on the other; the third element, soul, will often stand in between the two. We are still used to some such distinction between body, soul, and spirit, but we no longer think, as the Greeks did, of a continuum of elements from the most dense (earth) through the more refined (air and fire) and onward to something still lighter and less palpable that is what actually *lives* in living things. Any talk of soul or spirit was confronting one overriding challenge: to account for *life*. There must be something in us that enlivens the whole of us and makes all parts of us responsive, but leaves some parts of us (fingers, toes) able to be cut off and thereafter lifeless and inert. This life principle may be something active in air, for our breath stops at death, or something active within blood, which flows out of a cut and ceases to flow on death, or—to look farther afield—something related to living, flickering fire, warm as we are warm until we die.

Air has no obvious body, but it has volume and weight. Fire has no clearly defined body and rises upward, apparently weightless. Imagine the trajectory, ever farther from dense, inanimate stone through the lightness of mobile, life-giving air or living flame to some element far lighter and purer, alive with an inextinguishable life of its own. Eventually we will reach the point at which this supposed stuff really does not have a body at all. Keep going, farther and farther, towards a principle free from the last remnants of even the most impalpable matter. Keep going, I might have said, higher and higher, for as we leave matter behind, so we leave dense, ponderous weight behind. As we draw nearer in our imagination to the life principle, we imagine the purest of pure fire in the highest of all heights. And fire is the source of light; we imagine a brilliance far more dazzling than the sun's.

Somewhere on this trajectory we will need to place the human soul and the human spirit; whatever their intrinsic weight and density, they live on earth only in a "solution" of flesh. And right at the highest end of the trajectory, we will place God himself, pure Spirit, freed from all material content or vehicle. (The human spirit, clearly related to the divine, supreme Spirit, would be an element more free from earthly dross than soul.) When I distinguish matter and spirit in the following pages, I will be evoking this continuum between the dullest matter and the purest supercelestial Spirit, with due acknowledgment that this is not the way in which we would nowadays draw the distinction.

Now consider our whole world and all its palpable, material "thinginess." As we look for the spiritual we will be looking upward and inward, yes; but imagine finally this same world in the form it would have as the thought—the actual content of thought—of a divine craftsman. This time we are following our trajectory in reverse, downward and outward. Let that intellectual world gradually gain weight and solidity until finally it becomes our own. Within this thing-filled world, informing and animating it, is that intellectual world, invisible, refined, and all too easily forgotten; but without that intellectual world our palpable world (if its elements were to exist at all) would be mere chaos. Here, then, is a final way in which to think of the spiritual world—not as something or somewhere else, but as the entire living and life-giving thought that makes possible the world of which we ourselves, bodily and mutable and mortal, are part.

As ever, our interest is chiefly in the questions the Gnostics asked; we are unlikely to share their answers. The Gnostics had two tasks: to recognize their proper place in this cosmic continuum, both now and after their death; and, within this present life, to keep in proper balance—and under proper control!—all the denser and lighter elements of which they were composed. How could the Gnostics, embedded in this present life, realize the potential of their spirit? We have already invoked one resource that will be vital throughout the coming pages—the Gnostics used their *imagination* to envision themselves, their world, and the realms of the spirit in which they belonged.

* * *

Scholars distinguish between mythical and mystical thought. Mythical thought uses stories to give an account of the world as an object, an "it," and speak of its origins, the powers that rule it and its destiny, and (among its myriad constituent objects) the thinker. Mystical thought gives an account of the individual as a subject, an "I" and speaks of my relation to God, the universe, and myself. But the contrast is not a contrast of incompatibles. The greatest scholar of Gnosticism in the twentieth century,

Hans Jonas, argued that in the early centuries CE mythical thought gave to mystical thought the framework and the terms in which to think. The transfer was so effective, he suggested, because both expressed a particular way of being human in the world. In the Gnostic stories, myth and mysticism meet. Mystical mythology, mythological mysticism—in an explosive fusion of the two, the Gnostics found the limitless energy that fueled their imaginations, hearts, and minds. We too easily read about Mary Magdalene in these texts as a figure from ancient mythology, and so we miss her role as a part, a representative or a symbol, of *ourselves*.

The Gnostics speak to us from their own time in the voices of that time; we must attune our ears to these voices that reach us from cultures so far from our own. The Gnostics were making a sustained, brave, and honest attempt to describe what it is to be truly human and to enable their readers to *become* truly and self-consciously human as they listened, by learning who they had been, what they had become, where they had been or at what point they were inserted into the scheme of things, where they were hastening to, from what they had been redeemed, and what birth and rebirth were. Visionary journeys themselves, of which we are hearing so much, were icons of a lifetime spent in prayer and discipline, and of a gradual transformation into the glory, reflecting the glory of God, that shone out from such a life.

In *Pistis Sophia* Mary asks question after question. Jesus confirms she may speak freely. "And I will fulfill you," he promises, "in all powers and all Fullnesses from the innermost of the inner to the outermost of the outer; from the Ineffable himself to the darkness of the darknesses, so that you may be filled with all knowledge." Mary also gives answer after answer, and in the book's second half the Saviour marvels at her answers, because—by now—"she had completely become pure spirit."[25] To learn was to be transformed, to become one's true self at last and so to become divine.

6

WISDOM, EVE, AND MARY MAGDALENE
Fall, Recovery, and Restoration

> The same subject-matter is discussed over and over again by the heretics and the philosophers, and the same arguments are involved. Where does evil come from? Why is it permitted? What is the origin of man? In what way does he come?
>
> *Tertullian (160–225),* On the Indictment of the Heretics 7.5[1]

> Some people falsify the words of the Lord and make themselves bad interpreters of what was well said. Thus they overthrow many and on the pretext of Knowledge (*Gnosis*) divert them from the one who founded and arranged this universe, as if they could show something higher and greater than the God who made heaven and earth and everything in them.
>
> *Irenaeus (130–200),* On the Detection and Refutation of the Knowledge Falsely So-Called (Against Heresies), *Preface to Books 1 and 2, 1–2*

Mary Magdalene was not, for the Gnostics, just a figure in the history of this visible, palpable world who received a revelation on Easter Day. She could represent the Gnostic's progress into knowledge and so could guide Gnostic readers on their path; and she could embody on earth and so reveal the Saviour's companion whose higher forms were paired with him in heaven and beyond. Mary's various roles were vital in the Gnostic drama of the individual and the world; we will make sense of these roles when we make sense of that moral, cosmic, and theological drama as a whole. For a few pages, then, we will confront two of the great questions faced by every generation of thinkers in the ancient world. We will be making less mention of Mary herself in these pages. If you would prefer to move straight on to the Gnostic texts (Chapters 7–9), please do—and then bear with me when I rely there on the results of this more abstract chapter.

At the Head of the Gnostic River:
Simon and Helen

Can we name the first teacher whose teaching and life showed the hallmarks that his own followers, his detractors, and we (these many centuries later) might all identify as Gnostic? There is at least a candidate, Simon, from Samaria. We hear of him in the New Testament as a magician foiled by Simon Peter.[2] His teaching is described about 150 CE by Justin Martyr and in the 180s by Irenaeus; quite enough time has passed, of course, for his followers to have developed Simon's own philosophy beyond all recognition. "Nearly all the Samaritans," says Justin, "and a few among other peoples, acknowledge and worship Simon as the First God, and they say that a certain Helen, who accompanied him at that time but was formerly a prostitute in Tyre, was the First Thought which he brought into existence." The Simonians worshiped Helen as Athene, the daughter of Zeus who was born fully grown from her father's head. (No wonder the thinkers who enjoyed allegory described Athene as Zeus's First Thought.) Simon himself was worshiped as Zeus.

Helen had been a prostitute; the First God's all-creative power had fallen (into "prostitution" of her spirit in the world of flesh) and needed rescue by the First God himself. There was as well a Samaritan goddess Helen; she was linked with Persephone, dragged down to the underworld by the god of the dead. For Gnostics our material world was the underworld, the realm of the dead. Persephone's journey was readily imagined as a spiritual fall into this crude, deathly world of ours.

Simon and Helen are described in terms startlingly reminiscent of God and his Word in the prologue to John's gospel. As the Word recalls God's Wisdom, so does Helen the First Thought.

We are focusing, throughout Chapter 6, on the influence of Greek and Jewish thought on the Gnostics. But it has long been wondered how much they drew (as their opponent Hippolytus claimed) on Babylonian and other Eastern stories. Possible connections abound, glinting suggestively. The goddess Isis was said (in the fourth century CE) to have been a prostitute in Tyre. She was known as Wisdom, She was linked with Athene, with Persephone, and with yet another goddess, revered in Babylon, who had descended to the underworld and needed rescue by the supreme god. There were many streams running into the Gnostic river.[3]

One of our questions we might call—for reasons that will soon become clear—the question of the Greeks; the other, the question of the Jews. The ancient world distrusted any "new" religion; the Gnostics believed they were uncovering the structures that undergirded and linked the most venerable religions of the age and, by their fusion, were reinforcing the deepest claims in each.

We will go to the headwaters from which the questions flowed through centuries of thought, the first or most vital texts we have that address the questions. In each case the questions will evolve into questions about gender, in human life, in the universe—and in God. We are physically sexed and socially gendered. Is the universe informed by sexual difference, as we are? If not, is our character as sexed and gendered beings a distortion, something inessential to our true selves, which are as sexless and ungendered as the universe and the powers that rule it? Perhaps the contrast had to be refined. Perhaps the current divisions in human sex and gender are a part and symbol of the opposites pervading all creation, which will one day be overcome in a perfect, eternal, cosmic version of our present sexual unions. The Gnostics were heirs to these questions, which they answered in stories of male and female powers, unfolding in layer after layer of existence until at last they are embodied in man and woman—in Jesus and Mary Magdalene.[4]

How Could the Imperfect Emerge from Perfection?

Here, then, is the first question, the question of the Greeks: how could imperfection emerge from perfection? It will take its most vivid form as: how could the (mutable, corruptible) Many emerge from the (intrinsically perfect, unchangeable) One? The question was posed by Parmenides (b. ca. 515 BCE), poet, seer, and a foundational figure in Greek philosophy. Parmenides wrote of being carried up in a chariot to heaven. There a goddess instructed him in the ways of Truth and of illusory Appearance. Her claims sound very strange to us and would have to Parmenides' first readers too. In grand poetry, well suited to this revelation of pure paradox, Parmenides relays what he learned about true Being, That Which Is:

> But motionless in the limits of mighty bonds
> Being is without beginning and never-ending;
> For it is not right for Being to be incomplete,
> For it lacks nothing; if it did, it would lack everything.
> Therefore, all that mortals posited will be [mere] name:
> "Coming into being" and "perishing," "to be" and "not to be."

Parmenides, Fragment 8, from lines 26–40

What, then, is "true" in and about this changing world in which we live? What about it can we be said really to "know"? With these challenges Parmenides set an agenda for all subsequent Greek thought. Plato (429–347 BCE) postulated a realm of unchanging Being, in which exist the true and perfect "forms" of all that we apprehend. He first surmised that there exist forms corresponding to our concepts (such as Justice and Unity); he then saw that the arguments for these would also argue for there being forms of kinds (such as Cat and Dog) and of qualities (such as Blue and Green). These forms are the foundation of all knowledge. Plato, even when he himself had undermined the theory of forms, retained the conviction that beyond the mutable world (of which no real knowledge is possible) there is a realm of that which truly is; on this our world is modeled.

Plato wrote in the *Timaeus* of the world's creation. There is a cosmic Demiurge or Maker, who gazed on the Eternal and made a material copy or image of it, which is our universe. This Demiurge is *good* and devoid of all envy; he wanted the universe to resemble himself as closely as possible. Confronted with the visible world, shifting and unordered, he brought it from disorder to order. Is the Demiurge, then, really just "god"? No. The Demiurge engendered the self-sufficient and most perfect god and additional lesser gods. These, the gods of Greek mythology, he set to work on the creation of humankind. The Demiurge himself made the immortal principle of soul and then entrusted to the lesser gods the construction of the physical body and of the second, mortal, soul of our passions. So these gods "moulded" human beings. The superior sex was man; those men who lived a good life would, on death, return to a life in the stars. Anyone who lived badly would return to earth as a woman, and if she lived badly again, she would next return as an animal.[5] (We shall see far more of this androcentric bias.)

Is the world itself good? It is only an image of the Eternal, distorted and subjected to change. Plato wrote of our escape to the realms of the Eternal, sometimes with a wistful appreciation of this visible world (*Symposium, Phaedrus*), sometimes with little more than scorn for it (*Phaedo*). But this world is nonetheless still informed by the rationality and order of the Eternal; the philosopher can still be led, by glimpsing the beauty of the world's order, to look for the greater beauty that lies beyond. All that we have encountered in Plato we shall encounter again in the Gnostics, but their Demiurge is an evil figure, ignorant and envious. He understands nothing of the eternal world he is so badly copying; the world he makes is an incorrigibly dark place and most of its inhabitants are subject—and perhaps irremediably subject—to the turmoil of their passions.

Plato was always asking how knowledge of the unchanging truth is possible in this forever changing world. The heavenly world of eternal forms provided him with one answer. We are the reincarnation of souls that have seen the forms themselves and that, reembodied here, remember—however faintly and inaccurately—what they have seen. By the second century CE, when the Gnostics were absorbing Platonic thought, Plato's successors had located this realm of the forms in the great mind of the one Supreme Being, who was beyond existence itself.

Plato: The Myth of the Cave

Our world, then, and everything in it are informed by the eternal, unchanging forms, but are mere copies of these forms, derivative, imperfect, and transitory. What will it take for us to recognize this truth, to see through the total and compelling illusion that our world is the real and only world? Plato's most famous story was well known to the Gnostics. Plato's Socrates in the *Republic* compares us to people in a deep sunless cave, forced to face its back wall. Behind us are puppet masters manipulating their marionettes; behind them in turn is a fire. The fire casts the puppets' shadows onto the cave's back wall, where we see them. The puppet masters provide speech for each character; their voices echo off the cave's ceiling and sound to us, the audience, as if they come from the shadows themselves. What, for us, is *reality*? The puppets' shadows and the echoed voices—these are all we see and hear.

What, then, will happen if one of us breaks free, turns round, sees all this dramatic machinery, and walks past it up to the mouth of the cave? This explorer will discover the truth about that shadow play and come out into the real world. Even at night the light of moon and stars will be dazzling. The light of the sun will at first be blinding—no wonder our explorer starts by looking downward into ponds to see this brilliant world in reflection, and only gradually grows accustomed to the brightness of the landscape and of the sun itself. What will happen to such an explorer who returns to the darkness of the cave to alert the other victims of the puppeteers' deception? Once more blinded, this time by the unaccustomed blackness, our traveler will seem confused to the point of madness, telling an incredible story. So it is, insists Socrates, for the philosophers in this world of ours. They have actually left our earthly cave and seen the real world of eternal truths—and are derided for their pains.[6]

And what will help us to make the turn towards the truth? In the *Phaedrus* Plato's Socrates speaks of the soul as a chariot drawn by two winged horses. He imagines the gods traversing the heavens in such chariots and gazing forever and without interruption on the beauties of divine truth. Then he imagines the human soul, in which the two horses are wildly ill-matched; one is well-disciplined, the other passionate and almost beyond the charioteer's control. If they ever see a beautiful creature, the horses feel all the sensations and desire of *love*. The well-ordered horse longs to rise on its wings to heaven to see the true beauty of which the beloved's beauty is an image; the unruly horse longs for sexual union with the beloved, here and now. Socrates writes in wonderfully vivid terms of the soul's turmoil. The horses' wing feathers begin to grow, the wings itch and throb, the whole soul palpitates and rages with pain until soothed by the memory of the beloved and the beloved's beauty. Mary Magdalene in *Pistis Sophia* speaks of her own longing in such terms, as she rises towards the highest heights of dazzling light; her person-of-light moves her, joys and bubbles in her, and desires to go out from her to Jesus.[7]

We love the good and the beautiful around us; we see adumbrated in them the truly and eternally Good and the Beautiful and so grow to love these too. Such love is a *longing* for complete and transparent knowledge of the Good and the Beautiful. And those who dedicate themselves to the life and learning of a philosopher will find themselves becoming, in this present life, ever wiser, ever closer to the object of their longing, and ever more nearly divine.[8]

We long for what we love and lack. The objects of this love and longing are generally outside ourselves: people or things or the goodness and beauty that—however imperfectly—they embody. But does this longing disguise another, more intimate, lack within each one of us? In Plato's *Symposium* the comic-poet Aristophanes tells a delightful fable to account for the mutual desire of lovers for the union of their bodies. There were once, says Aristophanes, three human sexes, male, female, and androgynous. To envisage each individual in this first humanity, think of two humans with our present limbs, joined along the length of their chests and stomachs; their backs and sides formed a circle. Their genitals were on the "outside"; they procreated by casting their seed on the ground. Each such doublet was a single creature with two heads facing outward (away from each other), four arms, and four legs; to run, they could whirl around and around like acrobats, using all eight limbs for their cartwheels. The double men were offspring of the sun; the double women, of the earth; and the androgynous hybrids, of the moon.

Male and Female: The Greek Premise

Pythagoras (active before 500 BCE) already postulated the First Unit, which inhaled the Unlimited or Void and so formed numbers. Pythagoras formulated the pairs of opposites out of which everything in creation can be conceived. Here is his list:

Limit	Unlimited	Rest	Motion
Odd	Even	Straight	Crooked
One	Many	Light	Darkness
Right	Left	Good	Evil
Male	Female	Square	Oblong

Aristotle, Metaphysics A 5.986a.15

We might be inclined to imagine that such a schema is just the fantasy of an overorganizing mind. But it is an organization of *value*. In the left-hand columns, order and symmetry and stability stand alongside light and goodness—and the male. In the other column these perfections slip away into imperfection, into asymmetry and disorder and darkness—and the female. How then did our degenerate world of change and death emerge from the perfect and unchanging One? The first move was from One to Two. That primordial unity might be best described or envisioned as male, as androgynous, or as beyond the distinctions of sex and gender altogether—but it would quite certainly not be female.

Behind much Greek thought, and not just its formal philosophy, lies a premise about the world and its constituents that may be sketched as follows. Once more, a higher value is being ascribed to the (warm, dry, rising, spiritual) elements in the chart's top half than to the (cold, damp, heavy) elements in the lower.

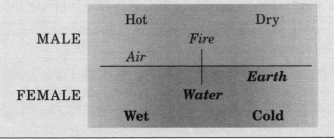

These doublets were so strong that they sought to scale the heights of heaven and fight the gods. Zeus, king of the gods, brought an end to their schemes. He sliced each of them lengthwise in half, sewed up the halves (with a knot at the navel), and turned their heads around to face their new front. But each of these new half creatures was desperate for reunion with its other half; when they met they would embrace each other longingly. Zeus took pity on them and moved their genitals to their new fronts, so that they could be united in love. Those who had been half of an androgynous hybrid became lovers of the opposite sex; those who had been half of a double woman became women who loved women; those who had been half of a double man became men who loved men. For Plato's Socrates, these last were the aristocrats of human nature, virile, brave, and destined for public office. The greatest blessing for individuals is the discovery of their own true beloved, with whom the lovers can once more be joined in their primordial union; next best is love for a compatible favourite.[9]

A single creature carved in two and longing for reunion with its other half. The image would be valued for centuries—and would become a vital ingredient in Gnostic thought: as an individual, what I am really missing, in love with, and longing to find is the rest of myself, so that I can once more be complete and the person I was made to be. As Plato's heirs, the Gnostics came full circle. For them this love will be fulfilled in knowledge, when I am drawn back upward to my spiritual counterpart, the real and spiritual me of which my bodily self is just a flawed and misleading image. So I will come to *know myself* with complete understanding—and therein to be wholly myself at last.

The *Gospel of Philip* is heir to Plato. Every Valentinian is envisioned as a female spirit due to be reunited with her own male angelic counterpart. And one couple represents this union: Jesus and Mary Magdalene.

How Could Evil Emerge from the Good?

And so we come to the question of the Jews: how did evil emerge from the good? Genesis begins: *In the beginning God created the heavens and the earth.* One good God, creator of everything, has replaced the pagan pantheons; his word of command is enough to secure all the elements' obedience. As the climax of the work God makes the Human.

> *And God said, "Let us make a Human in our image and in a likeness. . . ." So God made the Human, in the image of God he made him, male and female he made them.*
>
> Genesis 1.26–27 *(Greek version)*

God finished his creation on Day Six and he looked and, *Behold, it was very good;* on Day Seven, God rested.[10] Then we seem to hear the story over again. This time, we hear how God moulded the Human and breathed the breath of life into him, and the Human became a living soul. God placed Adam in the garden in Eden and out of Adam's side God took the material from which God himself would mould for Adam a fitting companion, the woman.

Such was life in paradise; it is not the life we lead now. How was that idyll lost? God gave Adam all but total freedom in the garden. He had imposed only one restriction: Adam was forbidden to eat from the Tree of Knowing Good and Evil. God had warned, *"In the day that you eat of it you shall be certain to die."* But the serpent beguiles the woman with the sight of the tree's fruit and the promise of godhead: *"God knows that on the day you eat from it your eyes will be opened and you will be like gods, knowing good and evil."*[11] The woman eats; Adam eats too, and God expels them from the garden. From now on the woman will bear children in pain and will desire her husband and he shall rule over her.

The rest of the Old Testament never refers directly to this story of the Fall. The narrative may well have been added long after the rest of the Old Testament reached its present form, as a prelude to the human histories that follow.[12] It soon caught the attention of Jesus's devotees. To describe what Jesus had achieved and who he had been, the New Testament's authors turned again and again to the stories of creation and the Fall. Mark's Jesus, after his fast in the desert, is at peace with the wild beasts and is fed by angels; here, right at the start of Jesus's ministry, Mark is hinting at paradise. The motif sounds again when Jesus speaks about divorce with reference to life in Eden. The New Testament ends with the descent of the New Jerusalem to earth; its river is bordered by trees of life such as the tree that stood in Eden, and its fruit, from which God kept Adam and Eve in Eden, is now to be eaten for the healing of the nations.[13] Paul dwells systematically on the theme:

> For since death came in through a human, so too through a human the rising of the dead. For just as in Adam all die, just so in Christ shall all be made alive. . . . The first human, Adam, was made into a living soul [Gen. 2.7]—but the second human into a life-giving spirit.
>
> 1 Corinthians 15.21–22, 45

The ancient Greeks had a clear sense that each species had its proper perfection, and the Jews believed that humankind, made in the image of God, had fallen from its perfection at the fall of Adam and Eve. Jewish thinkers steeped in Greek thought would put these two ideas together: humanity was surely called to recover, in God's good time, the perfection for which it had been created and to bear once more the bright, unsullied image of God. So far, so good. But what will humans be like, once they have recovered that perfection? Each will be a unity, matching the unity and completeness of the First Human. They might then be male by default or they might be androgynous, *but they will not be female.*

Once more a tide is flowing against Mary Magdalene.

* * *

To counter this insistent precedence of men over women, just one female figure stands out: Wisdom. King Solomon is made to say,

> I loved Wisdom and searched for her from my youth;
> I resolved to have her as my bride,
> I fell in love with her beauty.
> *Wisdom of Solomon 8.2*

Wisdom is infinitely attractive and can offer to her lover the supreme rewards of knowledge and understanding. "Search her out and seek her, and you will come to know her, and once you have hold of her do not let her go. For in the end you will find rest in her, she will turn out to be your joy." The Old Testament's book of Proverbs exhorts young men to value Wisdom and to shun the smooth-talking women who tempt them to adultery; this neatly sets an imaginary courtship over against the actual dangers of an empty head and wandering eye. Greek and Latin, with a range of words for different forms of love, can discriminate between those forms more readily than we can in English. Once we hear in the Jewish Scriptures and once in the Apocrypha of a passionate, erotic love for Wisdom: *Love her passionately, and she will protect you;* "I fell in love with her beauty." [14]

But far more is at stake than in any other courtship, for Wisdom existed before the beginning of the world:

> *The Lord created me for his works, the first of his ways,*
> *Before the aeons he established me, in the beginning.*
> *When he was preparing the heavens, I was there with him,*
> *And when he was making strong the foundations of the earth,*
> *Before he made the earth and the deeps.*
> *When he was preparing the heaven, I was there with him,*
> *And when he was setting his throne above the winds.*

I was with him, setting things in order,
Day by day I enjoyed myself in his presence, on every occasion,
When he took pleasure in the completion of the world
And took such pleasure in the sons of men.

From *Proverbs 8.22–31 (Greek version)*

Wisdom is not just an observer of God's work or a technician fulfilling his commands. She is God's own Wisdom, distinct but inseparable from God himself.

She is a breath of the power of God
And an outflow of the pure glory of the Almighty;
Therefore nothing impure can find its way into her.
She is a reflection of the eternal light
And an untarnished mirror of the active power of God
And an image of his goodness. . . .

The lord of all loved her,
For she was initiated into the knowledge of God
And is the one who chooses what he shall do.

Wisdom of Solomon 7.25–26; 8.3–4

This is poetry whose echoes we shall hear in page after page of Jewish and Gnostic texts. Philo calls Wisdom the daughter of God, the bride of God, and the Mother of all.

Wisdom will be a central figure in our coming chapters, the first of three distinct but inseparable female figures: Wisdom herself, who by her fall caused the creation of this fallen world; Eve, who by her so-called fall began, in defiance of this world's lesser god, the redemption of which the Gnostics are part; and finally, as the symbol of the individual Gnostic recovering from the fall and on her ascent to the realm of the spirit—Mary Magdalene.

Creation Revisited

We are ready now to look again at the stories in Genesis with the eyes and insights of a Gnostic Christian of the third century. This Gnostic (whether Jewish or gentile by birth) is steeped in both Platonic and Jewish thought, dedicated to the deepest possible understanding of the Old Testament, and devoted to John's gospel.[15]

By the second century CE, the shadows Plato had seen darkening the visible world were growing longer and deeper. Superstition was tightening its grip again on diffident minds and anxious hearts. Of course our world had always seemed dim by comparison with the brilliance of heaven, home of pure intellect and spirit, but our own sunlit, intelligible realm had once been contrasted too with the dark horror of Hades, underworld and realm of the dead. Plato himself had quoted the motto *sōma sēma* (Gk), "The body is a tomb."[16] By the second century, more and more people found our own world to be a Hades, a domain of the dead; hell had risen from the depths. The clarity of reason that had both ordered and illumined the classical Greek world seemed to have given way to dark, turbulent passions in the cosmic powers themselves and in the human minds that surveyed their handiwork. For Jews, two tragedies confirmed that the world had been abandoned to evil: the sack of Jerusalem in 70 CE and then its devastation in 135, both at the hands of Roman armies. The world was under the control of arrogant forces who were themselves deluded and who fueled delusion in the blind majority of humankind. Never had fog as dense as this blocked out the dazzling light of truth.

Christianity itself had been born from a Judaism that affirmed our present world and its value. Christians, with their longing for a better world than this world and their promise of a life to follow this life, soon encountered Greek thought, which had for centuries dwelt on an immutable world of truth and on the conditions for attaining it. Christians added the prospect—alien to Greek thought—of a God who would bring to an end the normal course of history to punish humanity for its infinite wrongdoings. And so Christians could endorse and reinforce the sense of turmoil threatening the world, and among those who felt this threat most deeply were the Gnostic Christians. The Gnostics needed all the knowledge and understanding they could get to remain stable and fearless under the world's apparent dominion by ignorance, violence, and death.

Studying the biblical stories of creation and the Fall, their leaders saw profound and subtle stories. The "surface" meaning of the stories, they were sure, was childish and shallow; such standard readings gave credit to the deceitful and deluded god who believed that this patently sick world of his creation was "very good" and who denied to Adam and Eve the knowledge that would show them otherwise. The Jews were misreading their own Bible and had simply failed to see what it really said about the real god and about their own. Most Christian leaders, in turn, had misread their own Jesus, who had not by his short life here saved this— obviously unsaved—world, but who was on an eternal mission to save the Gnostics *from* this world.

Our Gnostic Christian was sure that Plato had been right, that what was ultimately real was an eternal One. But Plato had been wrong too.

The Demiurge who made this physical world was not a good copyist of the ultimate and eternal good; he was deluded and arrogant and made a world of delusions. Moses, the supposed author of Genesis, had been right that God made the First Human in his own image. But Moses had also been wrong in details and misleading overall.[17] Layer after layer of creation must be unfolded and described, from the realms of pure intellect in the mind of God to our tawdry, physical world moulded by the Demiurge. The Gnostics saw symmetries and analogies everywhere, and the fallen human in a fallen world could still be brought, in the process of salvation, to see the patterns informing the whole universe. The layers of creation shared a single, repeated structure, and its fragments, glimpsed in any one layer, could be read into all the other layers.

Few of us now would analyze the created order as the Gnostics did, and none of us would expect Genesis, as the Gnostics did, to conform to that analysis. But the Gnostics were not carelessly or wantonly distorting Scripture; on the contrary, they read with scrupulous care and with deep questions in mind. Adam and Eve take, in different texts, different roles; and in its various forms this primordial past provides, for the Gnostics, the template of our present life and its route towards our final future. Here emerge a new Adam and new Eve: for Adam, read Jesus, and for Eve, read Mary Magdalene.

* * *

On Day One God said, *"Let there be light."* In Greek, "light" is *phōs;* so, with a slightly different pronunciation, is "man." By the time of the Gnostics, it was a commonplace to see a deliberate pun here. God created, as the first of all creatures, a man of light. But there is another man to follow, the Human of whom we will hear on Day Six:

> *And God said, "Let us make a Human in our image and in a likeness.". . . So God made the Human, in the image of God he made him, male and female he made them.*
>
> *Genesis 1.26–27 (Greek version)*

Here, of course, conventional readings recognize the climax of God's creative work. But that, insisted the Gnostics, is far from clear. This Human is a second man to be made and is made by a god who refers to himself as *us*. Who are these creators? Whatever happened to that single supreme God, the maker of everything? We seem to be hearing hints of some lesser creation by a lower god and his cohorts: such a creation as we heard of in Plato's *Timaeus,* when the great God entrusted to the lesser gods the manufacture of humans' bodies and their lesser, mortal, souls.

A very strange creation it is too, in Genesis 1.26–27. This god first seems to make the Human *in our image* and then *in a likeness;* this sounds like two creations, not one. Again, this god makes the Human first simply as a *him* and then—without a word of explanation—as *them, male and female;* once more we seem to be hearing of two creations. Perhaps an explanation was to hand in Genesis 2. In this second story of creation, the Human (Adam) is made first and then the Woman is moulded from his rib. Now if the Woman could be built up out of Adam, then everything specific to the Woman had once been in Adam too. So Adam had contained in a single person, beyond any distinction into male and female, all that was human. In one tradition of the Greek translation of Genesis, this thought came out of the shadows; here the crucial clause was translated, *male and female he made* [not *them* but] *him.*[18]

Wherever we look, the text is letting hints slip that there was more than one creation of a Human. Exactly how many creations in all and exactly how we should envision the Human created at any one stage remained open to dispute. In Appendix B, at the end of this book, I summarize three Gnostic accounts that (amid their strange complexities) give a striking role to the female powers in creation. One thing was clear. The Bible itself, properly read, disallowed any naïve impression that it was describing—in the story of an unambiguously single, uniform succession of events from the light of Day One to God's rest on Day Seven—the creation of every spiritual, mental, and physical being.[19] (We might now define one vital difference between John and Thomas, as follows. John wanted his readers to see themselves in the Eden of Adam and Eve on or after Day Eight. Thomas wanted his readers to become once more the Adam of Day Six, and so to grow into the glory of the Light-Human of Day One.)

The stories of creation were already suggestive, but the story of the Fall cried out for the careful reading that, so the Gnostics believed, the mainstream synagogues and churches were too frightened or too blind to give it.

The Fall: Guilt or Growth?

The Woman ate from the forbidden Tree of Knowing Good and Evil. What was wrong with her longing for this knowledge? Such discovery is part of growing up from childishness to adulthood. What sort of God would want his children to be kept in ignorance? Odder still, God tried to keep Adam from eating the fruit by a threat that appears to have been a bluff. God warned Adam that in the day he ate of the forbidden Tree of Knowing Good and Evil he would be certain to die. But it is not true. The serpent insists, *"God knows that on the day you eat from it your eyes will be opened and you will be like gods, knowing good and evil,"* and the serpent is right. As God himself says, when Adam and the Woman have eaten the fruit, *"They have become like one of us, knowing good and evil"* [20] There is arguably something heroic about the Woman and something unworthy about God. After the Fall, the Woman is at last named Eve (Heb. *hawwā*), recalling Life (*hayyā*), for she was the mother of *all living* (*kol-hā*). Eve, then, could be seen as the living spirit that gives life to humankind. Now we can see what in Adam was specific to the woman, taken out of Adam as his rib when man and woman were divided: the spirit or breath of life. And this life is lived out in the disruptive but vital, enlivening search for the knowledge of good and evil.

Let's watch Eve's action more closely. On a traditional reading she acts without Adam, as she should not; her unilateral action disrupts the whole created order and wins the threatened punishment from God. But now look from a Gnostic viewpoint. This world is made by a lower god, ignorant and jealous, who has tried to keep Adam and Eve from knowledge; it is Eve, Life itself, who has broken the bonds of ignorance. She is herself (or at least she seems to be) the creation of the lesser god, but she has set out on the search for knowledge and opens the way for Gnostics to follow.

The Gnostics found confirmation in Genesis of the truth clear to any Platonist, that there was a first, intellectual creation by God before our everyday world was made. And the Gnostics found analogous structures in the two creations. As there was a Fall in our world, so there had been a Fall within the conceptions of the Great God. With brilliant intuition, some Gnostics reckoned that it was precisely this Fall within the intellectual creation that gave rise to the lesser god and his creation of our everyday universe. A woman acting unilaterally in her search for knowledge caused the so-called Fall in our world, so a female power triggered disaster by her unilateral search for knowledge in the spiritual world. What a woman begins to undo, a "woman" had done in the first place. And what female power represented, in the spiritual world, the search for knowledge? *Wisdom.*

The Gnostics could read backward from Genesis, from the creation and the so-called Fall of Eve to the first stages of creation and the real Fall of Wisdom; and forward from the first restoration in the action of Eve to full restoration in the person of a new Wisdom and new Eve—Mary Magdalene.

The Valentinian Scheme of All Creation: A Simplified Version

The Work of the Great God

On Day One, God says, "Let there be light" = *phôs* = Man

The Light-Man, beyond male and female

The Descent of Being

From the Great God emerge successive pairs of spiritual Beings, male and female, and finally

The male Christ and the female Wisdom

Wisdom acts on her own, in her longing for God

Wisdom falls

The Boundary, dividing spirit from matter, restores order

Wisdom gives birth to the ill-formed Lesser God

The Work of the Lesser God

The Lesser God creates our everyday universe and within it

Adam and Eve, from Adam

Eve acts on her own, in her longing for knowledge of God

The Lesser God expels Adam and Eve from Eden

The Work of the Redeemer

From the Great God descends

JESUS, THE REDEEMER, to redeem the female Spirituals,

who long for knowledge of God

The Cross, dividing spirit from matter, restores order

The Ascent of the Redeemed Beings

The redeemed spirituals, beyond male and female

Valentinian Cosmology: A Theory of *Everything*

So how does the whole creative sequence begin? Let's hear one of the Gnostic stories told in these terms to account, in effect, for everything. From one generation to the next, we will be following a succession of pairs, each engendering the next such pair, and so eventually we reach our own physical world and our pairs of men and women. (We should not think of time passing between one spiritual generation and the next; there is a logic to the successive pairs, and the order of their unfolding is primarily conceptual rather than temporal.) Pairs and generation: we are about to hear how the Gnostics, speaking of the core of creation, spoke about sex. To clarify the stages of creation and redemption we will encounter, here in the accompanying chart is a (simplified and overschematic) summary of the Valentinians' history of creation. I need to ask your indulgence. Do not look at the chart as an instruction manual or technical diagram or even as a map, but as a (rather surprising) work of art, a painting that reflects and evokes by its orderly pattern the beauty and coherence of all creation. The cosmos as a whole, men and women and the individual's soul and spirit—each can be understood precisely and only when the others are understood.

The First Forefather—of both sexes or of neither—inhabited his own Silence or Solitude, in which he thought his own First Thought. Generation is under way. Forefather and his Thought are distinct, but inseparable. They engender Mind, which inhabits the realm of Truth and populates it with Reasoning Word and with the Life that is intrinsic to this Word. In this spiritual realm, whatever exists comes into being by the conjunction of male and female and their paired offspring. (The grammatical gender of the Greek nouns involved, masculine and feminine, match the "gender" of each power, male and female.) All these well-ordered, balanced pairs long for the knowledge of God, but across their harmony sounds a sudden, jarring discord made by the unilateral action of Wisdom tipping the whole order off balance as she strains upward by herself to see the Father. She is brought back into the essential symmetry of Being by union with her consort, Christ. But she by herself, without a father's input, is pregnant.

What could emerge from mother Wisdom without a father's collaboration? According to most of the obstetrics of the ancient world, the mother provided just the matter from which a child was made. The father's seed provided its shape and character; he made it what it was. The offspring of a mother alone, unformed by a father's contribution, could only be an ill-formed monster. Who then was Wisdom's child? The lesser god (known as the Demiurge or Creator) who would go on to create this ill-formed, misbegotten universe of ours.

So far, so good (or so bad). But we will want to look more closely at the First Forefather. He must be One. But is he utterly single and sexless, or is he the potential for male and female together? It is not surprising that Gnostic speculation took different forms here; the Gnostics needed to preserve *both* his singleness *and* his power to generate. The heresy hunter Hippolytus was determined to show that the Valentinians were really Pythagorean and not Christian at all. He described their First Father as a Monad, unbegotten, imperishable, incomprehensible, and (for those Valentinians who remained true to their roots) unwedded, unfeminine, and lacking in nothing. He has to acknowledge, nonetheless, that some Valentinians "think it impossible that from a male alone there could proceed a generation at all; so they reckon along with the Father of the universe, so that he may be a father, Silence as his spouse."[21] (The Gnostics are often described as dualists, sharply distinguishing two principles: on the one hand, spirit and goodness, on the other hand, matter and evil. The description is misleading. The Gnostics were the heirs of Plato: everything—spiritual and material, good and evil—is ultimately derived from the single principle of the supreme, incomprehensible One.)

This may sound like a wild cosmological fantasy. But we must keep in mind the chart's fifth column, for in all these patterns the Gnostics sought to describe as well the individual human being, a tiny copy of the constituents and structure of all reality. The Gnostics have suffered as the children of this abortive world, but all is not lost. Eve, acting unilaterally again but drawing her partner with her, launched the restoration of knowledge. Now it is for Jesus to open the way to the Fullness within and beyond this life. The Gnostics will, in reascent to the realms of spiritual reality, be reintegrated into the wholeness—of the individual and the cosmos—for which each Gnostic was made.

The disruption that Wisdom caused in the cosmos and causes in the individual is overcome at last. In this great drama, some Gnostics saw in the companions of Jesus a precedent for themselves and their relation with the Redeemer. One figure above all was suited to be the human image of that yearning Wisdom, now reconciled to the Redeemer and to order: *Mary Magdalene*. To her rich and varied story in the Gnostic texts we now turn.[22]

7

UNITED IN THE BRIDAL BEDROOM

Mary Magdalene, the Saviour's Companion

> There were three who always walked with the Lord: Mary his mother, and his sister, and the Magdalene, the one who was called his companion. For Mary is his sister, and his mother, and his partner.[1]
>
> *Of Mary Magdalene, we read that Christ or the Saviour* loved her more than all the disciples and used to kiss her often on her [. . .]. The rest of the disciples . . . said to him, "Why do you love her more than all of us?"
>
> Gospel of Philip 59.6–10; 63.30–64.2

Mary Magdalene as "companion" and "partner," often kissed by Jesus—what were the readers of the *Gospel of Philip* to make of this? What are we to make of it? If we speculate what word is missing in the manuscript, we will likely imagine an erotic frisson and guess that Jesus kissed Mary Magdalene often "on the mouth." No wonder the *Gospel of Philip* values, above all other symbols, the symbol of the bridal bedroom; here man and woman, united in love, surely echoed the marital union of Jesus and Mary. If there were those who resented the claims of and for women that women could wield authority in the churches, most of all they would have resented the long-remembered intimacy between Jesus and Mary, which still, a century after her death, lent such authority to her name. This is a gripping story of all too human love and jealousy, but is it really the story behind the *Gospel of Philip*?

Such ideas lead on to a second speculation. There is a popular impression that Jesus and Mary Magdalene can really be understood when we acknowledge in the records of their relationship all the contours of a "sacred marriage," familiar in the pagan mysteries, between a god and goddess or between a god or goddess and a mortal, and such marriage was a celebration of sexual energy. What the Gnostics found in the stories about Jesus and Mary they symbolized in the bridal bedroom of Gnostic ritual, and in the stories and rituals alike the Gnostics were celebrating human—and unashamedly sexual—love between man and woman. Here again is a vivid account of Jesus and Mary and rituals in the ancient pagan world, but are these really the connections shaping the *Gospel of Philip*?

The Gnostics did seem to their contemporary opponents to be copying the pagan mystery religions, so it is certainly appropriate for us to bring those mysteries into the frame. The mysteries, cults of initiation, were ubiquitous, their public celebrations were famously lavish, and in some settings (as at Eleusis, outside Athens) even the private rituals were watched by thousands of initiates. Some of those mysteries did involve at the heart of their rituals at least a symbol of sexual potency and perhaps, in some cases, a form of sacred marriage between divine and human, heaven and earth. The great festival at Eleusis marked the death and restoration of Persephone or Korē (Gk, "Maiden"), daughter of the grain goddess Demeter; the ritual, it seems, came to its climax in the sexual union of priest and priestess. We can look as well beyond the mysteries themselves. At the great Dionysiac festival in the springtime the honorary "king" of Athens appointed fourteen priestesses, headed by the queen, his own wife; the rituals culminated in the sacred marriage of the god Dionysus—perhaps played by the king—and the queen.

More hints glint at us. Dionysiac initiation involved a giant phallus. At initiation into the mysteries of Attis the candidate would declare, "I have slipped into the bedroom." At initiation into those of Sabazius, candidates would have a [metal] snake slipped through their clothing, representing "the deity gliding through the lap." One rite of Isis involved the preparation of a bed covered with linen, "which is unspeakable for the profane." Most telling—and most bizarre—of all is the story of a distinguished and famously virtuous Roman woman who was fooled by the priests of Isis into believing that the god Anubis wanted sex with her; her would-be lover was in fact an upper-class Roman, Decius Mundus, whose advances she had rejected. She duly went to the temple of Isis, spent the night there, and told her family and friends afterward of her night with Anubis—until Decius Mundus told her how much he had enjoyed their lovemaking. It was surprising but not, it seems, incredible that a god should summon a human for sex.[2]

So far, so good. But we should beware. The public parts of the mysteries were very public indeed, but the details and claimed significance of the private rituals were known only to initiates throughout all the pagan centuries and will never be known again. We should certainly not assume these rituals were a simple celebration of sexual life. The union of priest and priestess at Eleusis followed the "sacrifice" of a child to mimic and make up for the death of Persephone and to appease Demeter's wrath. Again, Dionysus, god of wine and of the frenzy to which wine can lead, had been dragged from his throne by the Titans, torn to pieces, and eaten; the red wine of his festival recalled his blood. The cult's sexual rituals symbolized Dionysus's return; the victim was appeased by being given a woman and was revitalized in his own virility. There was a dark and violent background to these celebrations.

Symbols of Union: Sex and the Language of Sex

Just glimpses have reached us of the sexual elements in such rituals and of their significance. Let's turn now to the Gnostics themselves. The *Gospel of Philip* was written for communities influenced by the great Christian Gnostic thinker of the second century, Valentinus. Valentinus came from Egypt to Rome around 136 CE. There was a range of differing stories and teachings among his followers, generated by different communities to answer the central questions of individual, social, and cosmic existence. As it stands, the *Gospel of Philip* is a collection of sayings ascribed to Jesus, parables and doctrines.[3] It was compiled in Greek (in an area where Syriac was well known) and translated in the second or third century into the Coptic version in which it has survived. We do not know at which stage it attained precisely its present contents or confusing shape; for convenience, I will call the final editors who brought it to its present form by the single name, "Philip."

The Syrian background is important. We have heard of Thomas's "solitaries," who seem to have renounced any sexual activity. The Syrian churches encouraged a rigorous asceticism, and they were quite prepared to speak of spiritual beauty in terms of physical beauty precisely to draw their members away from the dangers of the flesh to the glories of the spirit. We should never assume that the Syrian writers, when they used the language of sex, were writing about sex. The *Acts of Thomas* (another text linked, like the *Gospel of Thomas,* with Judas Thomas the Twin) includes a marriage song that Thomas sings just before the marriage of the king's daughter. It is just what we would expect in the celebration of a marriage:

> The maiden is the daughter of light,
> Delightful is the sight of her, radiant with shining beauty.
> Her chamber is full of light, breathing a scent of balsam and all
> sweet herbs.

Twelve are they that serve before her, having their gaze towards
the bridegroom,
And they shall be at that marriage for which the princes gather
together.

From the Acts of Thomas,
First Act (Greek version)[4]

But this Thomas is about to turn the marriage upside down. He will appear in the bridal bedroom and persuade the young couple to renounce all filthy intercourse in expectation of "that true and incorruptible marriage in which you will be groomsmen entering into that bridal bedroom which is full of immortality and light." His song has been sung not for the couple's physical consummation, but for their attendance at the marriage of the church to Christ the Lord.

The *Gospel of Thomas* had demanded that every woman, to be worthy of the kingdom, must make herself male in order to be ready to leave behind the turbulence of our sexed and gendered lives and be transformed, in visionary ascent, into the unsullied image of God borne by the First Human. Thomas mentions the bridal bedroom twice, most strikingly to claim it is the celibates who will enter the true bridal bedroom of the Spirit. For Philip, the bridal bedroom is a major motif. The present life offers an admission to the bedroom that is a genuine anticipation of the Gnostic's final entry into the bedroom of the spirit's "Fullness," when the Gnostic will be united with his or her angelic counterpart for the wedding banquet in heaven and then process from the banquet into the bridal bedroom, the Fullness itself, for the consummation of their union.

Philip is enthralled by the language he has to use. He acknowledges the different uses of the same terms with reference to the densely material and the spiritual realms, and he explores both the necessity of this use and its dangers—how this is the only way to convey what needs conveying and how easily people can misunderstand the meaning intended. Our antennae should be alert. Philip is both assessing and deploying the ambiguities of the language we use to speak about ourselves and our relation to others and to God. He can say what he means only by saying as well what he does not mean; the rituals he writes of can signify what they do only at the risk of seeming to the unwary to signify what they do not. "Names given to the world are very deceptive, for they divert our thoughts from what is correct to what is incorrect"; so with God, the father, the son, the holy spirit, life, light, and resurrection. And no language or ritual is more important for Philip, in itself and in its possible misunderstanding, than the language and ritual of the bridal bedroom.[5]

The Valentinians:
Brides and Children of the Bridal Bedroom

The bridal bedroom is the symbol of union and conception that Philip invokes to do justice both to baptism at the start of Christian life and to the consummation of that life in the spiritual realms. Philip envisions each individual Gnostic as a woman who must be reunited with an angelic counterpart in the Fullness as a wife is united with her husband on earth. It is natural to ask if Philip's communities had been drawn to this symbol of completion in the Fullness by one earthly union, above all, of which they had heard, the union of the bride Mary Magdalene and her bridegroom Jesus. To find out, we need to give to Mary Magdalene the place she is given by Philip in the gospel's great scheme of things, and in the chart on page 114 you will see where she belongs. As before, I ask you not to view the chart as a technical diagram, but to engage your imagination on all its different parts at once. We should not keep a sharp distinction between the figures stacked up in each of the chart's columns; each is an aspect of the others above or below it and can be understood only when they are.

Reality, for the Valentinians, is the interpenetration of three realms: the realm of the Fullness, a domain of the Spirit, which will at some stage be accessible to the Gnostic spirits; the heavenly realms, present home to angels and lower than the Fullness; and the realm of the flesh, in which our bodies trap us—a realm from whose temptations we can nonetheless be rescued to pass through the realms of heaven to the Fullness of the Spirit. And present in each is the Lord: in the Fullness he is Christ, in heaven he is the Saviour, and on earth he is Jesus.[6] And in each realm he has a female counterpart: in the Fullness, the Spirit itself; in heaven, Wisdom, whose lower self triggered creation by her unilateral action; and on earth—*Mary Magdalene*. Mary is not *just* Mary Magdalene; she is one member of a trio of Marys—or one-third of a single Mary—that is related to Christ in each of the three layers of creation. This is alien to us now; and it is just one of the strange ambiguities Philip found in the names of the most important people and powers with which his gospel had to deal. Philip finds a double sense in all the crucial terms he must use. "Truth did not come into the world naked, but it came in types and images; the world will not receive truth in any other way."[7] The truth that had come to the Gnostics' knowledge in Mary Magdalene had come in a type and an image that must be rightly interpreted.

The Valentinians knew as well as other Christians that there is a deep— and irresoluble—ambiguity in the status here on earth of initiated Christians. They are already freed from the powers of evil, but still tempted and buffeted

The Gospel of Philip: The Role of the Three Marys

Realm of the Fullness/Spirit	Christ	in a pair with	Spirit	who is **the mother of Jesus**, i.e., Mary
				The Bridal Bedroom
Realm of the Emerging Powers/ Heaven	The Savior	who rescues by coming to pair with	Wisdom (who had acted not in a pair)	who is **the sister of the Savior**, i.e., Mary
				Home of angels
Realm of Earth/ Flesh	Jesus	in a pair with (and so rescuing)	the Church of spiritual humans	as in Jesus's companion, i.e., Mary Magdalene
				Home of Angels' Human Images

on all sides; citizens already of heaven, but still all too frail; the heirs of immortality and of an everlasting life, but still destined to end the present life in death. There is an ambiguity built in to any mention of the Christian calling in this life and its final fruition in the next.

The ambiguity becomes all the more vivid when we are concerned with revelation, the actual disclosure of one realm in the terms of the other, of the hereafter and above in terms of the present and now. Philip turns questions of time into questions of meaning, probing the words used to describe structures and relationships in our ordinary life, which must be used to describe structures and relationships in a deeper life, which is nonetheless in intimate connection with our own. (The connection between these lives is itself an additional structure and relationship that those images must be used to describe.) To understand Philip's premises and aims, we might set aside the temporal sequence—the horizontal axis, as it were—of past, present, and future and chart our lives, instead, on the vertical axis of our dense physical world, then heaven, and then, at the highest heights, the Fullness. But we are still distinguishing what Philip would hold inextricably together. It would do no justice to a Valentinian to insist that he or she was at any one time on one and only one rung of any such spiritual, celestial ladder. We will continue to speak of movement onward (into the future, towards death and beyond) and of movement upward (away from the flesh towards heaven and the Fullness beyond), and in doing so we are speaking too of movement inward to the truth behind the illusions of this world—and inward to the realm of the Spirit within the Gnostics themselves.

Let's follow the Valentinians' theory of creation and the roles of the Marys within it. As we saw in the last chapter, creation was seen as the fruit of division after division, pair after pair. First Forefather reflected upon himself, and that reflection was his own Thought; their union in thought gave rise to the next generation of pairs, and so on. The principle remains steady: to each being there corresponds a counterpart, male is matched with female, and together they bring the next generation into being. And the members of each pair *belong together;* there is a match between them. They are the natural reflection of each other, true counterparts.

We have heard already of the Gnostic notion of the fall of Wisdom. Philip distinguishes two Wisdoms, higher and lower. It was the lower Wisdom who acted unilaterally in her search for knowledge, was sundered from the Fullness, and, despairing and barren, was rescued by the Saviour sent out from the Fullness. In one version of the Valentinian story, she saw the Saviour, broke out into praise—and in that praise created the angels.[8] The angels, then, were the constituents of heaven, between the Fullness and earth. To each Gnostic on earth there corresponds such an angel in heaven, the Gnostic's counterpart who *is* the Gnostic's true spiritual self: *"I tell you,"* says the biblical Jesus of his followers, *"that their angels in heaven forever look upon the face of my Father in heaven."* [9]

Wisdom, however, had given birth, without a father, to the lesser god who created our world. And as in the realms above, so, by analogy, on earth below. All non-Gnostics could be seen as the ill-formed product of Wisdom's unpartnered Fall. The Gnostics by contrast were the children of Wisdom and the Saviour, the earthly counterparts of their heavenly children, the angels. The Gnostics, therefore, were children of the bridal bedroom, of two parents. "As long as we were children of the female only, as if of a base pairing, incomplete and infants and senseless and weak and without form, brought forth like abortions, we were children of the woman; but when we have received form from the Saviour, we have become children of a husband and a bridal bedroom." [10]

And these children of the bedroom were also, in a different light, the bedroom's *brides:* "When we were begotten [*in baptism*] we were united." The children enter for union into the rooms of their own parents' union. Once more, scripture provided the inspiration. *"When I found him,"* sings the bride in the Song of Songs, *"whom my soul loves, I clasped him and would not let him go, not till I had brought him to my mother's house, to the room where she conceived me!"* As Wisdom was female, so too were the Gnostics; as Wisdom was given the Saviour as her partner, so the Gnostics were given his angels. "The Saviour and Wisdom," as Irenaeus describes the Valentinian theory, "are the bridegroom and bride, while the bridal bedroom is the full extent of the Fullness. The spiritual seed, being divested of their animal souls and becoming intelligent spirits, shall enter in within the Fullness and be bestowed as brides on those angels who wait upon the Saviour." For this reason, records Clement, "it is said that the women will be transformed into men, and the church here below into angels." [11] As femaleness was repeatedly deferred in the Gnostic accounts of the beginning, so femaleness is overcome or absorbed into maleness as the Valentinians approach their consummation and their end.

The Fullness (the place of the Spirit) beyond heaven, heaven itself (the place of angels), and our own earth are now structured in parallel. Once more we hear of that lower and barren Wisdom, paradoxically the mother of many. [12] Where this is described in the *Gospel of Philip* the text is broken, but its thrust is clear:

> As for the Wisdom who is called "the barren," she is the mother
> of the angels and the companion of the [. . .] Mary Magdalene

[. . .] loved her more than all the disciples and used to kiss her often on her [. . .].

Gospel of Philip 63.30–36

Wisdom is the Saviour's companion; they are united in heaven and give rise to the angels. Mary Magdalene is Jesus's companion; they are united on earth and a birth follows. "It is by a kiss," says Philip, "that the perfect conceive and give birth. For this reason we also kiss one another. We receive conception from the grace which is one another."[13] Mary Magdalene, an icon of the "perfect," is united with Jesus by the kiss of the bridal bedroom and so from his grace is herself engendered as its child.

Here is a reunion of male and female in proper partnership, which undoes the turbulent, unilateral work of the lower Wisdom. But such wisdom and such union are rare, and those who do not share it resent it. Philip describes the envy of the lesser powers when Adam was united with the Spirit; so the disciples of Jesus envy Mary Magdalene her intimacy with the Saviour.[14] She has once more taken the privileged place of the Beloved Disciple. At issue is not romantic intimacy, but wisdom.

The rest of the disciples [. . .]. They said to him, "Why do you love Mary more than all of us?" The Saviour answered and said to them, "Why do I not love you like her? When a blind man and one who sees are both together in darkness, they are no different from one another. When the light comes, then he who sees will see the light, and he who is blind will remain in darkness."

Gospel of Philip 63.36–64.9

Baptism: Entering the Bridal Bedroom

An interpenetration of present and future, promise and fulfilment is central to classic Christian doctrine. But the Valentinians put equal weight on the past as well, on the emanation of pairs—dividing and engendering—that had led from the First Forefather to this present world. Christ and his counterpart, the Spirit, were at the heart of the spiritual realms; the Saviour and Wisdom were central to the creation of this material world; and Mary Magdalene represented the Gnostics within this world who would be restored by union with their own personal counterpart, an angel of Jesus. The Spirit, Wisdom, the Magdalene: the mother, the sister, and the companion—and all of them known by the same name, Mary.

The Gnostics themselves exemplified the pattern of all creation from its very start, a pattern always being repeated but already—in its internal logic—completed. Mainstream Christianity has always emphasized that Jesus's life on earth, once for all time, was the vital turning point in God's relationship to his creation. The Gnostic's life, by contrast, did not echo just Jesus's one-off life, death, and resurrection, but the whole cosmic outgoing and return of which Jesus's earthly life was a paradigm. The once-only historical Jesus was certainly important for revealing the whole sequence. "It was not only when he appeared that he voluntarily laid down his life, but he voluntarily laid down his life from the very day the world came into being."[15] What Jesus did on earth, Christ and Saviour had been doing in the higher realms since creation began; what brought Jesus into being on earth was the same process of union that had engendered Christ in the Fullness itself. So Christ (qua Jesus) was a son of the bridal bedroom as well as being (qua Saviour) its groom.

> Jesus revealed [at his baptism] in the Jordan the fullness of the kingdom of heaven. He who was born before everything was born again; he who was already anointed was anointed again; he who was redeemed was once again redeemed. Truly, a mystery must be spoken. The Father of everything joined with the virgin who had come down [Wisdom], and fire illuminated him on that day [for fire was said to have descended on Jesus at his baptism] and revealed the great bridal bedroom. Therefore, his body [that is, Jesus's spiritual body] came into being on that day. It came forth from the bridal bedroom as that which has come into being from the bridegroom and the bride.
>
> *Gospel of Philip 70.34–71.11*

What was true of Jesus was true of his Valentinian followers. The angelic part of the Valentinians with which they must be reunited existed long before their physical birth here. "The Lord said, 'Blessed is he who is before he came into being. For he who is, has been and shall be.'"[16] No simply clicking clock—marking past, present, and future—could be calibrated to record this interlocking, overlapping sequence.

The baptismal beginning, as we have seen, adumbrates the final bridal union. "Some of them," we hear from Irenaeus, "prepare a bridal bedroom and perform an initiatory mystery rite, with certain invocations, for those who are being initiated, and they claim that they are effecting a spiritual marriage, after the image of the pairings above." So Philip links present and future status closely together: "We live either in this world or in the resurrection. . . . They are to acquire the resurrection in this life so that when they strip off the flesh they may be found in repose"; for "those

Companions and Partners: What's in a Name?

What did it mean to be the companion or partner of Jesus? *Koinōnos*—"companion"—is a word borrowed into Coptic from Greek, in which it denotes a person who shares with another in an undertaking that might be anything from a business enterprise to marriage. The word occurs twice in the *Gospel of Philip*: once, to speak of Mary Magdalene as the companion of Jesus, and later, in a damaged portion of the text, to speak of either Wisdom or Mary as the companion of the Saviour. Other words with the same stem, *koinōn-*, appear more frequently to designate sexual partnership; at least three times Philip uses them of adulterous relationships and once of human marriage. And then there is the Coptic *hōtr*, a word of overlapping meaning used as well for pairs yoked together. (Philip himself uses this of normal sexual intercourse among humans and animals.) Philip uses the two terms interchangeably: "There were three who always walked with the Lord: Mary his mother, and his sister, and the Magdalene, the one who was called his companion (*koinōnos*). For Mary is his sister, and his mother, and his partner (*hōtre*)."[17]

But this is only half the story. Philip also writes about the union of Gnostic and angelic counterpart, and with just the same words, *koinōn-* and *hōtr*. Three times Philip uses the *koinōn-* words to speak of the Gnostics' union with their angelic counterparts or of its anticipation in the bridal bedroom or of both at once. And Philip himself points out that *hōtr* is used of both the earthly union of husband and wife and of the—quite different—union fulfilled in the heavenly realm.[18] As we are seeing throughout this chapter, Philip finds in our palpable, earthly realm the images through which we can glimpse the realm beyond; he must use the language of the one to speak of the other.

who do not receive the light while they are here, they will not be able to receive it in the other place," after death. The Valentinians spoke of union in the bridal bedroom on "the Lord's Day," so by union they could refer at once both to the final consummation and to the weekly liturgy and Philip could write of unity with the angels here and now at the Eucharist.[19]

Irenaeus mocks the claim of Gnostics who believed themselves to be in the bridal bedroom already. It may well be true that there were converts who (as Irenaeus scathingly describes them) were puffed up to such an extent that they think they are neither in heaven nor on earth but that they have passed within the Fullness; and having already embraced their angels, they walk with a strutting gait and supercilious countenance, possessing all the pompous air of a rooster. Some among them say it is appropriate that the person who has "descended from above" exercise noble behavior, and this is the reason they put on a display of dignity in this supercilious manner.

Irenaeus, Against Heresies *3.15.2*

Irenaeus is condemning what utterly orthodox theologians would elsewhere praise: the dignity of deportment that befits the saints who are recovering the image of God in which they were created.[20]

A Kiss Is Just a Kiss?

Of Mary Magdalene, we read that Christ or the Saviour "loved her more than all the disciples and used to kiss her often on her [. . .]. The rest of the disciples . . . said to him, 'Why do you love her more than all of us?'" Perhaps this kiss represented a kiss within a ritual of the bridal bedroom, perhaps it was a public symbol of some such (private) ritual, or perhaps there was no connection between the kiss and the bedroom; we cannot now be sure.

Kissing was a liturgical form. We know from the New Testament of the kiss of peace exchanged in the liturgy. Paul's instruction to the Romans, *"Greet one another with a holy kiss,"* follows a list of both men and women.[21]

A kiss on the mouth could signify or portend the transfer of breath or life or the knowledge that will lead to life. Another Nag Hammadi text tells of Jesus praising James. Then, says James, "he kissed my mouth; he took hold of me, saying, 'My beloved! Behold, I shall reveal to you those things that neither the heavens nor their powers have known.'" At the end of *Pistis Sophia,* Book 3, Mary Magdalene kisses Salome before answering a question Salome herself has asked, and Salome responds, "The Saviour has power to make me understanding like yourself"; she surely stands for other followers too whom Mary's wisdom will enlighten. Master and pupil, in one mystical text, kiss before a mystical ascent. Those singing one Syrian psalm would say that immortal life itself had embraced and kissed them.[22]

The Valentinian imagery is dazzling. When the Father and a higher Wisdom join in the bridal bedroom, their child is Jesus's spiritual body, which the total of all the Valentinian brides and their angelic grooms, in consummated union, will eventually compose. When the catechumens are kissed at initiation, they are engendered as children of the bedroom of which they are, in anticipation, also the brides. When those initiates are finally united with their counterpart in the bedroom above, they become their final reintegrated male-female selves and restore in themselves the unity that Adam and Eve once were.

The Valentinians relished the wealth and density of this bridal motif. An inscription has survived from a grand Roman dining room of the second century. Its Valentinian owner expected banquets to be held in the room after ceremonies of initiation; the bath of baptism in a pool or stream would

---

Most striking is the Jewish mystical romance of Joseph and Asenath; the conversion of Asenath to Judaism makes possible the fruition of their love. The author is using their kiss to good effect:

> And Joseph put his arm around her, and Asenath put hers around Joseph, and they kissed each other for a long time and both came to life in their spirit. And Joseph kissed Asenath and gave her spirit of life, and he kissed her the second time and gave her spirit of wisdom, and he kissed her the third time and gave her spirit of truth.

> Joseph and Asenath *19.10–11*

We readily imagine the kiss of Jesus and Mary Magdalene in the *Gospel of Philip* to be simply erotic, but this drains it of the significance it certainly had. "It is by a kiss," says Philip, "that the perfect conceive and give birth. For this reason we also kiss one another. We receive conception from the grace which is one another." So the Gnostics by their rituals of initiation engender their own spiritual siblings.[23] By such a kiss, the new members were conceived as children of the bridal bedroom in which they will live from then on with the Son of God and in which, within the Fullness, they will be ultimately be reintegrated with their own angelic counterpart.

be followed by a procession, lit by torches and accompanied by a hymn, to the banquet. Here, as we would expect, are "bridal bedrooms." The term is describing either the baptism itself or the whole scene of the bath, procession, and banquet; these were all elements in a Roman wedding.

> Fellow brothers, celebrate for me with torches the baths
>   of bridal bedrooms.
> They hunger for banquets in our rooms,
> Singing hymns to the Father and praising the Son.
> In that place may there be flowing of a single spring
>   and of truth.[24]

The baths of baptism, the banquets of the Eucharist, and the bedrooms of marriage—all are evoked in one room that was likely the setting for the culmination of a single coordinated ritual. Was this ritual consummated in some specifically "marital" form? We simply do not know, and we cannot be surprised that outsiders—who could watch the torchlit procession from pool or river to the "wedding banquet" in this grand house—suspected that such suggestive display was a prelude to sexual activity. It was a brave church that tried in a "bridal bedroom" to do sacramental justice to our sexual and spiritual nature and to the revelation offered by each about the other.

Let's imagine, for a moment, how the following formula of initiation might have been heard by an initiate—and then by a caustic heresy hunter. This quotation is relayed to us by Irenaeus with characteristic indignation as the honeyed words with which Marcus, a follower of Valentinus, seduced women; but perhaps, in some such form, they really were words recited by a master over the candidates in a solemn service of initiation. (Marcus claimed to be investing the women with the power of prophecy; such power was often described in terms of sexual union between the prophet and the prophetic spirit.)

> "I am eager to make you a partaker of my Grace, since the Father of Everything continually sees your angel before his face. Now the place of your greatness is among us; it is right that we become one. Receive first the gift of Grace from me and by me. Adorn yourself as a bride expecting her bridegroom, so that you may be what I am and I may be what you are. Set the seed of light in your bridal bedroom. Receive from me a husband, and be receptive, while you are received by him."
>
> *Irenaeus*, Against Heresies *1.13.3*

This Life and the Next:
The Journey to the Holy of Holies

For Valentinians past, present, and future were all linked. There was, nonetheless, progress to be made in this life, and death still lay inescapably ahead. Irenaeus gives a full account of the "redemption" promised by the Valentinians. He reports that the term was variously applied, and not least to the Valentinian last rites, offered to the dying, when oil and water were again poured on the head and strange formulas were uttered "in order that they may become unassailable by and invisible to the principalities and powers, and their inner man ascend to the realm of the invisible. The dying were instructed what to say, when they encountered the powers: 'I am a son from the Father, a son in the preexistent one. . . . I go again to that which is my own, whence I came forth.'"[25]

We have heard such language before. The *Gospel of Thomas* had armed believers against the demons, around and within, who would endanger the visionary's journey to the sight of God. And in the *Gospel of Philip* we are again on the strange threshold between visionary journeys in this life and the ascent of the dead to bliss. Philip praises those who "come out of this world and so can no longer be detained on the grounds that they were in the world"; they are above desire and fear and envy and are not vulnerable to the attack of the powers. "The powers do not see those who are clothed in the perfect light, and so are not able to detain them." So much for this life. And for the next, "One will clothe himself in this light in the union."[26] Such a journey—in this life or the next—had an imagined route and an imagined destination, the bridal bedroom. At this point one set of images could converge upon another. A rabbinic tradition described the Holy of Holies in Jerusalem as the bridal bedroom of God, where he and his beloved people Israel belonged together in union. *Who is this,* asks the Song of Songs, *who comes out of the wilderness like pillars of smoke, perfumed with myrrh and frankincense? Look, here is the couch of Solomon!* There were rabbis who interpreted the couch as the Temple, filled with the smoke of incense. "And why was the sanctuary compared to a couch? Because just as this couch serves the engendering of children, even so the sanctuary: everything that was in it was fruitful and multiplied."[27]

So Philip, with the bridal bedroom in mind, had good reason to envision as well the Temple in Jerusalem and the movement there ever inward towards the Holy of Holies. "There were," he says, "three buildings specifically for sacrifice in Jerusalem. . . . 'The holy of the holies' is the bridal bedroom." As we would expect by now, Philip evokes the movement inward towards the heart of the Temple as the movement inward to the Valentinians's own spirit. Philip introduces a theme familiar from the *Gospel of Thomas*. Here is Philip's version: "He said, 'I come to make the things below like the things above, and the things outside like those inside.'" Philip refers to two "heavenly men" as well known to his readers: the lower, who is revealed, and the higher, to whom belongs the hidden world. But Philip insists, "It would be better for them to say, 'The inner and the outer.'" He reminds his readers how Jesus had spoken of his *Father who is in secret* and told his disciples to go into their chamber and shut the door and pray to their Father who is in secret—that is, says Philip, "the one who is within them all." But that which is within them all is the Fullness; it is of this that they say, "That which is above them."[28]

The journey is the journey of *visionaries* who are transformed by what they see to become what they see. "You saw the spirit, you became spirit. You saw Christ, you became Christ. You saw the Father, you shall become Father. So in this place you see everything and do not see yourself, but in that place you do see yourself—and what you see you shall become."[29] The Valentinian is already in this life being reintegrated into his or her original and destined unity within Christ's spiritual body. So the Valentinian is becoming a Christ, ready to enter the Holy of Holies, where Christ the High Priest belongs, and so to behold (as the High Priest does) the Father himself; and the sight will transform the Valentinian (highest mystery of all!) into Father.

Philip is quietly promising what Thomas loudly demanded—the movement towards maleness here and now, in his readers' visionary ascent towards union with their male angelic counterpart. But Philip's three Marys, nonetheless, play a vital role. Mary Magdalene has emerged from the Spirit's Fullness and Wisdom's heaven to take shape in this physical world; so had every Gnostic emerged into this world. Mary Magdalene had been united with Jesus here on earth; so every Gnostic had at baptism been united in anticipation with his or her male counterpart among Jesus's angels in heaven. Mary Magdalene represents on earth her namesakes of soul and spirit, in heaven and the Fullness; so the Gnostics awaited their final fulfilment, transcending both body and soul, in their ascent to the Holy of Holies.

In the Gnostics' beginning is their end. It was the disordered split of male and female that had led to crisis. "When Eve was still in Adam," according to Philip, "death did not exist. When she was separated from him, death came into being. If he enters again and attains his former self, death will be no more. His separation became the beginning of death."[30] This separation—and so death itself—is overcome in the union of the bridal bedroom, when Eve is reabsorbed into Adam and Adam recovers the "Life" he lost at their separation.

For a poignant testimony to the hope the Valentinians invested in their faith and its rituals, here is a second Roman inscription. A husband speaks, on a monument to his dead wife. It is in verse, and more elaborate verse than the translation can reveal—the opening letters of the lines, in Greek, spell SOPHIE. Once more the motifs converge from different rituals, all of them evoking in this life the consummation to be attained in the next. As Sophie ("Wisdom") will have been bathed and anointed and entered her "bridal bedroom" both at her baptism and at her marriage—so she has now rushed, washed and anointed at death, to the ultimate bridal embrace. "Sophie," writes the husband, "my sister, my bride," as the lover in the Song of Songs addresses his beloved. However they actually lived, he and Sophie were husband and wife:

> Yearning for the Father's light, my sister, my bride, Sophie,
> Anointed in the baths of Christ with imperishable, sacred oil
> You hastened to gaze on the Realms' divine faces,
> The great angel of the great counsel, the true Son;
> You entered the bridal bedroom and into the bosom of the Father
> You leapt, immortal. . . .[31]

The Symbols of Consummation

Images, symbols, and rituals—we have seen how rich and multivalent these, in Valentinian minds, could be. But everything is still in the mind, and we rightly ask, what did the Valentinians do with their *bodies*? And we have one couple, as ever, at the forefront of our mind. What did the Valentinians believe Jesus and Mary Magdalene had done together with their bodies?

The Valentinians were known to value marriage more highly than the ascetics did. The Valentinians drew a careful distinction between the true Gnostics shaped by spirit and those who could attain only to the level of salvation offered by the mean clothing of their half-knowing souls. Both groups shall attend the wedding banquet in heaven, where the angels already have their home. But only the spirituals, when mere soul can be shed and the spirit emerge from the chrysalis that has hidden it, shall pass into the bridal bedroom and attain to the vision of the Father in the intellectual and eternal marriage with their angels. In this setting, one detailed claim from Irenaeus may be well founded. He said there were Gnostics who used John's distinction between those *of* the world (the worldly) and those *in* the world but not of it (the spiritual): "Whoever,

Christian and Pagan: A Gnostic Sarcophagus?

The sarcophagus in Rome in the accompanying photo was believed by a great scholar of the 1920s to be Gnostic in origin. At each end two figures embrace, a standard motif in late antique art showing Eros (Love, with the larger wings) and Psyche (Soul, with the smaller). In the centre Jesus is flanked by a man and a woman, with a hanging behind them to symbolize heaven. The woman looks like a Muse, most probably Calliope (the Muse of heroic epic), the bearded, thoughtful man like a philosopher. But these are *pagan* motifs. To do justice to the sarcophagus, surely we should find a context in which all these figures, Christian and pagan alike, belong together—and we find it among the Gnostics. The winged figures recall the Valentinian image of all believers as female, awaiting their final union with their male angel; and Jesus is flanked by the Gnostic heroes Mary Magdalene and James. The sarcophagus, then, would have housed the bones of a Gnostic who had looked forward to angelic union in the realm of the spirit in accordance with James's and Mary's teaching.

Later scholars have been unconvinced. The sarcophagus remains an epitome of particular ancient beliefs, but probably not the Gnostics'. We are shown a Jesus who belonged between two symbols of ancient wisdom, a Muse and a philosopher, and who had fired the soul of the deceased with the divine love (Eros), which, as Plato had described centuries before, would raise the soul (Psyche) to heaven. Pagan and Christian are at one.[32]

Early Christian Sarcophagus: The Ascent of the Soul (marble, fourth or fifth century), Museo Nazionale Romano, Rome. Photo: Deutsches Archäologisches Institut, Rome (1957.0067 [Sansaini].

being *in* the world does not love a woman and unite with her, is not of the truth and shall not attain to it. But whoever, being *of* the world, does have intercourse with woman, shall not attain to the truth, because he has done so from lust. So those *of* the world must practice continence and good works."[33]

Clement quotes a vivid passage from a non-Valentinian Gnostic author. Clement's condemnation is careful; he recognizes that there is sound doctrine in here that has been distorted. "All things were one," reads the Gnostic passage, "but as it seemed good to its Unity not to be alone, an idea came forth from it, and it had intercourse with it and made the beloved conceive. In consequence of this there came forth from him an idea with which he had intercourse and made powers which cannot be seen or heard." This, Clement claims with disgust, was used among its believers to justify sexual love as a mystical communion. He contrasts the abuse to which the targets of his attack subject such doctrine with the "spiritual union" of the Valentinians. As we have seen, the Valentinians likely did endorse an actual sexual union between Valentinians themselves; driven not by desire—such as the misplaced desire of Wisdom for the sight of the Father!—but by the reasoning will, this was at once a physical and a *spiritual* union. Such union could lead, of course, to the birth of children, and one Valentinian text suggests that this was vital for the embodiment of the full number of Gnostics destined for ultimate reunion in the Fullness.[34]

How strange, then, that the Valentinian Philip seems to decry earthly, physically consummated marriage. He praises the marriage of the successive generations of spiritual beings, which led to the world's creation. "Great is the mystery of marriage," he says, "for without it the world would not have come into being." But then he decries its image, earthly marriage, as a "defilement." The true bridal bedroom, he says, is only for "free men and virgins"; Abraham's circumcision teaches us "that it is proper to destroy the flesh." Surely, then, Philip stands in the Syrian tradition of a radical renunciation of sexual activity: earthly marriage is a triumph of bestial flesh; his readers now "live with the Son of God" and can have no other bridegroom. (Valentinus himself put such value on continence in general that he argued that Jesus—apparently in part by an act of will—retained in his body everything that we would discharge from ours. This settles the question of whether Valentinus thought Jesus himself might have been sexually active; such a vision of Jesus's unbroken bodily integrity would allow no possibility of sexual emission.)[35]

So far, so good. But Philip has more to say than this. He denigrates earthly marriage, and yet in the very next lines he attends carefully and generously to the problem of sexual temptation; he is trying to do justice to our physical and psychological constitution as man or woman. He seems to envision a married couple protected from temptation by the union of each partner with that partner's own angel. This union would afford protection either against desire itself (making possible a chaste marriage, the couple "sitting next to each other") or against desire for other partners (making possible a loyal marriage shaped by the rational will of husband and wife).[36]

Philip seems ambivalent here, because he is. His churches were heir to the rigorist Christian mystics of Syria and were surrounded by the rigorist Gnostics of Africa. But they themselves were Valentinian, and Philip is finding a balance between rigorist and Valentinian ideals. We now associate sex with intimacy and excitement, commitment and parenthood. Philip placed it quite differently—in relation to the spiritual world where true union took place. The whole history of creation is a

A Strange Meal

Mary Magdalene, recipient of special revelations, was given some very strange disclosures indeed. According to the heresy hunter Epiphanius, a text known as the *Great Questions of Mary* relayed the following story. Alone with Jesus on the sacred mountain, Mary saw him produce a woman from his side and begin to make love to her; withdrawing from her before he came to climax, he then ate his own emission. "Thus we must do," he says to Mary, "that we may live."[37]

Jesus is clearly revealing himself as the new Adam from whom the new Eve is taken, but their union must not, by consummation, lead to the birth of additional earthbound generations. In the semen is soul or life, and so it must be consumed—and thereby afford more life—and not be wasted; but the physical bodies to which it might otherwise give rise are the work of the lower, demonic powers, whose purposes must be defeated.

Epiphanius follows the story with an account of various beliefs and proof-texts adduced by the groups that (he says) used the *Great Questions*. "If you do not eat the flesh of the Son of Man and drink his blood," says Jesus in John's gospel, "you have no life in you."[38] John was writing about the Eucharist, and the groups described by Epiphanius seem to have linked their ritual with the Eucharist too. Jesus's disciples had been horrified by his demand, and Mary story of divisions and unions and generation. With what images could the Valentinians hope to do justice to this saga? Precisely with the language and symbols *and reality* of sexual union. "Truth," writes Philip, "did not come into the world naked, but it came in types and images. The world will not receive truth in any other way." Philip evokes human marriage in its entirety—including its bridal bedroom and the consummation of marriage there—because he needs this whole symbol to expound the bridal union of Gnostics and their angels.

Philip treads a careful path between the conflicting claims for marriage he would have heard from married people and from celibates in and around his churches. On the one hand, for Philip, earthly marriage and its bridal bedroom are no better than a defilement, but, on the other, they provide the image, indispensable to our understanding, of the true bridal bedroom. On the one hand, marriage engenders children who may grow up to be Gnostic, but, on the other, spiritual children are conceived not

---

fainted at the revelation on the mountain. Any such practice was for most people as strange (even disgusting) then as it would be now.

These themes recur in *Pistis Sophia,* Book 4, and once more with Mary Magdalene to the fore. "We have heard," she says, "that there are some upon the earth who take sperm and menstrual blood and make a dish of lentils and eat it. Is this a seemly thing or not?" Mary is asking about a practice that her own reported vision on the mountain was used to authorize. But the Jesus of *Pistis Sophia*— clearly speaking for its authors—responds angrily, "Truly I say that this sin surpasses every sin and every iniquity."[39]

Mary is being used both by those who demanded and by those who condemned the practice. It is wholly unlikely that, if the ritual was ever actually enacted at all, Mary Magdalene had any part in its institution or suppression. Both sides were deploying her, two hundred years after her death, as the conduit of a supposed revelation. She was famous for such privileged disclosures and, as a woman, was well suited to ask her counterpart, Jesus, about such an instruction for men and women. (It is striking that menstrual blood was consumed as well as semen, so life was being ascribed to the woman's fluids as well as to the man's.) Epiphanius warns us how readily later leaders, in disagreement with each other and looking for an authoritative source for their teaching, could manipulate a figure such as Mary Magdalene.

by sex, but by baptism. On the one hand, there are real distinctions, in our sexual relationships, between the intercourse of husband and wife (in private) and prostitution (in public), and between specifically human marriage (controlled by reason and spirit) and the (unreasoning) indulgence of the appetites we share with the animals. But, on the other, these are chiefly important as clues to a higher distinction between the marital union of (even the purest) 'earthly marriage and the union of Gnostic and angel in the Fullness. On the one hand, earthly marriage is a genuine prophylactic, guarding Gnostics against temptation, but, on the other, there is a higher marriage awaiting the Gnostics from which they must not be distracted.

"The image [the Gnostic on earth] must rise again through the image [the bridal rituals]. The bridal bedroom and the image must enter through the image into the truth: this is the restoration." Those who do rise will acquire the name "Christian"; such a person "is no longer a Christian but a Christ."[40] For Philip, we *need* the flawed but genuine images our physical life offers us. So Philip freely uses suggestive language of Jesus and Mary Magdalene as companions before he himself, in the climactic section of the gospel, turns to the great erotic mystery of the "bridal bedroom." Even in marriage sexual activity is undertaken under cover of darkness; what a sad token of its inadequacy. Philip's readers are called to look forward to a different union, when they will be united light with light, not human with human, and in the light, not under cover of darkness. And they can live out some part of that life in its image within this life.

Philip ends his gospel with an extended meditation on the initiation represented by the bridal bedroom and on the future it portends for believers. The register of his prose changes. He is now offering not just description or analysis; he is *inspiring* his readers, with a lyrical evocation of the scene, to long for what they are offered. I have inserted some glosses in brackets:

> The mysteries of truth are revealed, though in type and image. The bridal bedroom, however, remains hidden. We shall go in there by means of lowly types and forms of weakness. The hidden things of truth have opened to us. The Holies of the Holies were revealed, and the bridal bedroom invited us in.
>
> He who will receive that light will not be seen, nor can he be detained [by the cosmic powers, on his route from this world to his final union with his angelic counterpart]. And none shall be able to torment a person like this, even while he dwells in the world. And again when he leaves the world, he has already received the truth [of the union] in the images [given form on earth in the rituals of

initiation]. The world has become the Eternal Realm, for the Realm is fullness for him. This is the way it is: it is revealed to him alone, not hidden in the darkness and the night [as befits the consummation of human marriage], but hidden in a perfect day and a holy light.

From Gospel of Philip *84.20–85.21; 86.7–18*

Philip Reclaimed by the Rigorists

Faced with such Syrian rigorism as we find in the *Gospel of Thomas*, Philip reacted in his gospel with self-conscious reflection on the nature of symbols and metaphors. He allows his gospel's symbols to become ever richer, ever more deeply interwoven, and so gives his readers a sense that they are utterly enfolded, in this visible, palpable world, with the signs of eternity. The language and rituals and intimacies of this world can (if only we will see them aright) reveal the truth about everything.

But those who read Philip responded in their turn. The *Gospel of Thomas* and the *Gospel of Philip* are preserved, one after another, in Codex II from Nag Hammadi. Here are the contents of the codex. If you would like to read in slightly more detail about the female powers in the *Secret Book of John* and *On the Origin of the World,* turn to Appendix B.

Secret Book of John[41]	A reinterpretation of Genesis's story of creation and the Fall
Gospel of Thomas	A gospel: making Mary male
Gospel of Philip	A gospel: transformative ascent into the bridal bedroom, from female to male
Reality of the Realms (*Hypostasis of the Archons*)	An "exposition" of Paul reinterpreting Genesis's story of creation and the Fall, with much about Wisdom
On the Origin of the World	A more elaborate account of the myths of *Reality of the Realms,* leading to an apocalypse of the last things
Exegesis on the Soul	A romance on the fall and restoration of the (female) soul
Book of Thomas the Contender	A dialogue of Judas Thomas with his twin, Jesus, in which he learns to "know himself" and so "the depths of the all": radically ascetic, warning against the fire of sexual and other passions

The *Exegesis on the Soul* is a short and theatrical account of the soul's fall and restoration. The premise for the whole treatise is set out in its opening words: "Wise men of old gave the soul a feminine name. Indeed, she is female in her nature as well; she even has her womb. As long as she was alone with the Father, she was virgin, and androgynous in form." But when she fell into a body, she was seduced and raped. From heaven the Father sent her husband-brother, the firstborn. She cleansed herself in the bridal bedroom and filled it with perfume. Then the bridegroom came down to her into the bridal bedroom, and he decorated it; united with one another, they became a single life. The first man and first woman were originally joined to one another when they were with the Father, before the woman led astray the man, who is her brother. And so the luscious descriptions continue, about the recovery of a "marital" union that is polemically free from any sexual contamination.[42] The whole codex ends with the *Book of Thomas the Contender* and its fierce condemnation of sexual relations: "Woe to you who love intimacy with womankind and polluted intercourse with them! Woe to you in the grip of the powers of your body, for they will afflict you!"[43]

For those who compiled Codex II, Philip would not be allowed to have the last word. His delicate, exploratory thought was relit in a far harsher light by the uncompromising stance of the *Exegesis on the Soul* and the *Book of Thomas the Contender*. Philip's Mary Magdalene had no part to play in this world of stern, ascetic masculinity.

8

THE *GOSPEL OF MARY*
Into the Inner World

> *Simon Peter, the leader of Jesus's disciples, calls upon Mary Magdalene to address them:*
> Peter said to Mary Magdalene, "Sister, we know that the Saviour loved you more than the rest of women. Tell us the words of the Saviour which you remember—which you know, but we do not, nor have we heard them."
> *Mary Magdalene does so. Now Peter, resentful, changes his tune:*
> Peter answered concerning these things. He questioned them about the Saviour: "Did he really speak with a woman without our knowledge and not openly? Are we to turn about and all listen to her? Did he prefer her to us?"
> Then Mary wept and said to Peter, "My brother Peter, what do you think? Do you think that I have thought this up myself in my heart, or that I am lying about the Saviour?"
> *Levi, another man among Jesus's disciples, breaks in:*
> Levi answered and said to Peter, "Peter, you have always been hot-tempered. Now I see you contending against the woman like the adversaries. But if the Saviour made her worthy, who are *you* to reject her? The Saviour certainly knows her without faltering. That is why he loved her more than us."[1]
>
> *From* Gospel of Mary *10.1–8; 17.7–18.20*

The conclusion of the *Gospel of Mary* is notorious. Simon Peter, leader of the disciples, has actually invited Mary to tell them what Jesus had told her alone. She does so; she mentions a vision of Jesus and tells, in Jesus's words, how the soul ascends to its proper home. Vision and account had both been granted to her alone. Peter changes his tune. Angry and resentful, he asks if Jesus preferred Mary Magdalene to the rest of his followers, men and women alike. Levi provides the answer: *Yes, he did.*

The authority of Mary Magdalene is disputed by Peter, but trium-
phantly vindicated; not even Peter can persuade his fellow disciples to
deny or ignore the privilege Jesus has given her. We interpret the conflict
readily: Mary surely represents the women called to leadership in the
Gnostic churches, Simon Peter the male leaders who resisted them. Yes,
perhaps. But this summary hacks the rich, varied foliage of the *Gospel of
Mary* back to the bare bark of just one of its limbs.[2]

The surviving portions of the gospel (in a fifth-century manuscript) are
not long. The Coptic text is a translation from Greek, and a few lines of
Greek text survive as well, from papyrus fragments discovered independently of the Coptic version. These lines in Greek do not give the exact
wording from which the Coptic translation was made; we have here two
(or even three) editions of the gospel, whose differences are fascinating
in themselves. We will be following the Coptic story and just glancing
occasionally at the Greek where it survives.

The gospel is a compilation in which different blocks of content are
relayed, as we shall hear, in different registers. We are bound to wonder
why it was compiled, why these blocks had greater cumulative value when
written up into a single—and dramatic—narrative. A particular challenge lies in Peter's change of tone. It may be an important part of the
point of the gospel, or it may betray the clumsy work of an unprofessional
editor. I suspect, myself, that it is the former and will be summarizing
the gospel from that point of view. Four sorts of knowledge are deliberately, programmatically presented in the course of the surviving text,
and it *mattered* to our authors who had access to these different forms of
knowledge and how.

The first pages of the Coptic gospel are simply missing. On the first
page to survive, Jesus answers a question with a motif we shall encounter again: in creation different natures are intermingled, and the time
will come when these different natures will be separated out. Now Peter
speaks up, to ask about the character of sin. Jesus builds on his last answer
by saying sin is the "adulterous" mixing of natures; the gospel's author
likely has in mind a noxious compound of dense matter and refined spirit
that causes a great passion and disturbance. The disciples, unsettled by
sin, can be reassured; sin will be undone when and where the different
natures within creation (finding their own level, as it were) are properly
resolved, unmixed and uncontaminated, into themselves.[3] Three times
Jesus urges those who can hear or understand to do so. As ever, this motif
signals teaching that is difficult to understand—an appropriate warning
to accompany this private instruction to Peter and the other disciples. This
is the first category of knowledge being offered by the gospel.

And now for the second. A scene in the gospel tells the story of Jesus's ascension:

> When the Blessed One had said this, he kissed them all, saying, "Peace be with you. Receive my peace to yourselves.[4] Beware that no one lead you astray by saying 'Look, here!' or 'Look, there!' For the Son of the Human One is within you. Follow after him! Those who seek him will find him. Go then and preach the gospel of the kingdom. Do not lay down any rule beyond what I appointed for you, nor give a law like the lawgiver, so that you are not constrained by it."
>
> When he had said this, he departed.
>
> Gospel of Mary 8.12–9.4

Most of this closing speech is a string of quotations and adaptations from the biblical gospels. *"Peace be with you,"* says the risen Jesus to his disciples on Easter evening and again a week later. Other sayings look back to Jesus's ministry before his death: *Look, the kingdom of God is within* [or *among*] *you. . . . They will say to you, "Look, here!" or "Look, there!" Make no move, nor pursue it. Seek and you will find. Follow me.* Jesus had preached the gospel of the kingdom; the Blessed One now sums up the rules that he himself had laid down, and he forbids any others to be imposed.[5] This is a telling reminder of the battles waged in the early churches between Paul's followers and James's over Christians' observance of the Jewish law. Simon Peter was linked—at least in Paul's presentation—with the Jamesian demands that the law be kept by Gentile converts. The *Gospel of Mary* suggests that when it was written there were still some factions linked with "the law" and the knowledge that the law represented. Our gospel extols, instead, the teaching of Jesus familiar from the biblical gospels and widely known. Here, then is the second category of teaching to be introduced in the gospel.

"The Son of the Human One is within you. Follow after him!" The Coptic phrase I translate as "the Son of the Human One" is itself a translation of the Greek phrase *ho huios tou anthrōpou,* well known in the New Testament, which is normally rendered there as "the Son of Man." That rendering disguises an important feature of the Greek phrase and of its Coptic equivalent. *Ho huios tou anthrōpou* is literally "the son of the human being," and for the Gnostics it recalled *ho anthrōpos,* the primal Human of Genesis 1.26–27; 2.7.[6] The New Testament's Son of the Human One is Jesus, both as seen in humility on earth and as envisioned on his throne in heaven. So who is this "Son of the Human One" who is, according to the

Gospel of Mary, within the believer? Our author evokes the vital analogy between the cosmos and the individual—the journey to heaven mirrors and gives words for the journey into the depths of one's own person. At the end of the first journey is the Son of the Human One, enthroned in heaven; the goal of the second is the Son of the Human One who *is* the innermost truth of the individual human undertaking the journey.[7]

But the disciples remain frightened by the prospect of persecution; they grieve and weep. They cannot yet see that their own route through "death" is the route through the separation of their different natures, adulterously mixed, into a proper distinction and the freedom of the spirit from the passion or suffering stirred by gross matter.

Now for a startling intervention:

> Then Mary stood up, embraced them and kissed them all, and said to her brothers, "Do not weep and do not grieve, nor be irresolute, for his grace will be entirely with you and will protect you. But rather let us praise his greatness, for he has prepared us [or, in the Greek, "bound us together," perhaps internally, in the cohesion of each individual; perhaps as a group] and made us into humans." When Mary said this, she turned their hearts inward to the Good, and they began to discuss the sayings of the Saviour.
>
> Gospel of Mary 9.12–24

Jesus had kissed (or greeted) the disciples; so does Mary. Jesus urged the disciples to follow the Son of the Human One within themselves; Mary reassures them that he has made them into humans. Mary, a woman, takes the role of Jesus, speaks as Jesus spoke, and reaffirms his instruction. Expectations are being deliberately overturned. Men were thought of as stable and rational, women as labile, tearful, and fearful, but here the men are making themselves womanly, and the woman is showing herself manly. She is becoming the true human being that is the Son of the Human One within her.

Mary has already stood up in a gesture of authority, spoken, and swayed the disciples to follow her instruction. She needed, it seems, no permission to do so. Now Peter invites her to teach again; he clearly expects (and is presumably expected) to exercise some control over the course of such a discussion. There is nothing combative or defensive in his approach:

> Peter said to Mary, "Sister, we know that the Saviour loved you more than the rest of women. Tell us the words of the Saviour

which you remember—which you know, but we do not, nor have
we heard them."

Gospel of Mary 10.1–6

Peter might be implying either that other women—less loved by Jesus
than Mary was—would not have had any such knowledge to impart or
that they would just have had less than Mary had. Mary is invited to
disclose teaching still more secret than the teaching already imparted
by Jesus before his departure; here is the third category of teaching the
gospel offers us, more secret than either of the first two. Mary introduces
a new theme in a grand, formal style:

> Mary answered and said, "What is hidden from you I will pro-
> claim to you." And she began to speak to them these words: "I,"
> she said, "I saw the Lord in a vision,[8] and I said to him, 'Lord, I
> saw you today in a vision.' He answered and said to me, 'Blessed
> are you that you did not waver at the sight of me. For where the
> mind is, there is the treasure.'"

Gospel of Mary 10.7–16

How intriguing. Mary saw Jesus twice in a single day. The first encounter was a vision; in the second she was able to discuss the vision with
Jesus himself. (We do not know if the second encounter was in the same
vision, a subsequent vision, or granted without any visionary privilege at
all.) Our author likely has two New Testament scenes in mind. At Jesus's
transfiguration three disciples including Simon Peter saw Jesus glorified[9]
and after the vision spoke with Jesus about it. The Mary of the *Gospel of
Mary,* then, has a standing as great as Simon's. And on Easter Day, according to John's gospel, Mary saw Jesus but initially failed to recognize
him. In the *Gospel of Mary,* by contrast, she is quite clear whom she saw,
and she herself launches the later conversation with Jesus. Our author is
deliberately ascribing to Mary greater insight and standing than John had
allowed her.

Mary's vision is a proper topic for discussion and (as we are about to
see) for analysis. It is a privilege, but one about which she can be properly
self-conscious and curious. "Where the mind is," says Jesus, "there is the
treasure." A famous saying from the New Testament has been pointedly
turned around: *"Where your treasure is,"* said the biblical Jesus, *"there
shall your heart be also."*[10] The biblical Jesus challenges the readers to
acknowledge to themselves where their "treasure" as an object of desire
is, inside or outside themselves; the *Gospel of Mary* is preparing to discuss the treasure available to an unwavering mind. Heart and mind were

more closely linked in ancient than in modern imagery (the heart was imagined as a seat of intellect as well as of emotion), but our author has good reason to emphasize the mind, for Mary continues,

"I said to him, 'Lord, now does he who sees the vision see it through the soul or through the spirit?' The Saviour answered and said, 'He does not see it through the soul nor through the spirit,

Good and Evil: The Planetary Powers of the Visible Heaven

The planets and stars above us, according to almost all ancient thought, shape our characters and destinies as the sun determines the seasons and the moon determines the tides. The planets and the zodiac may together be the source of our whole nature, from the physical (the lowest) to the rational (the highest), or may be the source only of the evil in and around us. The visible heavens, then, are either the source of the possibility of knowledge or are the ever present hindrance to knowledge. These contrasting emphases are clear in the lists below. Unsurprisingly, the Gnostics—as we shall see in the *Gospel of Mary* and *Pistis Sophia*—saw in these lower, material heavens nothing but evil.

	Numenius 2nd c. CE	Poimandres 2nd–4th c. CE	Servius 4th c. CE	Proclus[11] 5th c. CE
Saturn (father of Jupiter)	Rational	Falsehood	Torpor	Theoretical
Jupiter (king of the gods)	Active	Avarice	Desire for absolute power	Political
Mars (god of war)	Spirited	Audacity	Anger	Spirited
Sun	Perceptive	Arrogance	Passion	Linguistic
Venus (goddess of love)	Appetitive	Lust	Greed	Appetitive
Mercury		Evil cunning		Perceptive
Moon	Nutritive	Increase/decrease		Nutritive

but through the mind which is between the two—that is what sees the vision.'"

Gospel of Mary *10.16–23*

Against claims being made for the soul or spirit, the Saviour polemically endorses a view well known in the philosophies of the time—that the *mind* was the vehicle for the vision or understanding of God, just as it was the vehicle for the reflective understanding of oneself. In the *Gospel of Mary* the two aims converge: to know the Saviour is to know oneself, and to know oneself is to know the Saviour.

So far we have been given a cool lesson in the "faculty" that functions in a vision. Now follows a large gap in the text; four pages are missing. (There would have been more dialogue; perhaps Mary would have said when and how she learned what she relays in the next, climactic, section.) When we rejoin the story, Mary is still relaying words of the Saviour. But this is a new block of material whose tone we have not heard before. Gone is the dry analysis of sin and nature; now the language is rhythmic, almost incantatory, as Mary relays the Saviour's description of the soul's ascent upward, through and away from the powers of desire and ignorance and wrath. These are powers internal to the soul, corrupting it; desire wants the soul to be driven by desire, ignorance wants the soul to remain ignorant, wrath tries to rekindle the soul's old wrath. The powers address the soul, and there is a magic to be feared in their seductive words, to be countered by the soul's use of the same words in its subversive, clever replies.

We are being introduced to a fourth and final form of knowledge, the most personal of all. "From this time on," says the soul to the powers of wrath, "I will attain to the repose of the time, of the seasons, of the age [aeon], in silence." And with this, Mary herself falls silent, "since it was to this point that the Saviour had spoken with her."[12] Yes, since the soul represented by Mary has now been taken to the point of silence and of rest. What has been described to her by the Son of the Human One within her soul has been effected within her soul. The Mary relaying this secret teaching is a Mary who has been transformed by it herself, and readers are clearly invited to imagine—even to undergo—such a transformation in their turn.

From Respect to Resentment: Andrew and Peter

Mary represents both the Jesus whose instruction she imparts and the reader who is transformed by it. But the author does not imagine that

Mary's insight will be so readily attained by all who are offered it. The tone now changes again—for the worse.

> But Andrew answered and said, "Say what you wish to say about what she has said. I at least do not believe that the Saviour said this. For certainly these teachings seem to be according to a different train of thought."
>
> Gospel of Mary 17.10–15

The opposition to Mary has begun; it will get worse. It has been argued that Andrew is speaking in bad faith, that he is just looking for an excuse to silence Mary. But I doubt it. The character of the inner journey and the authority of any instructor who was to guide believers were matters of real dispute.

The Saviour had revealed to the disciples the confusion that ensues from the mixing of matter and spirit. In Mary's account an analogous confusion afflicts the individual soul—in the figures of Simon Peter and Andrew. Peter speaks out. It is worth seeing, here, both the Coptic text and the significant variations in the Greek fragments.

Greek	Coptic
When he was being questioned about such things [Peter said:] "Did the Saviour speak secretly to a woman and not openly, so that we might all hear something more remarkable? . . ." [or, "not openly; surely he did not want to show her to be more remarkable than us?"]	Peter answered and spoke concerning these same things. He questioned them about the Saviour: "Did he really speak with a woman without our knowledge and not openly? Are we to turn about and all listen to her? Did he prefer her to us?"
	Greek 21.11–15; Coptic 17.16–22

What a drastic change in Peter's attitude. He had asked Mary to reveal to the disciples what she alone had heard from Jesus; now he denies that Jesus would have spoken to a woman in secret at all. The Coptic text appears to make a distinction between the conversation of Jesus and Mary that the male disciples knew about but were not part of (and about which Peter asked Mary to speak) and a conversation about which they had never heard at all (the very idea of which offends Peter). We do not know, thanks to the break in the text, if Peter had been unsettled by Mary's account of her vision and of Jesus's teaching about visions, but he certainly resists this final, mystical, form of knowledge evoking the upward and inward journey of the soul.

What Andrew and Peter fail to comprehend in the *Gospel of Mary* is *themselves*. Andrew is as ignorant as the power of ignorance and Peter is as angry as the power of wrath—because they are both still under the dominion of these powers. Ignorance and anger, failing to see who Mary has become but sensing her authority, respond vehemently. Now even Mary is put on the defensive; she weeps. The leader of the disciples has done what the fear of death could not do and has made Mary unstable. She still, nonetheless, addresses Peter as her brother, as he had called her his sister.

> Then Mary wept and said to Peter, "My brother Peter, what do you think? Do you think that I thought this up myself in my heart or that I am lying about the Saviour?"
>
> Gospel of Mary *18.1–5*

Now for the next and final twist to the drama: Levi speaks up.[13] Levi uses the language of the mysteries and their initiates, "worthy" of illumination, perfectly known and securely loved by the deity. He is giving to Mary and her revelation the dignity of these famous (and in their initiations famously esoteric) cults.

Greek	Coptic
Levi said to Peter, "Peter, your angry temper is always with you, and now you are cross-examining the woman as her adversary. If the Saviour thought her worthy, who are *you* to scorn her? For certainly he, knowing her—without faltering—loved her.	Levi answered and said to Peter, "Peter, you have always been hot-tempered. Now I see you contending against the woman like the adversaries. But if the Saviour made her worthy, who are *you* to reject her? The Saviour certainly knows her without faltering; that is why he loved her more than us.
"Rather let us be ashamed and having put on the perfect Human, let us do what was commanded us: to preach the gospel, laying down no rule nor ordaining any law, as the Saviour said."	"Rather let us be ashamed and put on the perfect Human and acquire him for ourselves as he commanded us, and preach the gospel, not laying down any other rule or law beyond what the Saviour said."
When he had said this, Levi departed and began to preach.	When [. . .] and they began to go forth to proclaim and to preach.

Greek 22.18–32; Coptic 18.1–19.2

In the Greek Peter is just an ordinary opponent to Mary. In the Coptic, he is like one of the cosmic adversaries—ignorance and anger again!—

who attack human souls and seek to trap them under the domination of the lower powers. Ignorant Andrew and angry Peter typify in the outside world the dangers of ignorance and anger within. The Coptic Peter asks indignantly, "Did the Saviour prefer her to us?" The translator or editor is raising the stakes. To Peter's stark question Levi gives a stark answer: yes.

Powerless Vessels Made Strong

The *First Apocalypse of James* from Nag Hammadi addresses among other questions the standing of patently impressive women in Gnostic communities. The order of creation is as we would expect by now. The Lord said,

> "Nothing existed except Him Who Is. He is unnameable and ineffable. . . . Since you have asked concerning woman-hood, womanhood existed, but womanhood was not first. And it prepared for itself powers and gods. But it did not exist when I came forth, since I am an image of Him Who Is."
>
> First Apocalypse of James *24.19–25.5*

But this does not settle the practical question raised by women's courage in the face of danger. James asks,

> "Yet another thing I ask of you: who are the seven women who have been your disciples? And behold, all women bless you. I also am amazed how powerless vessels have become strong by a perception which is in them."
>
> First Apocalypse of James *38.15–22*

The Lord's reply is fragmentary, but may well have matched the women with the gifts of the spirit listed in Isaiah 11.2–3. James is under threat of attack, frightened and beleaguered, and it is not clear quite what Jesus recommends: "When you speak these words of this perception, encourage [or, be persuaded by] these four: Salome and Mariam and Martha and Arsinoe." The next lines are fragmentary, before Jesus says, "The perishable has gone up to the imperishable, and the female element has attained to this male element."[14] The text's communities are coming to recognize the strength of women, by finding in these women the calibre of men.

The Saviour knew Mary as the disciples did not and made her worthy of disclosures that would reach the disciples only through Mary's mediation after he himself had left their sight.

Levi picks up the themes we have already heard from the Saviour: the disciples, already made human by the Saviour himself, are to put on the perfect Human, to preach the gospel of the kingdom, and to impose no extra law or rule. Levi is rounding off the discussion. And so the main text of the gospel ends. What is the result of Levi's intervention? He has won the argument; Peter has been quelled. But Mary herself, in these final lines, is oddly diminished. In the Greek version only Levi himself heads off to preach; in the Coptic, "they" do so, but it is not clear if Mary is among them. Levi does not mention her name, and she does not speak again. She has spoken up within the circle of the disciples, her instruction has (eventually) been accepted—and then she is left to one side.

Mary Magdalene: Icon of Women in Authority

What, then, can we say about the structures—and not least the centres of authority—of the communities in which the *Gospel of Mary* was used? Such structures can be rigidly resistant to change; it is all too easy for those who have power to find good reasons why others should not share it. The text may well have been expanded (and so the story made slightly confusing) when a dispute over women's roles was growing more acute. Mary represents Christ, and so she represents the Gnostics who follow Christ and find him realized within themselves. Is she an icon specifically of the *women* among the Gnostics or among their leaders? Among other possibilities, Mary might typify gifted women who already led some Gnostic communities or the women who, according to some affluent and educated Gnostics (with access to the source texts and a scribe), should be authorized to lead. We will be returning to these possibilities in the next chapter, when we have surveyed the last of our Gnostic texts. For the moment, let's just notice that the text acknowledges two centres of authority: Simon Peter, the chairman in executive command, and Mary Magdalene, possessed of special knowledge and representing the Saviour.[15]

Mary, ideal believer and spokesperson for Jesus himself, is a *woman*. She has evoked the true convergence of the female soul and the Son of the Human One, so she has threatened any determinedly male believer working to realize the male Saviour in his own exclusively male self. The Son of the Human One has always been in her, the true Human she has had it "in herself" to become, whom the powers of desire and ignorance and anger have always kept from fruition in her own distorted vision of herself. But the text still leaves us with some tantalizing questions. In her discovery does Mary transcend her character as a (thoughtless, unstable) woman and grow into the character of a (stable, intellectual) man? Or does she, self-aware at last, become a fulfilled male-female figure and in her perfection restore the androgyny of the First Human? It is after all Mary's soul (Gk, *psyche,* feminine) that reaches rest, but it is her mind (Gk, *nous,* masculine) that has seen the Saviour, who is himself the saving mind.

The role of Mary Magdalene and its ambiguity are due, I think, to her role in John's gospel. The *Gospel of Mary* not only draws on John, but it finds there its chief inspiration. "Peace be with you," says the Blessed One to the disciples, "receive my peace to yourselves"; as John's Jesus had said, *"My peace I give to you."* The Saviour speaks alone with Mary Magdalene just as John's Jesus had spoken alone with a Samaritan woman and the disciples had been *amazed that he was talking with a woman.*[16] At least some Gnostics realized that in John's narrative the Samaritan woman understood Jesus more deeply than the disciples did, and in the *Gospel of Mary* the scene is set for just such another comparison. Above all, John's Jesus had appeared to Mary Magdalene by herself and had spoken to her on Easter morning. In the *Gospel of Mary* she is more highly privileged still, with insight and an unwavering mind. John's gospel had, after the raising of the readers as Lazarus, represented them in the person of the Beloved Disciple, but the disciple gives way at Easter to Mary Magdalene. The *Gospel of Mary* sees the link between the disciple and Mary and declares Jesus to have loved Mary above all others; Mary Magdalene has become the Beloved Disciple.

John's gospel has Mary Magdalene meet Jesus in a re-created paradise. This Holy of Holies can be inhabited only in the reception of John's own story and in the likely setting for that reception—the communities' liturgy. The story draws readers into the Eden, where, in their imagination and self-perception, they belong. Within this dreamlike landscape John insists on portraying, as the climax of his story, a relationship between two people, but the thread he had laid down through the whole length of the gospel, guiding his readers through *new birth from above,* encouraged his Gnostic readers to turn inward, to focus exclusively on their own deepening self-awareness. Such readers knew Thomas's ideas as well as John's and read John (Thomas's vehement opponent!) in a Thomasine sense. The goal was now the transformation of the innermost self of the individual Gnostic by union with Jesus. Luke's Jesus had already warned, *"Look, the kingdom of God is within* [or, among] *you. . . . They will say to you, "Look, here!" or "Look, there!"* The *Gospel of Mary* identifies the kingdom with the Son of the Human One himself and commands the believer to look only for this Son within and to ignore the illusion of any external person, thing, or place as the goal of their search.

John's Easter story is the trunk of a tree with many branches. Some of the tree's most vigorous branches grew into Gnostic stories; the story of Mary Magdalene grew with them. What deep mysteries did she learn, when she—before anyone else—saw the risen Jesus in the light of dawn on Day One? What might she have known that the men in Jesus's entourage never heard from him or saw in him? The *Gospel of Mary* ascribes to her alone the two most intimate forms of the four forms of knowledge exemplified within the text. One of these is technical, knowledge about knowledge; the other is the key that unlocks the door to the Gnostics' innermost being.

Within the story, Mary speaks out, is rebuffed, vindicated—and finally left aside; Levi has the last word. But our Coptic text gives to Mary, right at the end, her due. Into a world of men's voices and men's texts that shout down the teaching of women as improper in principle and heretical in practice, our author has sent this short story with a simple closing declaration:

THE GOSPEL
ACCORDING TO
MARY.

The *Dialogue of the Savior*:
Mary Magdalene, Who Understood Completely

> Mary said this as a woman who had understood completely [*or* the All *or* everything].
> The Lord said, "Pray in the place where there is no woman."
> Matthew said, "'Pray in the place where there is no woman,' Jesus tells us, meaning, 'Destroy the works of womanhood,' not because there is any other manner of birth, but because they will cease giving birth."
> Dialogue of the Savior *139.11–13; 144.15–21*

Our modern concern niggles at us still. Was there any place—let alone a leading role—in the Gnostic communities for a woman who did not attain the merits of a man? The *Gospel of Mary* has added nuance to the question. Authors in their stories could, it seems, deploy men (such as Andrew and Peter) and a woman (Mary Magdalene) to represent the contrasting qualities to be found in any one individual; and it is the woman (not the men!) who has shown the stability of the true Gnostic, who has won the visionary privilege it makes possible, and who now relays her knowledge to the uncomprehending men. The *Gospel of Mary* deploys individuals to typify qualities and is not the only text to do so. The *Dialogue of the Savior* deserves a careful look. It is far more imaginative and exploratory than its two famous sayings—quoted above—will ever reveal.[17]

The principal speakers, with Jesus, are Matthew and Judas and Mary Magdalene. Matthew and Judas are chiefly interested in cosmology, the future, and the place of repose and life to which Jesus's followers aspire. Matthew tells Jesus he wants to see the place of life and light, and asks, "Why do we not rest at once?" Judas wants to know what there was before the heaven and the earth existed. He asks Jesus about the movement of the earth, and he asks Matthew about a vision that he, Matthew, and Mary are given of the vast height of heaven and the terrifying abyss.[18] So much for Matthew's and Judas's concerns. Mary represents quite different priorities. She asks the men briskly, "Where are you going to put these things about which you ask the Son?" Mary speaks up for the reception of Jesus's teaching here and now; she is strikingly down-to-earth. The Saviour himself breaks in with an answer. It is fragmentary, but involves "putting these things in the heart," as the mother of Jesus had stored the memory of Jesus's early life in her heart.[19]

This pattern is maintained consistently through the dialogue. Our author is pursuing yet another possibility opened by John's gospel: to see all those—both men and women—who encounter Jesus as together, in an ensemble, representing the individual Gnostic. The male disciples have one set of interests, Mary another, and to do justice to a Gnostic they must be combined.

Judas speaks about the demonic governors of this world. Jesus reassures him that Jesus's followers who rid themselves of jealousy will clothe themselves in light and will enter the bridal bedroom. "How," asks Judas, "will our garments be brought to us?"

> The Lord said, "There are some who will provide for you, and there are others who will receive. . . . Who will be able to reach that place which is the reward? But the garments of life were given to a human because he knows the path by which he will leave. And it is difficult even for me to reach it."
>
> Mary said, "Thus with respect to 'the wickedness of each day' and 'the laborer is worthy of his food' and 'the disciple resembles his teacher.'"
>
> Dialogue of the Savior *138.20–139.11*

Mary is referring to three sayings of Jesus, versions of which have reached us in the New Testament itself.[20] Their full meaning is revealed, claims Mary, when they are brought into relation to the Jesus of the dialogue: there is jealousy enough for any day; the laborer who knows the path of Jesus is worthy of his reward, his everlasting garments; and even Jesus found it hard to attain his goal—no wonder it is hard for his followers. Mary grasps the links between the widely known sayings of Jesus and their esoteric meaning. The starting point is the esoteric teaching to which the widely known sayings are then applied, for the communities prided themselves above all on their secret knowledge. The editor now adds a striking comment in praise of Mary:

> She said this as a woman who had understood completely [or the All or everything].
>
> Dialogue of the Savior *139.11–13*

This is not itself a climactic saying, bringing the dialogue to its crescendo. On the contrary, Mary will later insist she wants to understand all things, as if she knows she has not already. Judas and Matthew then make characteristic interventions about the beginning and the end, and Jesus speaks up with praise for the men, "You have understood all things I have said to you, and have accepted them on faith." This total understanding is not Mary's alone.[21]

* * *

Watch the male disciples looking backward and forward; then watch Mary, speaking about our present condition and what we can see here and now. Mary is made to conform to the view of women that pervaded the ancient world, that they were at home specifically in our physical existence in this physical world. Within the story of the *Dialogue of the Savior,* it is not that she is right and the men are wrong; it needs both her perspective and theirs to reveal what readers need to see.

> Judas said, "When we pray, how should we pray?" The Lord said, "Pray in the place where there is no woman." Matthew said, "'Pray in the place where there is no woman,' he tells us, meaning, 'Destroy the works of womanhood,' not because there is any other manner of birth, but because they will cease giving birth."
>
> Dialogue of the Savior *144.14–21*

Now it is Matthew's turn to elucidate one saying by reference to another, this time to the saying about womanhood, from the *Gospel of the
Egyptians,* which we encountered when exploring the *Gospel of Thomas*
in Chapter 4. In the *Dialogue of the Savior,* Mary responds to Matthew's
interpretation. The tone of her comment is hard to gauge, but there is no
suggestion that she resents or will resist the dissolution of these works of
womanhood; she simply sees no end to them. Jesus speaks in turn and
effectively corrects Mary; however deep her understanding of the present

Echoes of History

On the one side, we have Mary Magdalene teaching the disciples,
and, on the other, Simon Peter, resentful of Jesus's love for Mary
Magdalene and of the authority it seems to give her. The argument was clearly real and mattered—but when and to whom? Let's
assume (tentatively enough) that the Greek versions of our Gnostic
texts were written down in their present form during the second
century and that they were translated into Coptic in the third and
fourth centuries. So we wonder whether the authority of women
was a live issue in the Gnostic communities in which our texts
were used in their present Coptic forms and whether it had been
an issue in Gnostic communities since the second century. We
can readily imagine each side in the argument invoking a hero
from the past—Simon Peter on one side, Mary Magdalene on the
other—and putting words into that hero's mouth to represent and
strengthen a position.

And let's go still farther back into the past. Did such factions, invoking Mary and Peter, have any evidence of their own that these
two *had* argued over women's standing in the years immediately
after Jesus's death? (It may seem odd, after all, to have spun the
debate out of thin air.) We may well wonder what memories had
been kept alive—however distorted, amplified, and recast—from
generation to generation, to be embedded in the second century,
perhaps a hundred years after Mary and Peter died, in the Greek
originals of our Gnostic texts.

We should take some notice of a second and perhaps similar case.
In Syria in the early third century a loose series of documents
about St. Clement of Rome was revised and expanded into a single
text known as the *Proclamations of Peter.* This was then subjected
to further revisions by different editors, who created from it widely

and however reasonable her conviction, she does not see what the future holds.

> Mary said, "They will never be obliterated." The Lord said, "Who knows that they will not dissolve [...]?" Judas said to Matthew, "The works of womanhood will dissolve [...] the governors [...]"
>
> Dialogue of the Savior *144.22–145.5*

---

divergent recensions of the same basic material. The whole set is now called the *Pseudo-Clementines*.

Among its heroes is Simon Peter. A recurring theme is Peter's struggle against his "enemy," a false preacher named as Simon Magus. (We have heard of Simon Magus already, in Chapter 6.) This enemy claimed to have been taught all he needed to know about Jesus from a single vision, and he preached to Gentiles without calling for their submission to the Jewish law. So who is really being attacked in this figure of Simon Magus? The name is a code in the text—for *Paul*.

Why was it worth writing up this bundle of texts in successive editions? Probably because a debate was running in the third century between two wings of the Syrian church. On the one side were missionaries (invoking Peter) who called for converts to maintain the observance of the Jewish law or to undertake it, and on the other were missionaries who taught Gentiles (as Paul had taught) a gospel free from the law's observance. And this replicates the split between Peter and Paul of which we know from Paul's letter to the Galatians. (Paul's letter is itself one of the sources used in the *Pseudo-Clementines;* it reveals as well that some Jewish Christians, if not Peter himself, clearly challenged the authority that Paul claimed on the basis of a call direct from God.)

The details of that first-century debate, as we read them in the *Pseudo-Clementines,* have been recast. The narrative is now shamelessly novelistic, Paul's identity has been disguised, and the two introductory letters (one of them ascribed to Peter) are a patent fiction. And yet the *Pseudo-Clementines* do echo, a hundred and fifty years after the event, a real disagreement between Peter and Paul. As we follow the trail of Mary Magdalene, this is a salutary tale. We may well be hearing, in the Gnostic texts, echoes of debates among the first followers of Jesus, and yet those echoes may well be so distorted as to have become, in any detail, hopelessly misleading.[22]

The Lord endorses Judas's claim, and then in a startling move he reverts to the theme of creation in the terms of the vision he relayed to his disciples early in the dialogue. Jesus is here actually describing a birth that involves no works of womanhood: "Now look! A true Word is coming forth from the Father to the abyss, in silence with a flash of lightning, giving birth."[23] The author, with his eyes on the "Word" of John's prologue, invokes the archetypal births—creation itself, the coming of Jesus, and the Gnostic's spiritual conception—as free from the works of womanhood.

Only fragments of the dialogue's following lines survive; they had both Mary and Jesus speak of works and dissolution. I suspect—but can only speculate—that Jesus spoke further about the consummation for which Matthew and Judas longed. *If* that is right, then at the climax to the world's history the disciples will reach the place hard even for Jesus to reach, Mary's worldly viewpoint will be abandoned alongside all the works of womanhood, and her voice will fall silent forever. So the combination of male and female, as the necessary constituents of an individual, will collapse once more into the maleness that this whole mixed-sex world has—for a short and turbulent period—interrupted. For Mary's insight and understanding to survive, we need to look elsewhere. In *Pistis Sophia,* the last of the Gnostic texts we will survey, Mary comes finally and unequivocally into her own.

9

FAITH-WISDOM

Ascent to the Highest Heights

> Jesus, the compassionate, answered and said to Mariham: "Mariham, you blessed one, whom I will complete in all the mysteries of the height, speak openly. You are she whose heart is more directed to the kingdom of heaven than all your brothers. . . . You are blessed beyond all women upon earth, because you shall be the Fullness of all Fullnesses and the completion of all completions."
>
> Peter leapt forward, he said to Jesus, "My Lord, we cannot able to suffer this woman [Mary Magdalene] who takes the opportunity from us and does not allow any one of us to speak, but she speaks many times."
>
> "My Lord," says Mary Magdalene, "my mind is understanding at all times that I should come forward and give the interpretation of the words which Faith-Wisdom spoke, but I am afraid of Peter, for he threatens me and hates our race."
>
> <div align="right">Pistis Sophia <i>1.17 and 1.19 [26.16–20 and 28.20–24];
1.36 [58.9–14]; 2.72 [162.12–18]</i>[1]</div>

Over and over in *Pistis Sophia* Jesus praises Mary. She is the text's heroine, a fitting foil to its hero, Jesus, and far more prominent than any of the male disciples. She speaks more than any of them and shows more insight. Of the 115 questions put to Jesus and explanations offered to him in the main body of the text (*Pistis Sophia,* Books 1–3), some 67 come from Mary Magdalene. Time and again Jesus lavishes praise upon her. *Pistis Sophia* leads us into an imagined world where Mary Magdalene stands head and shoulders above the male disciples. Surely this is the image of a real world where even male leaders (often grudgingly) acknowledged visionary or prophetic women, the heirs of Mary's insight and authority, as unsurpassed interpreters of Jesus's teaching.[2]

This long text is preserved in one manuscript, a Coptic translation of a lost Greek original, bought by Dr. Anthony Askew in London in 1772 and from his estate by the British Museum, where it remains to this day. The manuscript brings together two treatises that have become known as *Pistis Sophia,* Books 1–3, and *Pistis Sophia,* Book 4. *Pistis Sophia* is an odd juxtaposition of two nouns, "Faith" and "Wisdom." Faith-Wisdom herself, the Wisdom whose unilateral search for knowledge led to cosmic downfall, is a character in the book. (I will be calling the work *Pistis Sophia* throughout, and the character Faith-Wisdom.)[3] *Pistis Sophia,* Books 1–3 (to which we will devote our attention here), are themselves a compilation of texts that have been edited into a relatively homogeneous whole.[4] As a whole they tell a (slightly disjointed) story, and in this chapter we will do best to hear that story, in summary, from beginning to end. To do justice to *Pistis Sophia* we need once more to sense for ourselves something of the progress the text was intended to engender in its readers, for the story worked when it became the readers' own story, when the readers recognized themselves in Jesus's entourage, drawn higher and higher towards their spiritual home, the Treasury of Light.

We will encounter a familiar drama. Mary Magdalene is praised for her wisdom by Jesus and resented for her prominence by Simon Peter. Whose words will we really be hearing? Not the words of Jesus, Peter, and Mary from their time together two hundred years before *Pistis Sophia* was written. But that is nothing to regret. We are hearing instead the claims, the arguments, and the aspirations shaping the Gnostic communities that compiled and used *Pistis Sophia* itself. As we would expect by now, Mary Magdalene represents the ideal Gnostic, highly praised by Jesus. But we can be more precise. In *Pistis Sophia* Mary is both faithful and wise; she embodies Faith-Wisdom herself, as Faith-Wisdom should have been all along. Mary Magdalene hears of Faith-Wisdom's fall, agony, and restoration, but Mary herself never acts unilaterally, never lets her longing for knowledge delude her into Faith-Wisdom's catastrophic fall.

The Drama Begins: The Rescue of Faith-Wisdom

Pistis Sophia, Book 1, opens on the Mount of Olives, outside Jerusalem. Jesus has been with his disciples for eleven years since his resurrection, teaching them. Readers are told, right at the outset, that the disciples failed to know how little they actually knew; the readers themselves are being warned not to be overconfident. Jesus suddenly ascends in a blaze of light to heaven; the next day he returns, more dazzling still and authorized at last to reveal to them the full secrets of the higher realms. Jesus describes his journey to heaven through the lower realms. "He who has ears to hear," he concludes, "let him hear." Mary stares for an hour into the air, then asks Jesus's permission to speak. She is the first individual follower to be heard:

> Jesus, the compassionate, answered and said to Mariham: "Mariham, you blessed one, whom I will complete in all the mysteries of the height, speak openly. You are she whose heart is more directed to the kingdom of heaven than all your brothers."
>
> Pistis Sophia *1.17 [26.16–20]*

Mary dwells on that last demand of Jesus, "He who has ears to hear, let him hear." Adducing a "spiritual parable" from Isaiah, she speaks of those who can—and those who cannot—hope to know what needs to be known. Jesus praises Mary's insight: "Excellent, Maria. You are blessed beyond all women upon earth, because you shall be the Fullness of all Fullnesses and the completion of all completions." Mary needs more guidance. She asks him a question about fate. Jesus answers at length. Next Philip speaks up, then Mary again:

> Maria, beautiful in her speech, came forward. The blessed one prostrated herself at the feet of Jesus and said, "My Lord, suffer me that I speak in your presence, and be not angry because I trouble you many times, questioning you." [She asks her question.] Jesus answered and said to Maria, "Excellent, Maria. You ask well with an excellent question and you seek everything with certainty and with accuracy. Now indeed I will not conceal anything from you from this hour. . . . Hear now, Maria, and give ear, all you disciples."
>
> Pistis Sophia *1.23–24 [33.16–34.7]*

Jesus's long answer introduces the figure of Faith-Wisdom herself. To do justice to the epic drama in which the text is about to involve us, the chart on page 155 shows both Faith-Wisdom's travails in the spiritual realms and the Gnostic's journey towards the Ineffable Light, for they cannot be kept away from each other, in separate categories.[5] To understand the travails and the triumph of Faith-Wisdom was, for the Gnostics, to understand themselves; to follow the example of Mary Magdalene was to avoid or overcome those travails and to share her triumph. Once more the realms we would nowadays distinguish as physical and spiritual are stages on a single route. The realms of light for which Faith-Wisdom yearned were not, for the Gnostics, fantastical dreams; they were *home*. The Gnostics no more belonged in our densely material world than Faith-Wisdom did. The route upward and the route inward—the Gnostic could not travel one without travelling the other.

At the top of the chart is the Great God, the Ineffable, dazzling beyond measure, surpassing all human power of understanding. From this centre there flow outward and downward twenty-four realms of power. The first twelve are informed by the spirit and suffused with light; innermost is the Treasury of Light, from which come "the twelve saviours." The Thirteenth Realm—midway through the twenty-four, exactly halfway between ineffable light and dark chaos, and above the realms of the zodiac and fate—is vital to our story, for it is the proper home of Faith-Wisdom herself. Here is the first place of stability to which beleaguered and benighted Gnostics should aspire.

The Thirteenth Realm is alive with contrasting figures. They provide an imaginative account of the spiritual world, of its material instantiation in our everyday world—*and of ourselves, individual humans*. Our authors are not describing some alien world; they would claim to be describing, in their distinctive terms, *you* in all your rich complexity—your hopes, aspirations, and independence; the balances within and between your spiritual, intellectual, and emotional selves; your frailties and errors.

The Barbēlo inhabits the Thirteenth Realm. The Barbēlo is the body Jesus wore in the heights of heaven; he put part of its power into his mother, from which he was born as the earthly Jesus. The Barbēlo is also the mother of Faith-Wisdom herself and so, indirectly, of the human image of Faith-Wisdom—that is, Mary Magdalene. Mary Magdalene and the earthly Jesus are siblings; no wonder she will function as a Beloved Disciple, his mother's daughter, as the disciple himself had become his mother's son.[6]

Faith-Wisdom too inhabited that central Thirteenth Realm, longed for knowledge, and strained upward towards the dazzling glory of heaven. "I will go to that place," she said, "without my consort, and take the light, and create of it for myself realms of light, so that I shall be able to go to the Light of Lights which is in the highest height."[7] But darkness as well as light had a hold on the Thirteenth Realm. Here was Authades, "Self-Willed" (with a name also reminiscent of the domain of death, Hades). Authades aspired to be lord of the Thirteenth Realm and of those beneath it. Seeing Faith-Wisdom yearn for the higher spiritual realms and their light, he resented her aspiration. He generated powers to inhabit Chaos, chief among them the power whose light, shining in Chaos, would

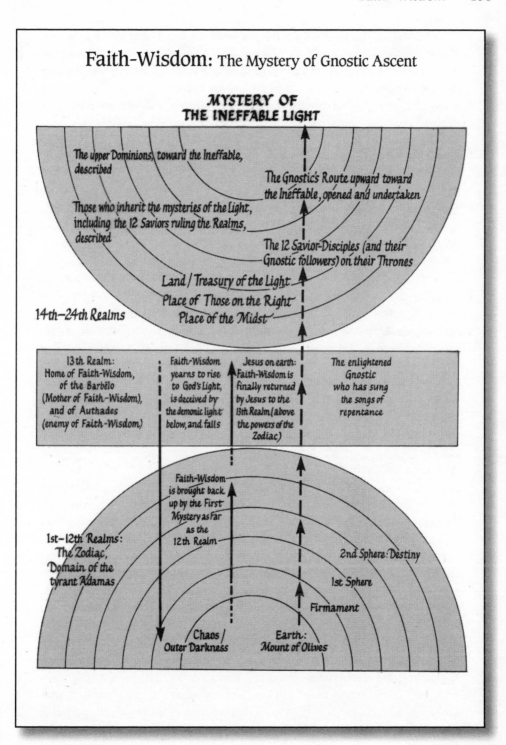

Faith-Wisdom: The Mystery of Gnostic Ascent

MYSTERY OF
THE INEFFABLE LIGHT

The upper Dominions, toward the Ineffable, described

The Gnostic's Route upward toward the Ineffable, opened and undertaken

Those who inherit the mysteries of the Light, including the 12 Saviors ruling the Realms, described

The 12 Savior-Disciples (and their Gnostic followers) on their Thrones

Land / Treasury of the Light

Place of Those on the Right

Place of the Midst

14th–24th Realms

13th Realm: Home of Faith-Wisdom, of the Barbēlo (Mother of Faith-Wisdom), and of Authades (enemy of Faith-Wisdom)

Faith-Wisdom yearns to rise to God's Light, is deceived by the demonic light below, and falls

Jesus on earth: Faith-Wisdom is finally returned by Jesus to the 13th Realm (above the powers of the Zodiac)

The enlightened Gnostic who has sung the songs of repentance

Faith-Wisdom is brought back up by the First Mystery as far as the 12th Realm

1st–12th Realms: The Zodiac, Domain of the tyrant Adamas

2nd Sphere: Destiny

1st Sphere

Firmament

Chaos / Outer Darkness

Earth: Mount of Olives

be mistaken by Faith-Wisdom for the light of the higher realms. So the lower powers could trap Faith-Wisdom at their own level. Authades's plan worked. From her place in the Thirteenth Realm Faith-Wisdom looked downward and mistook the light below her for the light of the Treasury of Light. She tumbled downward, and in Chaos the powers of Authades drained her of her own light.[8]

What was the fault of Faith-Wisdom? After all, she longed (surely an admirable longing!) to know God, and such knowledge would have raised her to be a more perfect image of God. But she acted unilaterally, with the self-will that Self-Willed wanted to stir in her. She was disrupting the ordered symmetries of God's spiritual creation. Longing to see reality, she became the individual of Plato's great myth of the cave who faces away from reality all unawares. Gnostic readers were to recognize, in the dangers facing Faith-Wisdom, the dangers facing *themselves*. The Gnostics inhabited a world created in consequence of a Fall and were forever in danger of a Fall themselves. The cosmic Fall had been triggered by the very yearning for knowledge that fueled their lives as Gnostics. The Gnostics, children of their age and its ideals, sought an ordered, stable, reflective ascent. Wrongly sought, the Wisdom they themselves wanted had brought about the world of death in which they were bound; this was the tragedy of the Gnostics' world.

First Wisdom, next Eve. Eve acted at first without Adam, but then brought him into her action, and together they attained the knowledge that the evil creator sought to deny them. Who, then, shall be the third female power, the embodiment of restored Faith-Wisdom, always at one with her counterpart and acting in obedience to him, making her way upward, way beyond the Thirteenth Realm, to the source of all that can be known and the light by which it can be seen? Mary Magdalene. And who will represent the Gnostics on this journey, both showing them the way and leading them along it to the heights? Once more, Mary Magdalene.

Faith-Wisdom herself—and so now the individual Gnostic—must be saved from the realms of darkness and brought to the light. Jesus tells how Faith-Wisdom, in her darkness, sang thirteen songs of repentance; he recites them. After each song, one of his followers offers to interpret it and adduces a passage from the Bible's Psalms or from the so-called *Psalms of Solomon* that matches the song of Faith-Wisdom verse for verse, sentiment for sentiment. Why need Faith-Wisdom sing such elaborate new songs if all she wants to say is already said in such simple and well-known passages? Precisely to cast light on the true significance of those familiar texts, which can now help the Gnostics rise from the thick, palpable atmosphere of chaos into which Faith-Wisdom and they had fallen and to

Interpreting the Songs of Faith-Wisdom: Jesus Praises His Followers

Here are the terms in which Jesus extols some of the disciples who interpret Faith-Wisdom's thirteen laments. Mary Magdalene is of course highly praised, but so are the others. At this elementary stage in *Pistis Sophia,* Jesus's followers are not just asking for illumination but displaying it. Mary breaks in four times and is clearly contrasted with the "humble" and reticent Martha, who speaks twice.

John kisses the breast of Jesus and is praised as "You Virgin who will rule in the Kingdom of the Light." Andrew is praised as "You blessed one," and Jesus anticipates what is to follow: "Truly, truly, I say to you, I will fulfill you in all the mysteries of the light, and every gnosis, from the Ineffable to the darkness of darkness . . . in order that you be called perfect. . . . In the place where I shall be in the Kingdom of my Father, you will also be there with me." Thomas declares, "I am sober, and my spirit is ready within me"; he admits he has held back from speaking "lest I cause anger in my brothers." Jesus praises him: "All the generations of the world will bless you upon the earth, because you have received of my Spirit, and you have become understanding and spiritual. And after this I will fill you with all the light and all the power of the Spirit." James also kisses the breast of Jesus, declares himself sober, and is told, "You will become first in the kingdom of heaven. But not only you, but also everyone who will perform my mysteries." Philip is the group's scribe, a telling reminder of the *Gospel of Philip.*[9]

pass, like her, ever upward towards the brilliance where they belong and where their thrones await them.

Jesus recites the first song, which Mary interprets. She has now spoken six times, Philip once, and nobody else except Jesus. Jesus recites the second song, and Peter leaps forward. "My Lord," he says, "we cannot suffer this woman who takes the opportunity from us and does not allow any one of us to speak, but she speaks many times." Jesus responds: "Let him in whom the power of the Spirit has welled up so that he understands what I say, come forward and speak." Jesus will not let Peter control the session. "Nevertheless," adds Jesus, "I see that the power in you, Peter, understands the interpretation. . . . You, Peter, speak the thought of Faith-Wisdom's repentance." Peter does so, and Jesus confirms in the disciples the authority that the biblical Jesus had given them: "He whom you receive on earth will be received into the light of the height; and he whom you cast out upon earth will be cast out of the kingdom of my Father which is in heaven." We shall hear more of Peter's authority—and of his resentment of Mary. It is no coincidence that the next three songs are interpreted by Mary, Martha, and Mary; Peter, however grand his status, must not overreach himself.[10]

The Disciples' Ascent

This first section of the book ends with its expected climax: Faith-Wisdom is rescued from the realms of Chaos. A great light-power comes to Jesus from the First Mystery, a second light-power shines out from Jesus himself, and in this dual strength he saves Faith-Wisdom. Here is *Pistis Sophia*'s account of the incarnation of Jesus. Three followers respond. First Mary Magdalene explains Jesus's dual nature; then Mary the mother of Jesus recalls (and she is undoubtedly the best person to do so) his childhood and his gestation and his links with John the Baptist; and finally John (the disciple, not the Baptist) explains the two aspects of the First Mystery, one looking inward and the other looking out. And for the whole next section of the book Jesus's own name disappears; the author refers to him as the First Mystery. Readers are growing in understanding as they read. As Faith-Wisdom has been freed from the darkness, so have they; they are able to see Jesus as the dual-natured First Mystery that he really is.

The First Mystery now retells, in similar terms but different accents, the story of Faith-Wisdom's rescue. Four times First Mystery speaks at length and asks his followers if they understand. Peter, James, Thomas, and Matthew respond in turn. A fifth time the First Mystery speaks, again quoting words of Faith-Wisdom herself; he asks for an interpretation from someone who understands. Mary comes forward: "My Lord, my mind is understanding at all times that I should come forward and give the interpretation of the words which Faith-Wisdom spoke, but I am afraid of Peter, for he threatens me and hates our race." The First Mystery insists again that anyone may speak who has been filled with the spirit of light, and Mary does so. Once more *Pistis Sophia* refuses to have the range of interpreters restricted by human authority.[11]

Mary Magdalene now turns the conversation in a new direction, from Faith-Wisdom, saved from the realms of Chaos and reinstalled in the Thirteenth Realm, to the realms far above. Mary is the spokesperson of the readers, and she acknowledges the special understanding they have been given in order to make progress from here on: understanding of the light, perception and greatly elevated thought, and superior understanding. From now on the questions put to Jesus come almost exclusively from Mary and (with far less frequency) from John. And Jesus, in replying to her, is replying to the other disciples and to the readers too. Jesus promises the world and far more: "Yet a little while and I will take you with your brothers and fellow disciples to all the places of the height. And you will look forth upon the whole world of mankind, and it will become the size of a speck of dust before you as a result of the great distance."[12]

Higher and higher Jesus will take them. Mary persists in her questions, insisting that "we question all things with assurance." Jesus confirms she may speak freely: "And I will fulfill you in all powers and all Fullnesses from the innermost of the inner to the outermost of the outer; from the Ineffable himself to the darkness of the darknesses, so that you may be filled with all knowledge." Mary knows her own power: "My person of light has ears and I receive all the words which you speak." The Saviour marvels at her answers, "because she had completely become pure spirit."[13]

Jesus warns that he is about to reveal additional secrets; he knows that his instruction is about to become hard to grasp. He urges his "disciples and companions and brothers" to be sober in the spirit that is in them and to bring forward the power of the perception of the light, for he is about to speak to them of the whole place of truth of the Ineffable. This is too much for the disciples; they despair. It is, as we would expect, Mary who speaks for them: "Have mercy on me, my Lord, for my brothers have heard and they have despaired because of the words which you have said to them. . . . What man in the world has power to understand that mystery?" Jesus reassures them: "That mystery belongs to you and to everyone who will hear you, and renounce this whole world and all the matter within it, and renounce every wicked thought within themselves, and renounce all the cares of this age."[14] Jesus opens before them—and before the readers—the vast landscape of salvation:

> Every person who will receive that mystery of the Ineffable and is completed in all its types and all its patterns, he is a person in the world but he is superior to all the angels and he will be superior to them all.
>
> Pistis Sophia 2.96 [230.3–8]

For over a page Jesus lists all the realms and rulers to which the initiate will be superior. This is not just description, but a ritualized, incantatory promise. Readers are to feel themselves drawing closer to the mystery, even as they read, and to sense the grandeur that awaits them. The initiate

> is a person in the world, but he is not of the world. And truly I say to you, that person is I and I am that person, and at the dissolution of the world . . . I will become ruler. . . . And all those who will receive mysteries in the Ineffable will become fellow rulers with me. . . . And truly I say to you, they are I and I am they. . . . I will give you the mystery of the Ineffable, namely: that mystery is I and I am that mystery. Now at this time, not only will you become rulers with me, but all those who will receive the mystery of the Ineffable will become fellow rulers with me in my kingdom. And I am they and they are I. . . . But because you will receive afflictions in the world. . . . your thrones will be joined to mine in my kingdom.
>
> From Pistis Sophia, 2.96 [231, 10–232, 22]

"I am they and they are I" is like the union formula, used by Marcus at the initiation of his prophets: "Adorn yourself as a bride expecting her bridegroom, so that you may be what I am and I may be what you are." We have heard of it from Thomas: "Whoever drinks from my mouth," promises his Jesus, "shall become as I am and I myself will become he, and the hidden things shall be revealed to him." It is recorded in a text of magical spells, and in a fragment of the lost *Gospel of Eve:* "He said to me, 'I am you and you are me; where you are, I am there.'" The promise of the biblical Jesus, to give thrones to his disciples and to have them forever where he is, has become the promise of a conscious, realized union of identity.[15]

Mary Magdalene, Pure Spirit

Mary is the most prominent of Jesus's interlocutors. Can she be "ranked" among the other men and women around him? "Maria Magdalene and John the Virgin," says the Saviour, "will be superior to all my disciples."[16] Mary Magdalene and John the Virgin, the Beloved Disciple in the story of his own gospel—woman and man are paired. John, like Mary, is a symbolic figure. At one point Mary, pure spirit, the pure spiritual one, asks about her antithesis, the counterfeit spirit. Jesus describes in detail the role of the true power of the spirit, which seeks the light; the soul, which seeks the place of mixture between light and darkness; and the counterfeit spirit, which urges the soul to all sinfulness and can at the person's death bring the delinquent soul to the judge, the Virgin of the Light. Pure spirit, in our human world, guides and illumines us; the counterfeit spirit tempts and entangles us. All the energy and effectiveness of the one is present—as an exact opposite—in the other. And who is listening to this account? Among the disciples is John the Virgin, the equal of Mary, who will himself sit on a throne beside the Saviour; he is hearing about another and greater power, the Virgin of the Light, who will sit in judgment on the world. Both Mary and John are, as it were, transparent, allowing the character of the spirit to be seen in and through them; but whereas John's role is only sketchily developed, Mary's is explored and exploited to the full.[17]

Other leaders among the men remain to be tested. Andrew does badly, Peter well. Andrew, apologetic and nervous, admits he cannot understand that people of this world will inherit the Kingdom of the Light. He is right to be anxious about his doubts; here—and in the whole of *Pistis Sophia,* only here—Jesus is stirred to anger by a disciple. He insists that he has himself brought the mysteries that would enable humans to inherit the Kingdom of the Light, and his disciples must urge the whole race of humankind to renounce the world and all the matter in it. Andrew has floundered; but the First Mystery has sent Jesus to forgive the sins of everyone, so he forgives Andrew for his ignorance. Will Peter be as forgiving? Jesus tests him to see whether he is merciful and forgiving as Jesus has commanded them. He orders Peter to banish a recidivist from the inheritance of the light, but Peter *refuses* to condemn the culprit: "My Lord, leave her again this time, so that we may give her the higher mysteries," and then it will become clear if she is suitable for the Kingdom of the Light. This is the Peter who has been given, in *Pistis Sophia* as in the Bible, the keys to the kingdom of heaven, and he will not lock the woman out. "For we, my Lord, are not only compassionate among ourselves, but we are compassionate to the whole race of mankind, so that they may be saved."[18]

Peter and Mary are vital figures, but—as we have heard—Peter resents her. He complains, early on, that Mary is speaking too much, and Mary says that Peter "hates our race" of women. Peter certainly does not stop her, and at times she speaks out quite openly on behalf of the male disciples: "Be not angry with me that I question all things with assurance and certainty, because my brothers preach them among the race of mankind and they hear and repent." Just once she overtly includes herself among the missionaries. She has asked about the dangers of death (not least from persecution); the Saviour, in reply, has assured all his disciples that a special mystery will free them from fate and from the material body, and that their soul will fly as a great outpouring of light to the height. Mary asks further about the power that the Saviour's mysteries give over the body and its suffering: "When we go to places of the country and they do not believe us and they do not listen to our words, and we perform a mystery of this kind [that is, a healing miracle] in those places, then they know truly that we are preaching the word of the God of All." Here, then, Mary includes herself explicitly among the missionaries.[19]

By now Mary is almost the only person other than Jesus to speak. Just once our author introduces another voice, seemingly to emphasize how deep is Mary's understanding. Salome asks Jesus, if the lower and evil rulers are the parents of the Gnostics on this earth, how could the Bible say, "He who shall leave his parents shall die the death"? Surely the Gnostic should *want* to leave the malignant parents of this fallen world behind. Now Mary intervenes. The power of light wells up in her; she asks and gets Jesus's permission to answer Salome's question, embraces Salome, and gives the answer. With a further embrace Salome exclaims, "The Saviour has power to make me understanding like yourself."[20] Jesus has enabled Mary to understand, and Mary enables Salome; there is a chain of capacity passed from woman to woman.

This Mary Magdalene is, in our physical cosmos, what Faith-Wisdom herself should have been in the intellectual cosmos. Mary insists over and over that she asks in assurance, not in doubt; she is as faith-ful as Faith-Wisdom. She always asks Jesus's permission to speak, so she never acts unilaterally. She is given in anticipation the sight of the Treasury of Light, which Faith-Wisdom sought. Mary, sober and illumined, is the exact opposite of Faith-Wisdom, turbulent and distraught.

A soul that understands Faith-Wisdom and her drama is on the way to understanding itself, its perils, and its salvation. The ascent is evoked in an incantation that invites readers to imagine the burden of their fleshly desires growing lighter and lighter as they envision their own ascent, well before they discard the burden of the flesh itself. They are invited to recognize themselves and the role they play within an all-embracing system of analogies that makes sense at last of the world they live in day by day. The text could work its magic when its readers heard all Mary Magdalene's questions and absorbed all Jesus's answers and so found themselves growing into their own proper relation to Faith, to Wisdom and to Jesus himself.

Spiritual and Executive Authority:
Different Roles for Different Leaders

In *Pistis Sophia* Mary Magdalene is once more the figure most intimately linked to Jesus, and this intimacy is once more a literary and pedagogic device. You may be wondering if, throughout these chapters on the Gnostics, my emphases have been too literary. Because only texts have survived from the Gnostics, I may seem to have imagined them forever in thrall to texts. In many circumstances, such a charge would be well founded, but not here. The Gnostics *were* obsessed with the stories preserved in sacred texts, and from them they devised ever more elaborate stories of their own. The Gnostic myths were self-consciously generated over the course of decades, in texts that were edited, fused, translated, and reedited; as traditions they may seem, at first sight, to have evolved like the bardic stories of Homer, but they were being deliberately woven into stories as heavily symbolic as the Narnia cycle by C. S. Lewis. In the stories of Mary Magdalene we are hearing a vast symphonic response to the stories of the old and new creation that found their most beautiful expression in John's Easter narrative.

These texts, nonetheless, belonged in the lives of individuals and (we may suspect) in the public life of churches. We would dearly like to know who commissioned and paid for the creation of these texts, and then who used them and authorized them for use by others, and finally how the texts were actually used. The *Gospel of Thomas* was designed to test and tease its users into understanding. The *Gospel of Philip,* for much of its length a slightly confusing compendium of instruction, has been given an inspiring end for its users' benefit. The *Gospel of Mary* may have been written up as a short and subversive text, commanding respect for all its teaching and thereby for the Mary who relayed the climax of that teaching—and thereby for authoritative and visionary women who had teaching to relay in the Gnostics' own churches. *Pistis Sophia* was probably edited into its present form (a long and expensive task) for use in catechesis.

We need to envision the evolution of Gnostic communities. To get some sense of the possibilities, we might compare the first followers of Jesus, from Easter through Paul's day to Matthew's and John's. Jesus's own friends were Jewish; during his life and after his death they attended their local synagogues. Some among them tried persuading their fellow Jews that Jesus was the Christ. They told stories about him, composed hymns ascribing to him a cosmic role, developed a ritual of initiation for others who came to acknowledge him, and met regularly for exclusive, ritual meals in honor of him—and all of it while they were still attending their synagogue. Gradually tensions grew. Pagans already attracted to Judaism were even more attracted to its new Christian version. The synagogue's leaders may at first have tolerated or even encouraged this new devotion, but the "Christian" leaders would have been claiming that trust in Jesus was indispensable for salvation and that his servants had an authority overriding that of all other leaders. The time came when such a synagogue either went Christian or the Christians (both Jewish and gentile) left and founded what we would call a church.

Now scroll on through several decades. Imagine Valentinus around 135 CE, disciple of a disciple of Paul and encouraged to think he might become bishop of Rome. He did not *mean* to be a sectarian. Valentinian texts were designed to supplement (not to be substitutes for) the New Testament and to reveal its inner truths; the Valentinian rites of initiation were designed to bring out, not to override, the significance of baptism, anointing, and the Eucharist. But tension grows; and when the Valentinians claim that their insights are *indispensable* for any believer's self-understanding, local churches with a strong Valentinian presence will either go—in their leadership and teaching overall—Valentinian, or the Valentinians will leave and set up their own. And during this process, perhaps over the course of decades, a Valentinian text such as the *Gospel of Philip* gets commissioned, composed, written up, authorized, and used; then it evolves, travels, and is translated to meet the changing circumstances of various churches, scattered through the Mediterranean, over the next two hundred years and more.

So much for the Valentinians. When we turn to the more "extreme" forms of Gnosticism, we may need to reimagine the trajectory and to envision the formation of quite new groups that claimed to embrace all the world's true, hidden wisdom by their loyalty to ancient Judaism, Platonism, numinous magic—and the great Jewish philosophical magician Jesus. Here were groups illumining all the great traditions by light cast from each onto all the others, a method whose success was evidence in itself of a single supreme fount of all truth and its knowledge.

Mary Magdalene herself plays more than one role in our texts. Sometimes she represents the women who were leaders in some Gnostic churches, sometimes all the women in those churches, sometimes—as an ideal female spirit—all those churches' members. She is frequently in dispute with Peter, but the variety of her own roles leaves us uncertain exactly which of her "characters" Peter is opposing in any one text. He might represent those within the same churches who resented women leaders or who resented women Gnostics, or he might, as the patron of mainstream churches, represent those who opposed all apparent Gnostics. To decide, from case to case, we need to envision some *practicalities*.

We have engaged our imagination on the Gnostics' myths and mysticism. Now we come right down to earth, to imagine the ways in which these Gnostics may actually have structured and lived out their communal lives. We are not going to end up with firm answers, but with a clearer view of the chequerboard of possibilities on which the answers once lay.

We need to acknowledge a variety between different Gnostic churches as wide as the variety we have found between the different texts. At one extreme, the *Gospel of Thomas* apparently faces the question of women's membership and defends such membership (against those who would deny it entirely) on the draconian basis that women must make themselves male. By contrast, in the *Gospel of Mary,* Mary Magdalene can even take the role of Jesus himself, and initially without being resented by the men. So what stirred the men's resistance here? Mary is actually *overtaking* the men in privileged insight; she is the new Beloved Disciple. Those who controlled the churches for which the *Gospel of Mary* was (subversively?) composed did not (it seems) try to suppress the insight and teaching of women, but they did want the authority to harness it.

The Gnostic communities varied; so did forms of authority. We are used within modern churches to leaders who hold, in one person, both spiritual and executive authority.[21] But we should not assume that the roles have always been so readily combined. There was the authority to formulate and teach doctrine, to preach to the members and to act as their spiritual mentors and guides; and there was executive authority to appoint additional leaders, to discipline members, and to run the churches' finances.

We can track some of these distinctions within the Bible itself. Paul, a maverick resented by the longer-established apostles, insisted he was father, mother, and brother to the members of the family of God. But he could only be in one place at a time. In his absence, who was running the administration of his churches? Letters were being written, messengers were travelling to and fro, authority was being exercised and delegated. It is surely telling that Paul, who generally did not baptize people himself, did baptize the wealthy Gaius, host to the whole Corinthian church; Crispus, the leader of the synagogue; and Stephanas, who had acted as ambassador for the Corinthians to Paul.[22] These men—educated, literate, and prosperous—were going to be important figures in Paul's churches. But the charismatic gifts of prophecy and speaking in tongues did not necessarily rest on them. Paul had to deal in 1 Corinthians with prophetic men and women who were not seeking overt executive power within the church for themselves; and by the same token they thought of themselves as quite free from the control that Paul's executive delegates were trying to impose on them.

In the Gospel of John we hear of the Beloved Disciple. He sat beside Jesus on the last evening before his death, was eyewitness to the crucifixion, was declared by Jesus to be the son of Jesus's own mother, and had been promised by Jesus, *"I want him to remain until I come."*[23] This promise had been understood to mean that the disciple would not die. His years would become a clock for his churches, trickling away like the sand in an hourglass; before the grains all passed through the neck, Jesus would return. This would in itself have given the disciple, in his lifetime, a stature enjoyed by no one else. And then there is Peter. Three times Peter had denied Jesus, and three times in John's last chapter Jesus commands him to feed Jesus's sheep; Peter is restored to intimacy with Jesus and is commissioned for the future. John presents Peter as the shepherd, a figure of nurture, protection, and control, who feeds the flock of Jesus, the true Shepherd. The Beloved Disciple, on the other hand, knows all that is to be known of Jesus and compiles the gospel. These are different—and potentially competing—roles.

The thread can be followed farther though the early decades of the churches. The biblical Jesus asks his disciples, *"Who do you say I am?"* Peter answers, in Matthew's account, *"You are the Christ, the son of the living God."* Matthew's Jesus praises and commissions Peter: *"On this rock I will build my church, and the gates of hell shall not stand out against it. I will give you the keys of the kingdom of heaven."* The *Gospel of Thomas* revisits the theme. Jesus's disciples ask who shall be great over them when Jesus has gone. Jesus replies: "Wherever you come, you will go to James the Just for whose sake heaven and earth came into being." Jesus himself then poses just such a challenge as Matthew's Jesus had posed: "Make a comparison to me and tell me who I am like." Thomas is setting out to redress the balance so heavily tilted by Matthew in Peter's favor. Peter answers first: "You are like a just angel." Then Matthew himself: "You are like a wise philosopher." But it is Thomas who does justice to Jesus's standing: "Master, my mouth will not be at all capable of saying who you are like." For this reply Thomas wins Jesus's highest praise; he is entrusted with three words so secret that they cannot be relayed to the other pupils. James, then, is the leader; Thomas is the privileged recipient of divine truths. Between them they have all the authority the churches need.[24]

The biblical book of Revelation, as we have heard, condemns the followers of Nicolas, apparently linking them with the false prophetess Jezebel and with the *deep things of Satan;*[25] a man's followers were invoking the teachings of a woman prophet who spoke of *deep things* as the Gnostics spoke of the Primal Depth. We have already heard of Apelles, who recorded the prophecies of Philoumene and on them based the doctrine of his new sect; he was the interpreter and executive, she was the mystic. We have heard of the women prophets Prisca and Maximilla, who inspired the Montanists. We know too of at least one woman among the Montanists who was known as an "elder"; her authority was (it seems) not based on prophetic power, and the distinction was worth making on an inscription. There were different roles to be filled by different leaders.

As we leave the Gnostics behind, we do well to imagine the scenes set in *Pistis Sophia* and the *Gospel of Mary*. They were likely based on scenes familiar in the churches that used the texts. Mary Magdalene is clearly portrayed as teaching within a church's meeting. It is less clear how often in our texts she is portrayed as preaching outside it. The *Gospel of Mary may,* in its Coptic version, envision Mary among the missionaries. It is in *Pistis Sophia* that Mary, just once, speaks clearly (not of the men's but) of "our" preaching to unbelievers.

We wonder, therefore, how widespread was the preaching of women— or the pressure to allow women to preach—on missions outside their church's own assemblies. The churches' organization was likely modeled on the organization of well-known social units. Here may lie the reason for that apparent restriction on the women's role. *If* these churches saw themselves as extended families, then the role of women within them will have been based, even if loosely, on women's domestic roles, and a matriarch, speaking up among the family elders within the home, is distinct from a woman preacher active out on the streets beyond it.

And so back to the *Gospel of Mary*. One leader presides over the meeting and gives permission to the church's members—men and women—to speak. A member—a woman!—describes a vision she has had of Jesus and then expounds, still on the authority of Jesus himself, the character and effect of a heavenly journey. The president and his assistant are bemused, then angry; this is not what they expected the woman to say at all. Another leader speaks up in the woman's favor; the meeting could soon break down into an exchange of personal insults. From fifteen hundred years ago, this fragmentary text gives us a perfect, lively vignette of church life; and for all the distance we have explored between the ancient Gnostics and ourselves, none of us would be surprised to encounter such a clash of gifts and roles today.

Farewell to the Gnostic Mary Magdalene

It is moving to watch from our vast distance the Gnostic attempts to follow foundational teachings through to their conclusion in doctrine and practice. I am no Gnostic. (Far from it.) But in the Gnostics' ever more elaborate constructions, at once mythological and mystical, there was an honorable attempt to account for *everything*. Gnostic myth revealed to the Gnostics their present place in that totality; Gnostic mysticism took them along the route in that totality towards their final, dazzling destination. The Gnostics saw how *strange* was the knowledge that faith required and offered, and they sought to make such knowledge possible. They fearlessly confronted the problem of evil's devastating presence in the world supposedly made by a good and omnipotent God. (After all, a faith that says, "Evil is just a mystery, beyond our comprehension," *may* look like a faith that is too dishonest or frightened or obtuse to look for understanding.) The Gnostics sought an account of evil; the mainstream churches accused them of pride. Adam and Eve had dared, against God's express command, to eat from the Tree of Knowing Good and Evil. For the mainstream churches, this was pride at its worst, in human rebellion against God. For the Gnostics, it was the moment at which humans came to adulthood as thoughtful, self-conscious, rational beings who would not be subject to a false god or to his self-proclaimed delegates on earth.

The Gnostics found in Mary Magdalene an invaluable icon. For the Valentinians of the *Gospel of Philip,* who emphasized the typologies of the threefold Christ and his pairs, Mary was the Saviour's consort on earth as the Spirit was in the Fullness and Wisdom was in heaven. Since every spiritual individual (whether man or woman) was imagined as a woman on her way to union with her angel bridegroom, Mary Magdalene herself could be the model Gnostic, winning ever greater insight from Jesus in her ascent through the realms towards the final bridal bedroom, the ultimate Holy of Holies. In the *Gospel of Mary* she takes the role of the Beloved Disciple and of Jesus himself. For those behind the *Dialogue of the Savior* who explored the possible conjunction of male and female outlook in the individual male-female Gnostic, Mary represented the female as the men in Jesus's entourage represented the male. In *Pistis Sophia* she is the earthly embodiment of Faith-Wisdom herself as Faith-Wisdom should always have been, and so she is both guide and model for the individual Gnostic.

In all these portrayals, the Gnostics' Mary represents the human being who rises to the threshold of divinity; in the same stories Jesus represents divinity descending to the threshold of the human. And so it will be for large parts of Christian history: the human soul has sung with a woman's voice, God with his Son's.[26]

Within the ancient androcentric world, Mary Magdalene and all the works of womankind were generally doomed to shine with a provisional splendour and then to be absorbed into maleness or utterly dissolved. Yet on her way—to absorption into the male, or to the highest heights, or both—Mary Magdalene made her mark in all these texts specifically *as a woman*. Some Gnostic authors—despite opposition from within their communities or from outside—*did* acknowledge the challenge that Mary mounted against an easy assumption of patriarchy, *did* set her up as an icon of human ascent towards the divine, and *did* insist that the authority she had from Jesus could be gainsaid by no human leader. We can catch from these texts only uncertain glimpses of the communities—and of the centres of authority within these communities—that produced and used them, but there is at once a care and a passion for Mary's roles that still enlivens these texts after nearly two thousand years. She should not and she will not be silenced.

"If the Saviour made her worthy," said Levi, "who are *you* to reject her? The Saviour certainly knows her without faltering. That is why he loved her more than us."

Gospel of Mary *18.10–15*

Part Three

THE TRAVELS
OF MARY MAGDALENE

Jesus Is Anointed
The Three Stories Summarized, in Their Order in Jesus's Life

Luke 7.36–50 An unnamed "sinful woman" who would in later centuries be identified as Mary Magdalene	*John 12.1–8* Mary the sister of Martha and Lazarus	*Mark 14.3–9* (closely followed by Matthew 26.6–13) An unnamed woman
In Galilee,	In Bethany, just outside Jerusalem	In Bethany,
during Jesus's ministry there,	six days before the Passover of Jesus's death,	two days before the Passover of Jesus's death,
in the house of Simon, a Pharisee,	with Lazarus among those dining, and Martha serving,	in the house of Simon the Leper,
"a woman who was, in the city, a sinner,"	Mary (Martha's sister),	an unnamed woman,
having brought an alabaster jar of perfume,	having got a pound of perfume, expensive and made of pure nard,	having an alabaster jar of perfume, valuable and made of pure nard,
standing behind him, by his feet, weeping, began to wet Jesus's feet with her tears,		
wiped them with her hair and was kissing them, and anointing them with the perfume.	anointed Jesus's feet with the perfume and wiped them with her hair.	broke open the jar and poured the perfume on Jesus's head.
Jesus criticizes Simon and declares the woman forgiven.		
	Judas Iscariot is (or rather pretends to be) angry at the waste; the money it cost could have been given to the poor.	Some disciples are angry at the waste; the money it cost could have been given to the poor.
	"Leave her alone," says Jesus, "so that she can keep it for the day of my burial.[1] You have the poor always with you, but you do not always have me."	"Leave her alone," says Jesus, "you have the poor always with you . . . but you do not always have me. What she could do, she has done. She has, in advance, perfumed my body for burial."

10

FROM THE MAGDALENE
TO LA MADELEINE
The Evolution of Mary Magdalene

> As Martha and Mary turned and went away, the Redeemer met
> them. So was fulfilled what was said, *When I had gone on a
> little way, I found him whom my soul loves* [Song of Songs 3.4].
> But the Redeemer answered and said, "Martha! Mary!" They
> said, "Rabbouni," which in translation means, "My Lord!"
>
> *Hippolytus (170–235),* Commentary
> on the Song of Songs *25.1–2*

> She whom Luke calls the sinful woman, whom John calls Mary
> [of Bethany], we believe to be the Mary [Magdalene] from whom
> seven devils were ejected according to Mark [16.9]. And what
> did these seven devils signify, if not all the vices?
>
> *Pope Gregory the Great (540–604), Homily 33,
> sermon preached in Rome on 21 September 591*

We have been attending all through this book to the New Testament,
the Gnostic texts, and the questions, insights, and aspirations that
shaped them. Let's now look forward, for a few pages, to follow just our
principal themes through the succeeding centuries.

Hippolytus of Rome (whose voice we have already heard vehemently
opposing the Gnostics) wrote a commentary on the Song of Songs. He
saw and explored the hints that John had added to the Easter story, that
Mary Magdalene (with Martha, according to Hippolytus) was to Jesus as
the woman in the Song of Songs was to her beloved:

> The Redeemer said, "Do not go on touching me, for I am not yet
> ascended to my Father." But she clung to him and said, "I will not

let you go, until I lead you in and bring you into my heart." *I will not let him go, until I lead him into my mother's house and the treasury of her who bore me* [Song 3.4]. Since the love of Christ is gathered within her, in her body, she will not let him go. O holy woman, who clung to his feet, so as to be able to fly upward into heaven!

Hippolytus, Commentary on the Song of Songs 25.2

Eve had been tempted by the Tree of Knowing Good and Evil; now an Eve clings passionately to Christ, the Tree of Life. When he rises to the Father as a new sacrifice, he may take her with him, for now she is clothed not with fig leaves to cover her shame, but with the Holy Ghost. Here is a grand moment, when the women are described as "apostles to the apostles."

These women offer us a good testimony, they who were apostles to the apostles, sent by Christ. To the women, first, the angels said, *"Go and tell the disciples, 'He is going ahead of you to Galilee; there you will see him.'"* And so that these apostles should not doubt the angels, Christ himself met the apostles, so that these women might be apostles of Christ and through obedience might make up for what was lacking in Eve. O new consolation! Eve was named an apostle!

Hippolytus, Commentary on the Song of Songs 25.6–7

Hippolytus invokes the bride of the Song, in its different verses, in different but overlapping ways. The result is a rich, multivalent symbol for the people of Israel before Christ, for those who (from among the Jews and the Gentiles) have become followers of Christ, and for those Jews who have not acknowledged Christ. *Tell me, you whom my soul loves, where do you graze your flock, where do you rest at midday?* Interpreted: the Jews complain that God has gone to the heathen nations, but it is in their power to confess their sins and be forgiven. *At night I sought him whom my soul loves.* Interpreted: so did the women who came at night to Jesus's grave; Martha and Mary fulfilled the Song's saying either alongside the synagogue or (in a different version of Hippolytus's text) as a symbolic duo in themselves, "Mary and their synagogue."[2]

Most significant for us is the convergence of the woman's or women's voice with that of Hippolytus and so of his readers. For most of this next paragraph, either could be speaking:

Look at me, bound fast to the feet—and not with a chain that I am trying to break—I am holding fast to the feet of Christ. Don't let me fall back to the earth, don't let me be tempted, for the serpent is trapping me and is trying again to arrange a Fall through me, is straining again to defeat Adam. Take me up to Heaven! O blessed woman, who will not be separated from Christ!

Hippolytus, Commentary on the Song of Songs 25.3

And why is Martha named with Mary? We know from the New Testament that Jesus freed Mary Magdalene from seven devils, that she saw Jesus die, brought ointment to his tomb to anoint his body on Easter Day, and was the first to see him risen from the dead. So far, so good. But we know too of Mary of Bethany, the sister of Martha and Lazarus, who anointed Jesus in the week before his death. Hippolytus has earlier identified the woman who anointed Jesus not as Mary of Bethany, but as her sister Martha. It is a striking move. Hippolytus has surely identified the biblical anointer, Mary of Bethany, as Mary Magdalene, and the former's sister, Martha, is now the latter's sister too; now this Martha comes with her sister, the composite Mary, to the tomb of Jesus.[3]

Mary Magdalene and Mary of Bethany—do these names in the gospels speak of two Marys or of one? As we shall see in a couple of pages, it was a fateful coincidence of names.

Brides of Christ

The Song of Songs is sensuous to the core:

> *Let him kiss me with the kisses of his mouth;*
> *For your breasts are better than wine.*
> *And the scent of your oils is above all fragrances.*
> *And your name is oil poured out;*
> *Therefore the young women love you.*

Song of Songs 1.2–3

Origen (185–254) of Alexandria in Egypt, heir to Clement's thought and the greatest scholar of the early churches, addressed the Song in a commentary that has echoed through Christian history ever since: the Song, Origen explained, is a wedding song of a bride who was being married to Christ, the Word of God, and burned with heavenly love for him.

Imagine, first, the bride as the Church; such imagery did triumphant justice to the prospect of perfect union restored between Christ and his people. Origen saw in the Song a second bride as well, the believing soul, united in mystical marriage with its lord. By the end of the fourth century such "brides of Christ" were almost exclusively consecrated virgin women, whose marriage to Christ was consummated in and through their lifelong chastity. The humanity of Christ is his soul, and his full union with that soul will be manifest in the union of individual souls with Christ at the end of our earthly time. So the virgins will have their final reward, when (writes a follower of Origen) "their eyes will see the Lord, their ears will hear his words, their mouth will kiss their Bridegroom and their nose will take in his sweet perfume. Virgin hands will touch the Lord, and the purity of their flesh will give him joy."[4] This is a melody familiar from the *Gospel of Philip,* but transposed into a different key. The consummation promised to Valentinian men and women, probably married—and imagined as female spirits—is now promised specifically to women dedicated to chastity.

Origen and his followers used sublimely erotic language to overcome eroticism. The soul, said Origen, is led by a heavenly love and desire when it once perceives the beauty and glory of the Word of God; the soul falls in love with the Word's splendour and receives from him some dart and wound of love, the saving wound, and thereafter will burn with the blessed fire of his love. It is as if the Word is armed with Cupid's arrows. How dangerous, then, the Song could be. If anyone fleshly reads it, who does not know how to listen to the names of love purely and with chaste ears, he may twist everything he has heard from the inner man to the outer and fleshly man, and it will seem that because of the spirit he is impelled and moved to the lusts of the flesh. So the Song is properly sung just for and by the soul who is mature and ready for marriage and for her entry to the house of God, the bridal bedroom.[5] With such a soul, the reader will not misunderstand this talk of our "love" of God, so Origen claims he can without danger speak of loving God with a passionate, "erotic" love and can even say of Christ, "My love [the object of my passion] has been crucified."[6]

* * *

Origen followed Hippolytus's lead in understanding the fragrant oil with which Christ was anointed as oil offered by Christ himself. *My spikenard gave off its* [or, *his*] *scent;* so, said Origen, the bridegroom wafts his scent back to the bride. "We need not think it strange that Christ [that is, the Anointed] should be the spikenard and yield its scent and be the ointment which makes those anointed by it to be Christs [that is, Anointeds] themselves, as it says in the psalm, *Do not touch not my Christs* [Ps. 104.15]."[7]

Once more we are not far from the world of the *Gospel of Philip*, "Become not a Christian, but a Christ."

Origen read the gospels as carefully as anyone ever has. He noticed, just as modern scholars do, all the differences in detail between the different stories of Jesus being anointed. Origen was certain that Scripture could not lie. Jesus must, then, have been anointed on three different occasions and (so different are the women's circumstances) by three different women. He draws a moral from the distinction between Jesus's feet and his head. Good works done for others—giving in charity, visiting the sick, humility, and kindness—may be done either from a love of natural and human justice or from a love of God; and if from the love of God, then they do constitute a good oil that may be poured, often for the remission of sins, over Christ's feet. Far more precious is the faithfulness that is of no benefit to other humans, but only promotes the glory of God. This is the ointment that anoints the head of Christ and runs down through his whole body, the Church; and this is the special work, not of penitents such as the sinful woman, but of perfect saints such as Mary of Bethany.[8]

These distinctions between the women were maintained and exploited in the Eastern churches. In the Western imagination those several women who anointed Jesus will become all one woman with one poignant biography: Mary Magdalene.

The Mediaeval Magdalene: Three Women in One

It was a beguiling possibility, for readers of the biblical gospels, to conflate several of the gospels' different women into one. In 591 Pope Gregory the Great preached the sermon in Rome that settled Mary's fate in the West for fourteen hundred years: "She whom Luke calls the sinful woman, whom John calls Mary [of Bethany], we believe to be the Mary [Magdalene] from whom seven devils were ejected according to Mark [16.9, in the verses added later to Mark's gospel]. And what did these seven devils signify, if not all the vices?" Gregory's sermons circulated for centuries in the West, bound in collections and authorized for annual delivery. Mary Magdalene was now both the nameless sinner and Mary of Bethany. So she acquired a family, for Mary of Bethany (who attended to Jesus's every word) was the sister of Martha (who busied herself with practicalities) and of the Lazarus whom Jesus raised from the dead. How fitting that the woman who anointed Jesus in his lifetime should be just the woman who brought ointment to anoint his body after death: Mary Magdalene. Gregory makes the most of the connections between her old sins and new life.[9]

It is clear that in the past Mary Magdalene, intent on forbidden acts, had applied the ointment to herself, to perfume her flesh. So what she had used on herself, to her shame, she was now offering to God, to her praise. Everything about her that she had used for pleasure, all this she now offered up as a sacrifice. She offered to God every service in her penitence which she had disdained to give God in her guilt.

Pope Gregory the Great, Homily 33

Thereafter, throughout western Europe, Mary's story was told as follows. She was a prostitute who repented of her way of life. Driven by her love for Jesus, she came uninvited to a party, stood at Jesus's feet, washed his feet with her tears, dried them with her hair, and anointed them with perfume. Jesus declared her past sins forgiven and drove from her the seven devils—representing all seven of the deadly sins—which had led her into wrongdoing. From then on she accompanied Jesus and helped from her own resources to maintain him and his entourage; and she dedicated herself wholly to his teaching and its contemplation—much to the annoyance of her more practical sister, Martha, at one meal in their own house, when Mary sat at Jesus's feet and left Martha to prepare and serve the meal alone.[10]

Mary supported Jesus out of her own means, so she clearly had a substantial income. It was no surprise, then, that Mary and Martha had a second home, at Bethany, a short way southeast of Jerusalem. Their brother, Lazarus, fell ill there and died. Jesus arrived too late, but he commanded the tomb to be opened, and he called to Lazarus, who came out alive from his grave. This Lazarus was among those at a dinner given for Jesus in Bethany. Martha, characteristically, was serving. Mary brought in a jar of ointment. She anointed Jesus's feet with it and wiped them with her hair; she anointed his head too. Once more she has anointed Jesus, this time not with the bitter tears of penitence, but with the beautiful perfume of gratitude; not just on his feet, in deep humility, but on his head as well. Jesus linked her action with his own impending burial.[11]

Within days of this dinner, Jesus had been betrayed. As he died, who stood loyally by the cross? Just one man from his followers and a group of women, among them, Mary Magdalene. She watched Jesus being buried and on Easter morning returned to the tomb with more ointment, this time to anoint his whole body. But the body was gone. As the light rose, she was given the greatest privilege of all—to her the risen Jesus first appeared. He commissioned her to give the news of his rising to his male disciples.[12]

It is a stirring story. This Mary Magdalene became a model for various parts and forms of Christian life. She was the sinner who repented, the contemplative figure who chose to hang on Jesus's every word and so chose *the good portion*,[13] the active figure who more than once brought ointment for Jesus, and the believer commissioned to tell others of his resurrection. So she represented all Christians, men and women.

But this was not all. She was as well a *woman,* and the sin she regretted was sexual. As a prostitute, she represented the sexual temptation the celibate men who ran the mediaeval church could only fight, never wholly defeat; as a penitent, she acknowledged and renounced the power of her own allure. So she represented for those celibate men both the danger that all women posed and the way—through women's own life-long penitence—to its resolution. Mary Magdalene, in one of her many roles, became a weapon in the self-defense the church's celibate leaders mounted against the power of women in general and against the sexual appeal that those leaders took to typify it.

And this Mary—with her profound, exemplary story of restoration—was created by the mediaeval church itself. The gospels themselves do not even suggest (let alone state) that she was one of the women who anointed Jesus, nor, therefore, that she was the sinful women in Galilee or the Mary of Bethany who listened so carefully to Jesus's teaching.

Most striking of all the stories is Luke's, of the woman who anointed Jesus's feet with perfume at a meal hosted by one Simon the Pharisee. The greater the detail in which we envision the scene, the more revealing the story becomes. It was a gesture of wild extravagance to anoint a person's feet with perfume; and surely a gesture with erotic overtones for a woman with long, loose hair to caress a man's feet and rub them with ointment. Don't her actions reveal her profession? She was surely a prostitute. So the story was read for centuries, but no longer. As we have seen, there is no evidence that the woman is Mary Magdalene; the story really belongs in this book as an appendix, and that is where we will attend to it, in Appendix A.

We are dedicated nowadays to the search for historical truth—what actually happened—and so we might view this composite Mary with some disdain. But our forebears looked to the biblical past for inspiration, in evidences of God's grace and judgment at work, in examples to follow and avoid. Scripture offered innumerable patterns of good and evil and their outworking, ready to be discovered and explored and offered for the guidance of the faithful. We shall be hearing shortly of St. Bernard of Clairvaux (1090–1153). From Bernard's circle came a long biography of Mary Magdalene. Its author draws over and over on the Song of Songs.

Mary Magdalene: Becoming Venus

By the sixteenth century, artists were painting Mary Magdalene as a patently erotic figure. Clothed only in her luscious hair, writhing in the agonies of her penance, she was more likely to stir viewers' sexual fantasies than any sorrow for sexual sins. Mary Magdalene, repenting her loves, was becoming Venus, goddess of love. When did an artist first make this link? Far earlier and with far more delicate a sensibility than we might expect.

Among the most famous churches in Italy is the Basilica of St. Francis at Assisi. It was decorated in an astonishing campaign—covering almost every wall and ceiling with frescoes—by Giotto (1276–1337) and his pupils. There is an Upper and a Lower Basilica, and in the Lower there is a Chapel of Mary Magdalene, decorated around 1308. The ceiling, simply vaulted, comprised four lunettes, three-dimensional "triangles," whose flat base was the top of a wall, with two rising sides converging at the centre of the ceiling. Two of these lunettes appropriately show Mary Magdalene being taken up to the heaven beyond the chapel's ceiling. In one she

Mary Magdalene Taken to Heaven in a Shell (fresco, ca. 1308),
by Giotto (1276–1337) and assistants. Photo: Lower Basilica of St. Francis,
Assisi / Franco Cosimo Panini Editore S.p.A.

is in profile, half length, covered by her hair; her hands are raised in front of her in prayer; she is carried on a cloud by four angels. In the other she is shown, upper torso, in a shell, once more supported by angels (see illustration, opposite page).

Both these figures have behind them a long artistic history; both are derived from portrayals of Venus, goddess of love. The first is inspired by mediaeval attempts to reproduce the most famous of all paintings of Venus in the ancient world, the *Venus Emerging from the Sea* by Apelles, brought to Rome by the emperor Augustus and described by Pliny. The second is inspired by ancient sarcophagi showing Venus in a shell, supported by putti; such a Coptic coffin of the fifth century is shown in the illustration above. The artist in Assisi, it seems, feels no conflict as he proudly appropriates the greatest of classical precedents for his theme; to do justice to Mary Magdalene rising to heaven he programmatically reminds his viewers of Venus rising from the sea. Mary rises as the Christian soul will rise, transformed by Christ's love into the loving Beloved.

The Birth of Venus, Coptic (limestone, fifth century), Louvre, Paris.
Photo: Louvre, Paris, France / The Bridgeman Art Library.

He was not writing simply to describe the love of Mary for Jesus, but to stir such love into life within his readers.

> Happy is the one who has heard all this concerning Mary Magdalene with pleasure. More happy the one who has believed and remembered it with devotion. Yet more happy the one who has marveled at Mary's holiness, and reverenced her with love and burned to imitate her. And most happy by far the one who has been so moved by and who has taken such delight in the surpassing fragrance of Mary's deeds that he has followed the example of her conversion, has imprinted in himself the image of her repentance and has filled his spirit with her devotion, to the degree that he has made himself a partaker of that best part which she chose.
>
> The Life of Saint Mary Magdalene
> and of her Sister Saint Martha, *lines 1736–48* [14]

The historical doubts lingered among those who knew Scripture well, but this did not prevent the use of Mary's immensely rich, symbolic history. Domenico Cavalca (1270–1342) wrote a biography of Mary in which he managed a careful balance, elaborating the stories of Scripture and alerting his readers when he did so: "I do not trouble myself about chronology in my meditations; it delights me to tell of the Magdalene and what she did at this time according to my fancy. . . . While I think of her I must perforce think of Jesus and his mother." [15]

The New Devotion

Our generation has heard of Mary Magdalene among the Gnostics—and of Mary Magdalene in France. We do well to turn our eyes briefly to Burgundy in France, in the twelfth century, and in particular to St. Bernard of Clairvaux, for he was at the heart of a new devotional movement that swept through Europe, touching the imagination and emotions of the faithful to their depths. Believers were to bring the life and death of Jesus vividly before their eyes. In their imagination they were to watch and even to play the parts of those around Jesus: those who loved him, who were forgiven and healed by him, who followed him and then betrayed, abandoned, or denied him; those who stood at the foot of the cross in tears and watched him die; and those who saw him, risen in triumph, on Easter Day. All that Jesus's dearest friends had felt, believers were to feel too: sorrow for their own wrongdoings, trust in his forgiveness, and

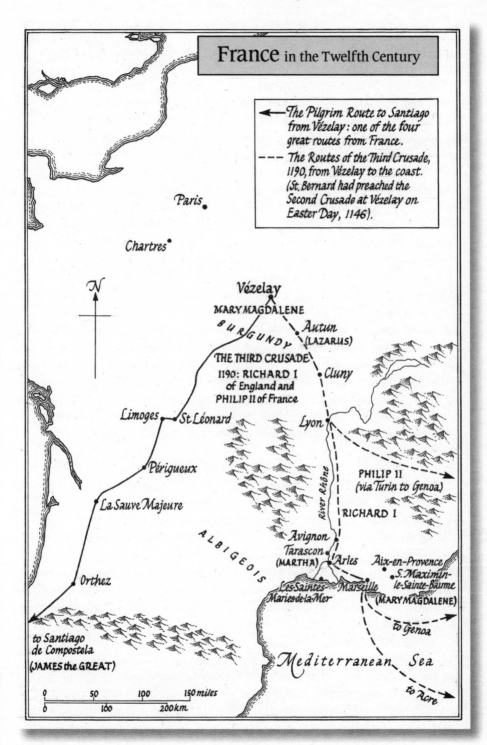

France in the Twelfth Century

⟵ *The Pilgrim Route to Santiago from Vézelay: one of the four great routes from France.*

– – – *The Routes of the Third Crusade, 1190, from Vézelay to the coast. (St. Bernard had preached the Second Crusade at Vézelay on Easter Day, 1146).*

Paris

Chartres

N

Vézelay
MARY MAGDALENE
BURGUNDY
Autun
(LAZARUS)

THE THIRD CRUSADE
1190: RICHARD I
of England and
PHILIP II of France

Cluny

Limoges   St Léonard

Lyon

Périgueux

River Rhône

PHILIP II
(via Turin to Genoa)

La Sauve Majeure

RICHARD I

ALBIGEOIS

Avignon
Tarascon
(MARTHA)   Arles   Aix-en-Provence
S. Maximin-
le-Sainte-Baume
(MARY MAGDALENE)

Orthez

Les Saintes-   Marseille
Maries-de-la-Mer

to Genoa

to Santiago
de Compostela
(JAMES the GREAT)

Mediterranean Sea

to Acre

0   50   100   150 miles
0   100   200 km

grateful, life-giving love in response to his love. Sermons, tracts, plays, and paintings—all were used, in the coming centuries, to stir and channel the fervor of the faithful.

Most of us now can imagine the scene of Jesus's death only with an effort and can imagine ourselves *into* the scene—as part of it—only at the risk of an embarrassed self-consciousness. To do justice to the Mary Magdalene of the Middle Ages, we need to entrust our cautious, rational minds to a world of vivid imagination. This world was given shape by the sites themselves of Jesus's life, by the re-creation of those sites in western Europe, by the presence in Europe of the relics of saints who had walked this earth with Jesus, and by the splendours of the church's liturgy. In the twelfth century these centres of holiness, already ancient, were reenvisioned, and so they helped to fuel the new form of devotion, intense and personal, that swept through Europe; and in its vanguard—as a model of Christian life—was the tearful, penitent, dedicated figure of Mary Magdalene. Her story took on new and elaborate forms, and her prestige spread throughout Europe, for she was an icon of love's different forms and their coexistence in each one of us.

Those who could make a pilgrimage could see the very settings of Jesus's life and death. To stir the devotion of those who could not, the sanctity of the Holy Land was re-created in western Europe. In Bologna were the Seven Churches at St. Stefano, a site linked with Jerusalem by 887; each of the churches evoked a scene of Jesus's suffering. A legend in Pisa claims that the main mediaeval cemetery, the Camposanto, was filled with earth that had been brought from the Holy Land by Bishop Lanfranchi; burial in the Camposanto was (vividly and literally) burial in the Holy Land.

Most sacred of all the sites linked with Jesus's life and death was the Church of the Holy Sepulchre in Jerusalem, a round church built by the emperor Constantine on the supposed site of Christ's burial. In the Middle Ages, round or octagonal churches were built in Europe to re-create the shape and the sanctity of the Holy Sepulchre.[16] I am writing this book from one such church, the Temple Church in London, built by the Knights Templar and the grandest of the round churches to survive in England. To walk into our round church, in the Middle Ages, was to walk into Jerusalem.

By the twelfth century, elementary dramas were enhancing the liturgies of the church's great festivals, and they would become ever more elaborate. Some developed the character of Mary Magdalene as an easy-going, lascivious woman, but others took more care. An Easter play recorded at Vic in northeast Spain builds up to Mary Magdalene's sight of Jesus.[17] Mary speaks in a rare poetic meter best known from a secular song of the

The Cathars and Mary Magdalene

In the twelfth century new versions of the Gnostics' beliefs reached western Europe from the Middle East and broke out in a new form as the Cathar movement. It was a time of enormous intellectual excitement. New notions were burgeoning of the love that men and women might offer to each other and to God, and the pressures that gave rise to St. Bernard and the mystics gave rise as well to the great heresies.

The Cathars, victims of the church's Albigensian Crusade, were believed to claim that Jesus and Mary Magdalene had been lovers. On 22 July 1209, on the Feast of Mary Magdalene herself, the Cathars' town of Béziers in southwest France was torched by the papal forces, and up to fifteen thousand people were killed. It seemed only too fitting at the time "that these disgusting dogs were taken and massacred during the feast of the one whom they had insulted."

The Cathars' claim was not quite what we might expect. They drew stark distinctions between good and evil and the realms of each. Imagine, first, a higher world in which the real drama of Christ's life and death was played out. The Cathars thought (so we hear) that "Christ was born according to the flesh from the Blessed Virgin and truly suffered and was crucified, killed and buried and rose on the third day, but he [the typical Cathar] thinks that all this happened in a higher world and not in this one. . . . In that world all humanity incurred death on account of sin . . . and when their bodies had been buried their souls descended necessarily into hell, that is to this world, and Christ descended to this hell to help them."

There are two gods. The evil god of the Old Testament lied to Adam and Eve about dying, slaughtered the people of Sodom and Gomorrah, and drowned the whole world in the Flood. The Cathars "said in their secret meetings that the Christ who was born in the earthly and visible Bethlehem and died crucified in Jerusalem was the evil Christ and that Mary Magdalene was his concubine; she was the woman taken in adultery (John 7.53–8.11). The good Christ never ate nor drank nor wore real flesh; he appeared in the world only in a wholly spiritual manner in the body of Paul; that's why we said 'the earthly and visible Bethlehem,' for the heretics imagined another earth, new and invisible, where, according to some, the good Christ has been born and crucified."[18]

These reports (from the Cathars' enemies) are not easy to interpret in detail, but there is no precedent, in this construction of two worlds, for the modern stories of a human Jesus living on this earth as we understand it and being in love with Mary Magdalene.

time in which a woman dreams of her dead lover and tries in vain to clasp the apparition. This Mary, who has lost her Jesus, evokes in every line the Song of Songs: *"While the king was in his place of rest, my spikenard gave off its scent. . . . My beloved came down into his garden. . . . I opened the door to my beloved, but he had turned away and had left."*[19]

> MARY: The king had already gone to his place of rest
> And my scent of spikenard filled the air;
> I entered the garden where he had come down,
> But he had already left and turned away.
> So I go out looking for him, through the night,
> Turning now here, now there, I find him nowhere.

The play presents the angels as the watchmen of the Song of Songs:

> MARY: The watchmen with burning zeal are running
> towards me;
> When I have passed them, I will find my husband!

She does, indeed; for the play, here following John's story almost to the letter, has Jesus appear as the gardener and Mary answer him:

> GARDENER: Woman, why are you weeping? Who are you
> looking for?
> MARY: They have taken my Lord, and I do not know
> where they have put him.
> If you have taken him, tell me and I will remove him.
> GARDENER: Mary, Mary, Mary!
> MARY: *(Answer again)*
> Raboni, Master, Raboni![20]

The Relics of Mary Magdalene: Provence and Vézelay Compete

With sufficient resources and ambition, it was possible to realize in a sacred place and sacred drama something of the sanctity of the holy places themselves. But sanctity—and its power—could be far more readily transported in the relics of the saints. Saints in their lifetime on earth had healed in the name of Christ (as the New Testament itself bore witness)[21] and could still, in heaven, be invoked to heal the sick. Their relics were conduits of their saving power. We can still capture some sense of the sacred landscape—physical and imaginative—that these saints and our forebears inhabited together.

Where, then, is the body of Mary Magdalene? The Eastern churches believe that Mary died in Ephesus and was buried there; her body was later taken to Constantinople (by the emperor who took Lazarus's body from Cyprus to Constantinople too). But in the West she had far more bizarre adventures to undergo. Their centre was the Burgundian abbey of Vézelay. It is impossible to map with any confidence the movements of the supposed relics of Mary, which are still, to this day, in Vézelay (and the following paragraphs make no claim at all to be discussing Mary's actual body), but here is a plausible outline.

The first community at Vézelay, for women, was founded in 859 by Count Girart and consecrated to the Virgin Mary, Peter, and Paul. Around 877 this gave way to a second community, for men, led by Abbot Eudes. Among Eudes's friends was Badilon, who had travelled to the East and then joined the community at Vézelay. Girart and Badilon will feature again in far later elaborations of the story, and it may well be that Badilon did bring some relic back from Constantinople or the Holy Land. If he did, the relic was disregarded for over a hundred years.[22]

We must turn our eyes, for a moment, down to the south of France, to Provence. In the early fifth century a certain Lazarus was bishop of Aix. In the centuries following his death, he was confused with the Lazarus of Bethany—the brother of Martha and of the Mary who was by now firmly identified as Mary Magdalene—whom Jesus had raised from the dead. The bishop's tomb in Marseilles came to be regarded as the tomb of that quite different Lazarus. In 972 the bishop of Autun in Burgundy removed the body of "Lazarus" from Marseilles to Autun; within a few years, Lazarus's head had been moved on from Autun to Avallon, another Burgundian city. It was time for Vézelay, only a few miles from Avallon, to see the potential in its own relics of this family from Bethany—the relics of Mary Magdalene brought back from the East by Badilon.

By the early eleventh century, Vézelay was in need of reform, a task that fell to its abbot, Geoffrey. Geoffrey revived every part of the abbey's life. Early in his rule, 1037–43, it was said that the body of Mary Magdalene had been brought from Judea to Vézelay by Girart and Badilon, and by 1037 miracles at Vézelay were being ascribed to her.

In 1049–50 Geoffrey was present when the pope deposed the corrupt Abbot Arnould of Pothières (sister house to Vézelay), and he knew the bishops who had benefited from the popularity of two churches, at Verdun and at Besançon, consecrated by the pope in honor of Mary Magdalene. Geoffrey saw every reason to adopt Mary Magdalene, the

Clad in Her Hair Alone:
Mary Magdalene and Mary of Egypt

In two small panels painted by the Flemish artist Quinten Massys (1466–1530), Mary Magdalene is on the left and Mary of Egypt on the right. The panels were almost certainly the wings of a triptych; a central panel, now lost, would have shown the figure—probably Jesus—whom they are kneeling to worship. The ensemble would have been portable and suitable for private devotion. Massys has made the two Marys almost identical. We can tell which is which only by their attributes: Mary Magdalene has at her feet the jar of ointment from which she anointed Christ; Mary of Egypt has the small loaves that sustained her for years.

Long before Massys painted, Mary Magdalene had been imagined in the form of her namesake, Mary of Egypt, as a penitent living in the desert. Mary of Egypt was a classic penitent. Lavishly promiscuous in Egypt (although not quite a prostitute—she gave herself free of charge), she made her way to Jerusalem by servicing young men on board ship. She tried to enter the Church of the Holy Sepulchre, was prevented by a strange force, and came to a dreadful recognition of her sinfulness. At the command of the

Virgin Mary she left Jerusalem. As she did so she was given three coins with which she bought three loaves of bread. In one version of her story, she ate half of the first before crossing the Jordan; the rest lasted her for the next seventeen years; thereafter she ate no earthly food at all. In another version, the loaves renewed themselves. These are the loaves shown by Massys at Mary's feet.

She headed from Jerusalem for the river Jordan. She received Communion, then crossed the river (symbol of baptism), and lived for the next forty-seven years alone in the desert (symbol of God's austere, purifying power). Shortly before her death she walked over the waters of the Jordan (back to the normal world of human life), received Communion once more, and ate three lentils. At her death, back in the desert, she was buried by a lion, for she was at peace with the wild beasts (as Adam and Eve had been in paradise) and was at one with Christ, the Lion of Judah.

Massys shows both Marys covered with hair. Mary Magdalene, as soon as she was identified as the woman who washed and anointed Jesus's feet, was bound to be imagined with hair almost to her waist, long enough to wipe the feet dry. But Mary of Egypt? Just before her death, she was met by the monk Zossima during his Lenten retreat in the desert. He was amazed to see any human there. "It was a woman, and she was naked, her body black as if scorched by the fierce heat of the sun, her hair on her head was white as wool and short, coming down only to her neck." So how did Mary Magdalene—let alone the short-cropped Mary of Egypt—both come to be imagined with hair covering the whole body? Both have been assimilated to a third, quite different, saint, St. Agnes of Rome. According to a legend current by the fifth century, Agnes was determined to preserve her chastity as a bride of Christ. She refused to marry her suitor, was denounced to the local prefect as a Christian, and was thrown naked into a brothel. Her hair grew miraculously to protect her modesty.

Mary of Egypt and Mary Magdalene—the two were easily merged into one. The so-called *Apostolic Life of Mary Magdalene,* from the eleventh century, knows of the confusion and resists it, saying the story of Mary Magdalene's years in the desert "is very false and is borrowed by creators of fable from the deeds of the Egyptian Mary."[23] If Massys even knew of any such grumbles, he sensibly ignored them to create his enchanting pair of saints.

Mary Magdalene and *St. Mary of Egypt* (oil on panel),
by Quinten Massys (1466–1530).
Photos: Philadelphia Museum of Art: John G. Johnson Collection.

reformed sinner, as the patron of his abbey's reformation. In 1050 Mary Magdalene was recognized as one of the patrons of Vézelay.

Back south in Provence, this version was contested. It had long been said, in the East, that the enemies of the biblical Lazarus had put him in a leaky boat with his sisters, and that they had floated safely to Cyprus, where he became bishop. In the West, the story evolved in the eleventh century. Lazarus and his sisters, it was now said, were put into a boat without oars or rudder, and they landed in southern France. Lazarus became bishop and was buried in Marseilles. His companions were (of course) buried in Provence too, Mary Magdalene among them. This was an effective story, blessing the city with the presence of the saints while they were still alive and ever since.

Vézelay met the difficulty. Its new story, also emerging in the eleventh century, would win the day. Mary had indeed come to Provence in her lifetime and had been buried in Aix; in 749 her bones, in danger of desecration during the Saracen invasions of Provence, had been rescued by Badilon and brought to safety in Burgundy. So Vézelay triumphed.[24] In 1058 the pope formally declared that the abbey held her bones and declared her to be its sole patron. For a century or more, Vézelay was the starting point for one of the great pilgrim routes through France to Santiago de Compostela.[25]

There was still room for refinement. Had the saints really reached Provence in that miraculous but random way? According to one biography from the twelfth century, the apostles in Jerusalem, after the death of the first martyr Stephen, divided up the church's missionary fields. France and Spain were entrusted to Maximinus, one of the seventy followers of Jesus and now at the head of twenty-four bishops. Mary Magdalene joined him; so did Martha and Lazarus, himself now bishop of Cyprus. They landed at Marseilles.[26]

As legends grew about Mary, so they grew too about her companions. The supposed relics of Martha of Bethany were discovered and enshrined in 1187 at Tarascon, where (it was said) she had tamed a dragon (*tarasque*); her relics there include her fingers, scull, and body and the little cross of incorruptible wood with which she touched the dragon. The tomb of Maximinus is said to be at St. Maximin, with additional relics of his body at Avignon and Aix. In the eighteenth century there was still a chapel at Aix, said to have been built by Maximinus and to be the place where Mary Magdalene died after her last Communion; any woman who entered the chapel would die the moment she did so.

Such legends lasted. In the early nineteenth century the parliament of Aix condemned to be burned a book showing that Lazarus had never

The Tomb of Mary Magdalene?

In Marseilles, in the Church of St. Maximin (Maximinus was one of the companions of Mary, Martha, and Lazarus on their journey), is a sarcophagus identified throughout the Middle Ages as Mary Magdalene's. Much of the damage to its reliefs was caused by pilgrims eager to take home with them some sacred souvenir of the Magdalene. The sarcophagus is in fact from the Gallo-Roman period (around the fifth century CE). The reliefs on the front include, at the right end, a badly damaged scene of Pilate washing his hands and declaring himself innocent of the blood of Jesus. This was a standard subject for such sarcophagi, but in this case was misread as Mary Magdalene washing the feet of Jesus.

Early Christian Sarcophagus: The (So-called) Sarcophagus of Mary Magdalene
(Gallo-Roman, fifth century), Church of St. Maximin, Marseilles, France.
Photo: Deutsches Archäologisches Institut, Rome (1960.1656 [J. Boehringer]).

been to Marseilles. And in 1848 E.-M. Faillon made a vast compilation of documents, *Monuments inédits sur l'apostolat de sainte Marie-
Madeleine en Provence,* with a passionate commentary, to disprove such
subversive claims.[27]

Vézelay 1146: Preaching the Crusade at the Shrine of Mary Magdalene

On Easter Day 1146, in a field at Vézelay, Bernard of Clairvaux preached
to the king of France, his queen, his court, and a crowd of thousands.
Bernard's theme was the Crusade to recover the Holy Land, proclaimed in December 1145 by a former disciple of Bernard himself, Pope
Eugenius III.

Relics: Value and Power

Relics attracted intense devotion. Hugh of Lincoln (d. 1200) collected them avidly. On a visit to Fécamp, whose monastery claimed
an arm of Mary Magdalene, Hugh took hold of the relic, unwrapped
it (with the help of a knife) from the cloths of silk and linen that
covered it, and tried to break off a piece with his fingers. It was
too hard, so he bit the piece off with his molars. He justified his
action: "If a little while ago I handled the most sacred body of the
Lord of all the saints with my fingers, despite my unworthiness,
and when I partook of it [at the Mass] touched it with my lips and
teeth, why should I not venture to treat in the same way the bones
of the saints?"[28]

The power of supposed relics could not quite be assured—especially if a story was told to discredit a shrine by a rival. The monks
of Vézelay gave a piece of Mary Magdalene to the Dominicans at
Lausanne. It soon won fame for its power to heal. We hear a dark
story, however, from the Dominicans at the rival shrine of St. Maximin in Provence, whose claims to have the body of Mary Magdalene
had by this time (early fourteenth century) trumped those of Vézelay.
A man possessed by a demon came to the Dominicans at Lausanne,
hoping to be cured. The friar-sacristan began the exorcism by swear-
ing on Mary Magdalene's strength, but the devil responded loudly,
"Clearly, friar, you do not know what you are talking about; I tell
you, you are lying, because that is not the body or relic of Mary
Magdalene, so I am not leaving this man of yours!"[29]

Above the gathering towered, on the hilltop, the newly rebuilt abbey church of Vézelay, dedicated to Mary Magdalene. The crowd was far too large to be accommodated in the church, so a platform had been built in the field for Bernard, the king, and their entourage. Bernard was just the abbot of Clairvaux, but his fame and authority extended over all of Europe.

To preach a Crusade at Vézelay—there could be no better setting. Neither the text nor any summary of Bernard's sermon has survived; let's just do what we can to evoke the atmosphere in which it was delivered. Vézelay's most precious possessions were the bones of Mary Magdalene. In her own lifetime Mary had come west from the Holy Land to France, to rescue from the devil the forebears of Bernard's congregation. Now that congregation could go east to rescue the Holy Land from the Saracens. Mary Magdalene had repented of a sinful life; it was time for Bernard's audience to repent of their own luxurious lives. Mary Magdalene had been forgiven all her sins; Crusaders, the pope had declared, would win remission from all theirs.

Mary Magdalene had her reward: she was the first person to see Jesus, risen from the dead, on Easter Day. Here, on Easter Day, the knights and people of France could pledge themselves to the service of that risen Christ. Their fathers, in the First Crusade, had captured Jerusalem and begun to restore the church that marked the site of Christ's death, burial, and rising. The sons could finish the fathers' work and tread the very ground on which Mary Magdalene had watched Jesus die, seen him buried, and met him on Easter morning.

We can catch the tone of Bernard's preaching from the letters and sermons he wrote in the following months. When a soldier committed himself to the Crusade, he would receive a small cross made of cloth, to be sewn onto his clothes.

> I have called you a blessed generation; you have been caught up in a time rich in remission and are found living in a year so pleasing to the Lord. . . . Take the sign of the cross and you will obtain remission of all the sins you have confessed with a contrite heart. The cloth of the [cross] is worth nothing, if it is sold; if it is worn on a faithful shoulder, it is worth the Kingdom of God!
>
> *Bernard of Clairvaux, Letter 363*

At Vézelay, we are told, Bernard had a pile of such crosses. (This was a moment for which Bernard and his allies had prepared themselves well.) His words, however, stirred so many to "take the cross" that his supply was soon exhausted; he had to make more from his own habit. So many people crowded onto the platform that it collapsed. Nobody was hurt—surely, it was believed, a miraculous sign of God's favor for the enterprise.[30]

The Second Crusade was under way. The words and passion of Bernard could launch it, but they could not save it from military and political disaster. It is all the more telling that decades later, in spring 1190, the kings of England and France—Richard I "Lionheart" and Philip II—gathered their armies at Vézelay for their own departure on Crusade.

Vézelay—the bones of Mary Magdalene, a great church, and two Crusades. We have come a long way from the Mary Magdalene of the New Testament. From those meagre beginnings, her cult grew to pervade all Europe. Nine hundred years after Bernard's sermon, the abbey at Vézelay still soars, visible for miles around, above the hills and vines of Burgundy.

* * *

The language of the Crusades was the language of love: love of vassals for their liege lord Christ, who had been robbed of his patrimony and called for his honor to be satisfied. *"He that loves father or mother more than me,"* said Jesus, *"is not worthy of me. . . . If anyone wants to be a follower of mine, let him renounce himself and take up his cross and follow me."*[31] Odo of Deuil began his account of the Second Crusade with solemn words, "The glorious Louis undertook to follow Christ by bearing his cross in order to be worthy of him." To take the cross was to show one's love for Christ.

So intense was the relation between feudal lord and vassal expected to be, that the poets of love, writing among their own liege lords, described the lover's duty to his lady in terms of the vassal and his lord. These poets took up too the poetry of the Crusades. Burgundy was home to the first of the lyric and epic romances, emerging in Bernard's own lifetime. These poems tell of soldiers who sought love and praise from the woman they adored. The poet Jaufre Rudel may well have heard Bernard preach at Vézelay; his patron, Hugo VII, Lord of Lusigan, certainly did. Here is a verse from one of Jaufre's best-known poems. Who is he praising in this song to his distant lover? A woman, Jerusalem in the hands of the Saracens, or paradise? Or all three? If a woman, then what exactly was the enjoyment that Jaufre hoped for? The love poets of the time spoke of a yearning passion, but they hovered—lightly and often ambiguously— around the question of whether sexual consummation was to be expected, hoped for, or even dreamed of. Jaufre knew, as Bernard knew, how the different forms and expressions of our love feed on and fuel—and sometimes compete with—each other.

Never in love shall I have joy
Unless I enjoy this love from afar.
So true is her worth and so perfect
That there in the Saracens' kingdom
I would for her be a prisoner proclaimed.

> *Jaufre Rudel,* "Lanquand li jorn" *8–9, 12–14* [32]

Jaufre wrote a poem for Hugh VII, whose wife Sarrazina had recently died. Jaufre plays neatly on her name to evoke all possible women, Christian, Jewish, and Saracen. Again he sings, all at once as lover, Crusader, and Christian, yearning in each persona for the unattained object of his passion:

Love of a far-off land,
For you my whole body yearns;
It is no wonder I am on fire,
For never was there Christian woman more noble,
Nor Jewess nor Sarrazina.

> *Jaufre Rudel,* "Qan lo rius" *9–10, 16–19*

The life of the aristocratic warrior was, in the romances, lived in the service of love. The monk, through his service of love, fought a war of the spirit fit, in Bernard's conviction, for the aristocracy of his age. Such warfare might become more than just spiritual. The Knights Templar, at once warriors and monks in a hybrid as startling then as it would be now, had been founded by Burgundian knights, and Bernard himself secured the order's future by writing its rule and a treatise, *In Praise of the New Knighthood.* These possibilities of love—in romance, knighthood, and monastic life—were images of each other, forever alike but forever distinct. They shared one language, a language enriched by its use in the service of all possibilities. Together they illuminated Europe like a starburst of spiritual and poetic energy.

The Embrace of the Crucified Christ

Bernard himself was as sensitive as anyone of his age to the call and power of love. He composed, in a series of sermons, the most famous of all commentaries on the Song of Songs. The soul is to be set on the endless royal road of a proper self-transcendence: "a searching never satisfied, yet without any restlessness . . . that eternal, inexplicable longing that knows no dissatisfaction and want." [33] How was Bernard to speak of this love in which all the concerns of the flesh have fallen away? By speaking of marriage, of Bridegroom, bride, and the kiss of the Bridegroom of the Song of Songs. To speak of the soul united with God, beyond all flesh, Bernard uses the language of flesh united with flesh.

Jesus, says Bernard, had been anointed first on the feet, with the sad and bitter perfume of repentance. Then the same—or, Bernard notes, a second—woman anoints Jesus on the head; this is the perfume of God's blessings upon humanity and of the praise offered him in return. And third? There is the ointment that Mary Magdalene brought to Jesus's grave to anoint his whole body. But Jesus is risen; his corpse has no need of ointment. This final perfume, then, is the love with which the faithful anoint Jesus's Body, the church.[34] The soul that speaks in the Song of Songs, says Bernard, had been disloyal to her husband. She longed to be able to return to him and to be allowed, through her tears, to kiss his feet, as the sinner in Luke's gospel, through her tears, had kissed the feet of Jesus. Next the

Mary Magdalene and Mary the Mother of Jesus

We have been shining our spotlight on Mary Magdalene herself. Jesus himself is beside her; Simon Peter flits in and out of the glare. Almost nobody else has been seen in the pool of light at all. Such isolation, however, is misleading. In any survey of mediaeval devotion Mary Magdalene should be viewed in relation—even in tension—with two other figures, both of them present with her at the death of Jesus: Mary the mother of Jesus, and John the Beloved Disciple. *There stood by the cross of Jesus his mother and the sister of his mother, Mary of Clopas and Mary Magdalene. So Jesus, seeing his mother and the disciple standing by, whom he loved, says to his mother, "Woman, look, your son"; then he says to the disciple, "Look, your mother." And from that hour the disciple took her into his own home.*[35]

The Virgin Mary is the mother of Jesus and, as the new mother of the Beloved Disciple, the mother of all Jesus's disciples for all time. She is the mother both of Christ and of all Christians, and so she embodies the church. The Virgin Mary had by the Middle Ages been credited with a cosmic role. Christ was the condensed and concentrated presence of the whole creation, which he would redeem; so in his mother the power must have been present, condensed and concentrated, that engendered all creation. That is, the soul longed to kiss the hand of her beloved. And finally? *Let him kiss me,* starts the Song of Songs, *with the kisses of his mouth.* Such language (and gestures) of intense affection had become common in the courtly friend-ships and knightly rituals of the late twelfth century. The Song could now evoke both erotic and feudal attachments, for Bernard was writing for a new breed of monks, who had entered monastic life when they were already adult and experienced in the ways of the world.

Bernard wrote the most sensuous prose for monks who had to fight, every day, the dangers of sensuality. The faithful soul becomes, as it should, once more like the Lord, who created it. So it will think of mar-riage to that Lord. "When you see a soul leaving everything and clinging to the Word, ruling her life by the Word, conceiving by the Word what it will bring forth by him, you know that the soul is the spouse and bride of the Word." Such marriage involves bride and Bridegroom and, for some,

Virgin Mary undertook what God's creative Wisdom had under-taken, bringing God's plan to fruition. As the Virgin is a mother, so too she is a spouse; she was perfectly conformed and obedient to God's will and so should be seen as the second and perfect Eve, pure virginal spouse of the second Adam.

And Mary Magdalene? This Mary is the individual believer who has renounced all other men and the sins that were leading her to damnation and can now be linked only to her beloved Jesus. She who once flouted God's will is now dedicated to obedience. By the Middle Ages there were stories that the Beloved Disciple and Mary Magdalene were the groom and bride of the marriage at Cana,[36] but the disciple heard Jesus's call and devoted himself to celibacy and the gospel.

Now imagine a classic scene of the crucifixion. Jesus is in the centre. The Virgin is placed just where, in all depictions of her glorification, she is enthroned in heaven: below Jesus and to his right. (She sits between her son Jesus and all her children in the church, for whom she intercedes.) At the foot of the cross the Virgin is often seen fainting into John's arms; Mary Magdalene is distraught. Here are Jesus's mother, his dearest friend and new brother, and the woman who loves him. Mary Magdalene and John were once engaged to each other. What a change. Now John, the ideal believer, is given a new home with Jesus's mother, the church, and attends to her; Mary Magdalene, the penitent believer, is wild with passion and has eyes only for Jesus.[37]

the children born of preaching and an active life. "The soul is affected in one way when it is made fruitful by the Word, in another when it enjoys the Word itself. A mother is happy in her child; a bride is even happier in her bridegroom's embrace."[38]

Bernard himself knew of Christ's embrace—he had a vision in which Christ lifted his arms from the cross and drew Bernard to him. The motif was well known to Bernard's generation, but it would take a mystic of Bernard's intensity to appropriate and live out the imagery within himself. "Rush to the embrace," urged a lament of the Blessed Virgin Mary. "While he hangs on the cross, he offers himself with outstretched arms to the loving for a mutual embrace." Who at the crucifixion itself represented the believer, longing for such closeness? Mary Magdalene. "Oh, most blessed cross," she cries out, in the biography we have already encountered by Domenico Cavalca, "would I had been in your place, and that my Lord had been crucified in my arms, my hands nailed against his . . . so that I had died with him, and thus neither in life nor death ever departed from him."[39]

There is much to regret in the churches' use of Mary Magdalene, but we miss its essence if we think of her as the representative only of women. On the contrary, she was an icon of all believers, all in equal need of forgiveness. This does not absolve the churches of their historic misogyny; it remains the bitter case that a *woman* became the churches' icon of the sinfulness we all share. But she became too the symbol of a life forgiven and transformed. If we remain only angry about the churches' abuse of Mary, we will miss all there is about her that anger cannot see.

Anselm (1033–1109), archbishop of Canterbury, had been the first hero of the twelfth-century church and of its newly emotional forms of devotion. He composed a prayer to Mary Magdalene, beautifully wrought. He declares himself to be a penitent sinner, longing to be fired with the love of God that filled Mary. Then he turns on Jesus himself and asks how he could be so callous to Mary on Easter morning, keeping his identity hidden and reducing her to ever more desperate sorrow. It is a brave move. Anselm is inviting readers to join in this challenge to Christ, as they recognize what depth and length of sorrow they may be called to undergo before their own tears of penitence can turn to tears of joy.[40]

Anselm's motifs were taken up by an anonymous twelfth-century author whose sermon on Mary Magdalene (long ascribed wrongly to Origen) was widely circulated for four hundred years. It was almost certainly composed by a follower of St. Bernard and for an audience who knew the scene vividly from Easter plays. The author conducts a dialogue with Mary. He praises her courage and her love, which gives her that courage, but when he urges her to take comfort from the sight of the angels at the tomb he gets a brusque response: "I seek not for angels, but for him who made me and angels." He speaks to Jesus too, asking him to see "not the error of the woman but the love of thy disciple." (The author was a child of his time and could play on Mary's manliness: "O unspeakable love of this woman! O marvelous audacity of a woman! O woman, no woman.")

Jesus had promised to answer those who called upon him, to be found by those who sought him, and to open the door to those who knocked. But "thou [Mary] callest him and he heareth not; thou seekest him, and findest him not; thou knockest, but he openeth not.—Alas, what meaneth this? Alas, how is all turned upside down." Jesus had asked on the cross, "My God, why hast thou forsaken me?" But Mary asks, "Where is my sweet Lord? Why hast thou, my health, forsaken me?" She is the desolate lover of the Song of Songs who lost her beloved: "I will rise truly, I will go about, I will search in all places I can. . . . Who shall show me whom my soul loveth, where is he bestowed? I beseech you, tell him how I pine with love, consume with sorrow, and that there is no dolour [sorrow] as is my dolour. . . . Turn again, my beloved; turn again, my heart's desire and dearling." So on Easter Day she speaks up with Jesus's own words from the Lenten liturgies, heard only days before. Jesus had asked (from Lam. 1.12) if there were any sorrow such as his sorrow and had urged his own people, "Turn, O Jerusalem, to the Lord thy God."

So Mary's complaint—which is the *reader's* complaint—against Christ is heard. Only right at the end does the author turn the tables on the reader:

> Learn of Mary to seek for Jesus in the sepulchre of thy heart. Roll away the stone from the door of the sepulchre of God, remove all hardness, take away all worldly desire from thy heart and search diligently whether Jesus be in it. And if thou find not Jesus in it, stand without and weep. . . . Keep looking; and if he ever appears, do not presume ye know him, but ask him to show himself to thee. Stand at the tomb of thy heart and bow down with humbleness and by Mary's example receive no comfort of Jesus except ye receive Jesus—and he will reveal himself to thee.
>
> An Homilie of Marye Magdalene[41]

This is a powerful, supple deployment of Mary Magdalene. No messengers (from the church!) would do; the readers were encouraged to be demanding, to require of the church the evidence for the resurrection that

Crucifixion (tempera on panel, 1426), by Tommaso Masaccio (1401–28).
Photo: Museo e Gallerie Nazionali di Capodimonte, Naples, Italy / Giraudon /
The Bridgeman Art Library.

At the Foot of the Cross

In Masaccio's *Crucifixion* (painted 1426, now in Naples) Jesus's mother and the Beloved Disciple flank the cross, weeping. The composition is formal, symmetrical, and traditional. They and Jesus stand out against a gold background. This event is not set in an earthly landscape; in its church the scene would have shimmered in the glory of candlelit gold. We are the privileged viewers of a heavenly scene, revealing to the believer more than just the history of Jesus's once-for-all death.

At the foot of the cross itself, Mary Magdalene kneels. She is disproportionately small. We see only her back—a huddled mass of bright orange fabric and long hair, her arms upraised in grief. Her head is next to the feet she once washed with her tears. Her arms frame the legs of Jesus and echo his own outstretched arms, for she is suffering her own crucifixion. She is facing the cross as the viewer faces it and kneels before it as the viewer, in prayer, would kneel. Mary Magdalene draws the viewers into the picture and represents them there; as she mourns the death of Jesus, so do they.[42]

This is a small panel (83 x 63cm.), painted as the apex to a large altarpiece whose central panel (now in London) is a regal depiction of the Virgin Mary enthroned with Jesus, with four angels—two playing musical instruments—by her feet. Beneath that primary scene was a narrow panel, *Arrival of the Magi*. Additional panels of standing saints and their lives flanked the central ensemble.

The viewers' eyes were drawn up past the Magi and past the Virgin and Child to this topmost scene of the crucifixion. (It was inevitably seen from below; Masaccio has, with only partial success, foreshortened the neck and head of Jesus to allow for the viewpoint from which the figure will be seen.) Mary Magdalene is drawing us with her up to heaven as she goes there through her devotion to Jesus at his death. But at this highest point she brutally disrupts, with her violent, vivid figure, the symmetry of the scene and the harmony of its colours.

The poet Jacopone da Todi (d. 1306) wrote an interlude for Good Friday in which he encourages his audience to recognize themselves in the Magdalene. It could serve as a commentary on Masaccio's figure:

> And I, sad Magdalene, threw myself at his feet
> at which I made a great gain, for I purged my sins.
> To his feet nail me, and never lift me up again.[43]

the church proclaimed. But, at the last, caught quite off guard, readers are urged to see themselves as the place of death that lacks the Christ they are so loudly looking for outside themselves.

Bernard could feminize himself by a brave imaginative and literary effort—quite unnecessary for a female mystic such as Mechtilde of Magdeburg (1207–82). In a dialogue between the soul and God, Mechtilde has the Lord declare that the soul is his and nothing can come between them. The soul responds with an outpouring of erotic praise, "Lord, now I am a naked soul and thou a God most glorious! Our twofold intercourse is love eternal which can never die. Now comes a blessed stillness, welcome to both. He gives himself to her, and she to him." The mystic recovers the likeness of God, strips herself of "self," and lets love flower in undivided possession: "For God, the soul is a free and open way, into which he can plunge from out of his furthest depths; and for the soul, in return, God is the way of freedom, towards the depth of the divine being, which nothing can attain save the depths of the soul."[44]

Such union was readily associated with the Eucharist, when the believer's body at Communion ingests "the Body of Christ." Hadewijch, a contemporary of Mechtilde and part of the same movement of lay-men and -women, analyzes with great care the stages of union she had experienced at Communion. First Christ came in the form and clothing of a man, as he had been when he instituted the Eucharist; then he gave himself to Hadewijch in the shape of the sacrament in its outward forms: "After that he came himself to me, took me entirely in his arms, and pressed me to him; and all my members felt his in full felicity, in accordance with the desire of my heart and my humanity. So I was outwardly satisfied and fully transported." This deeply erotic union is still, for Hadewijch, an outward union of limbs and heart; she has not yet absorbed Christ into her whole self. "Also then, for a short while, I had the strength to bear this; but soon, after a short time, I lost that manly beauty outwardly in the sight of his form. I saw him completely come to naught and so fade and all at once dissolve that I could no longer recognize or perceive him outside me, and I could no longer distinguish him within me. Then it was to me as if we were one without difference. . . . After that I remained in a passing-away in my beloved, so that I wholly melted away in him and nothing any longer remained to me of myself."[45]

Margery Kempe of Norfolk, England (ca. 1373–1433), was heir to such mystical thought. Her many fits of tears were mocked as the crying of an actress or a hypocrite, because, for all her protests that she longed for chastity, she continued to bear her husband children. In 1413 Margery made a pilgrimage to Jerusalem, and in the Church of the Holy Sepulchre she "wept and sobbed as plenteously as though she has seen our Lord with her bodily eyes suffering his passion." Margery meditated on the deposition of Christ's body from the cross, imagined Mary Magdalene asking the permission of Jesus's mother to kiss his feet, and longed to be able to touch Jesus's body as Mary Magdalene had. She stood in the place where Mary Magdalene had stood when Christ said to her, "Mary, why are you crying?"

A woman's body could make possible the expression and experience of the most intimate closeness to Christ. Margery Kempe believed that Christ acknowledged her as his spouse, with all the nearness that implied. She records Christ saying to her, "Daughter, you desire greatly to see me, and you may boldly, when you are in your bed, take me to you as your wedded husband, as your dearworthy darling, and as your sweet son, for I will be loved as a son should be loved by the mother, and I will that you love me, daughter, as a good wife ought to love her husband." Forms of intimacy are multiplying: Jesus is father, husband, and son; Margery is daughter, wife, and mother. "Therefore you may boldly take me in the arms of your soul and kiss my mouth, my head and my feet, as sweetly as you will."[46]

Most modern scholarship—until recently dominated by men—used to speak freely of the sublimation of sexual desire in the intense devotional life that burgeoned in the twelfth century. In recent decades it has been brilliantly argued that this distorts the devotional experiences of mediaeval women. The gospels seem to call for nurturing virtues alien (then as now) to men's upbringing, self-image, and aspirations. To make possible a growth in such virtues, male theologians needed drastic conversion in themselves and called for it in others; pride in the strengths, possibilities, and standing of mediaeval manhood had to be renounced in favor of humility and obedience.

Bernard knew what inner warfare a monk could face. But he realized as well that he and his monks were paradoxically feminine; as the woman had seemed to waste the money spent on the ointment she applied to Jesus, so Bernard's monks, spending their lives in penitential or grateful meditation, seemed a wasteful extravagance. Bernard imagines the Lord himself coming to Bernard's defense. "Why," asks Jesus, "do you trouble this woman? He is not a man, as you think, who can put his hands to great works, but a woman; he is doing a good work for me. If he ever makes progress, from being a woman to being a man—and a perfect man—then he can be employed on the work of perfection."[47]

For men, the body's urges were a danger; rescue lay in the spirit alone. A deep divide was defined between the two, body and spirit; men saw humanity as a realm of stark contrasts and of permanent warfare between

Mary Magdalene (wood, painted and gilded, ca. 1460), by Donatello (1386–1466).
Photo: Scala, Florence: Florence, Museo dell' Opera del Duomo © 1990.

Donatello's Mary Magdalene

Donatello (1386–1466) carved his figure of Mary Magdalene for the Baptistery in Florence around 1460. John the Baptist, clothed only in animal skins, had lived in the desert and called for repentance; it was fitting that a baptistery should house a figure of Mary Magdalene, who had gone out to the desert in penitence and was clothed only in her hair. Her statue, nearly life-size, was once highly coloured; her flesh was painted in the tints of flesh, and on her hair some gilding survives. She is a gaunt figure, but still shows the fine features and elegant proportions of her youth; she is both a frightening reminder that human life comes to this and a humbling reminder that, for penitent believers, it should.

Once seen, never forgotten. For whom did Donatello make this extraordinary statue, and why did he create quite so harrowing a figure? No record has survived of its commission. Donatello may have made it in thanksgiving for his recovery from illness. Its character was likely influenced by the teaching of Antoninus, archbishop of Florence and the centre of a movement for moral and religious reform at the Dominican convent of San Marco. Antoninus lived in austerity himself and established charities for the poor. He was spiritual adviser to the Medici dynasty and a broker between rival factions in the city. He was also a prolific author. He wrote a devotional and an ethical guide (both for members of the Medici family) and a chronicle of the world's history that included the story of Mary Magdalene and a treatise on confession—one copy of which, still in Florence, is bound with a copy of Mary's own supposed confession of her sins. His book of systematic theology was influential for centuries.

The Dominicans had adopted Mary Magdalene. In 1295 they had been made the guardians of her shrines at St. Baume and St. Maximin in southern France, and soon afterward she was declared a patroness of the order. Antoninus doubted that Mary Magdalene had been as evil as some preachers and writers claimed; she was just an example of woman's immodesty. So she became all the more accessible as a model for women's confession and penance and for the contemplative life, which Antoninus encouraged women to adopt.

Mary Magdalene features in several Florentine paintings and statues of this period, all showing her as a haggard penitent. One of them, Donatello's, is among the greatest sculptures of its own or any generation.[48]

them. But the virtues of gentleness and nurture, which men diagnosed as gifts of the Spirit, hard to secure and all too easily lost, women recognized as the gifts with which they were born and the virtues to which they were trained from childhood. Christ had sacrificed his own life for believers, and—in the Mass—gave his own blood for them to drink and his body for them to eat. A woman, even if she was not herself a mother, had a vivid sense of how a mother endangered her own life to give birth to her children, fed those children with her own milk and prepared food, every day, for her family. For a woman, her body was not a danger to the spiritual life of men or of herself; it was the vehicle for that life and for its deepest expression.[49]

Mary Magdalene represented the penitent, grateful, adoring believer at the foot of the cross, but we cannot assume that men's experience, if and as they made this role their own, was the same as women's. Our own age is acutely alert to women's and men's sensibilities; we ask if they are complementary or interchangeable, if they are distinguished from each other by nature, by culture, or both. Our eyes are open, therefore, to recognize the differing viewpoints from which women and men gazed on Jesus in the religious life of the Middle Ages.

Perhaps, nonetheless, we can find some presuppositions in common: in particular, the proper commitment of the whole person—body, heart, and mind—to the believer's relationship with Christ. Our forebears in the Middle Ages could envision in the passionate yearning for Christ a primary—*the* primary—form of human love: love for the lover's creator and saviour, for the beloved who is love and life itself and who himself has loved the lover through all eternity. The lover longs to be close to this beloved, cares for this beloved, invests every ounce of hope and trust and love in a future undertaken and undergone with this beloved, and finds in these a meaning and point in life which life otherwise lacks. And all this is brought to nothing by the death of the beloved. No wonder there are poems, written to express Mary Magdalene's sorrow at the death of Jesus, which seem to us to be aching and achingly beautiful love poems; that is exactly what they are. And most of those that have reached us were written by men.

> With my love my life was nestléd
> In the sun of happiness;
> From my love my life is wrestéd
> To a world of heaviness.
> Oh! Let love my life remove,
> Since I live not where I love!

Robert Southwell (1561–95), from *Marie Magdalen's Complaint at Christ's Death*

Tradition and Truth

There had been occasional objections, through the Middle Ages, to the identification of all the women who anointed Jesus as one and the same Mary Magdalene. In 1518 the Dominican and humanist Jacques Lefèvre d'Étaples published a treatise, *On Mary Magdalene*. He argued that Luke's anonymous sinful woman—Mary, the sister of Martha, and Mary Magdalene—were three different women. Bishop John Fisher of Rochester (1465–1535) later recalled his own reaction to this treatise:

> How many difficulties would confront the whole church if Lefèvre's opinion were ever to be accepted. How many authors would have to be rejected, how many books would have to be changed, how many sermons formerly preached to the people would have to be revoked! And then, how much uneasiness would arise among the faithful, how many occasions for loss of faith. They will soon doubt other books and narratives, and finally the mother of us all, the Church, who for so many centuries has sung and taught the same thing.

Lefèvre admitted, in the second version of his book (1519), what opposition he faced:

> Strong, I admit, are the authors, and their number is great, but the gospel is stronger than any number of authors. Strong too is an ancient custom, even a false one, and it often claims for itself, although erroneously, the Church's authority. Yet the truth is stronger still.[50]

Only in 1969 did the calendar of the Roman Catholic Church free Mary Magdalene from association with Luke's sinner and with the sister of Martha. Even now the saga has not ended well. In 1974 the Roman Catholic festival of Mary Magdalene was downgraded; she is now honored with just a memorial, one of the lowest forms of such liturgical dignity.

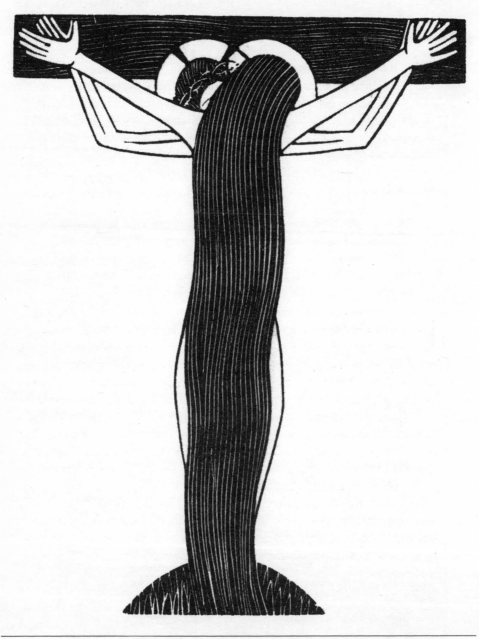

The Nuptials of God (wood engraving, 1923), by Eric Gill (1882–1940).
Photo: V & A Images / Victoria and Albert Museum.

THE NUPTIALS OF GOD

> *I heard what seemed to be the voices of a huge crowd ... :*
> *"Alleluia! The reign of the Lord our God Almighty has begun;*
> *let us rejoice and give glory to God, because this is the time for*
> *the marriage of the Lamb; his bride is ready. . . ."* The angel
> said, "Write this, 'Blessed are those who are invited to the
> wedding feast of the Lamb.'"
>
> Revelation 19.6–9

Jesus is suspended on the cross, his arms outstretched. But we see almost nothing of him, for against the whole length of his body a woman stands between him and us, the viewers. She has her back to us. Her hands press against Jesus's hands, her torso covers his. She herself is clothed only in her hair, which hangs down to her feet. Jesus's head hangs down to his right; the woman's leans into his neck, her face against his. The two bodies are as one; she shares his posture and his suffering. The scene is erotic, but not coarse; it is tender, intimate, and quite still. This moment of love is the moment of death. At this climax to Jesus's passion, all passion is spent. As Jesus said moments before he died: *"It is completed."*

At Easter the churches celebrate with a ringing claim, "This is the season when heaven is wedded to earth, and all creation is made new." But the Good Friday marriage depicted here is a painfully human story of love and loss. The woman's hands are raised in a loving touch, but her outstretched arms form as well a classic gesture of lamentation. How little we see of Jesus himself; the woman is guarding his wounded body from our gaze. The moment is his—his sacrifice, his death. But the woman makes him her own, and with a loyalty indifferent to all danger she comes between her loved one and any stranger's eyes.

This is Eric Gill's wood engraving *The Nuptials of God* (1923).[1] We have heard of Mother Church and her children, the souls of the faithful, as forming together the brides of Christ, and we have heard too of the startling intimacy that could be sensed between Christ and the soul. But why should Gill show the church or the soul clothed in nothing but her own luxurious hair? Gill's woman may embody the church or the soul, but she represents it in the unmistakable figure of *Mary Magdalene*.

Mary Magdalene is in Christian tradition many things, but (without careful redefinition or miraculous intervention) she is certainly not a virgin; she is a penitent prostitute.[2] Gill's Mary Magdalene is naked in a frankly erotic, adult embrace; the title of Gill's engraving draws our thoughts towards the mystical marriage of Christ and his people, the image itself towards a thoroughly earthly union of Jesus and Mary Magdalene.

Of course we might imagine the childlike, perfected soul of a believer as naked, for we were born naked and at death our soul itself will be deprived of the body's clothing. Adam and Eve were naked in their innocence; only at the Fall did they come to be ashamed and to look for clothing. Truth, when unadorned and undisguised, is naked; so is true virtue, free from guilt and shame and any need of artifice. Who else are naked? Lovers in a sexual embrace, alert to every special sight and every touch received and given. Mary and Jesus may be unraveling the effects of Eve's and Adam's Fall, but to many modern eyes, used to linking the Fall with sex, the pair seem at this most poignant moment to be reliving the Fall, not undoing it. This is just what Origen did *not* mean when he wrote in his commentary to the Song of Songs: "My love [the object of my passion] has been crucified."

The biblical images of marriage between God and his people come to their climax at the end of the book of Revelation, right at the Bible's end: *I saw the holy city, the new Jerusalem, coming down out of heaven from God, prepared like a bride adorned for her husband.*[3] The bride in Gill's engraving is already, at the cross, free from all adornments and in her bridal bedroom.

Humans are made (according to the Bible) in the image and likeness of God; we may think of our capacity for love as distant echoes of God's own being as love itself. But Gill's woman? She is almost a mirror image of Jesus's *body*, and the match between them is the match of their bodies in an irreducibly sexual union. Gill's image will likely surprise us; it may well shock us too. But Gill is doing nothing new. As we have heard, Mary Magdalene was for centuries evoked as an icon of the individual believer, sinful, penitent, and redeemed. Over centuries she was shown in paintings and sculpture at the foot of Christ's cross, and in sermons, poems, and visions she was imagined—still as the individual believer—closer still to her beloved Lord. In *The Nuptials of God* Gill has distilled Europe's age-old dream about Mary Magdalene into a beautiful simplicity.

We have attended more carefully to the love that Gill portrays here than to the death. We should redress the balance. By dying, according to classic Christian doctrine, Jesus destroyed death. Gill accompanied the engraving with a long poem on the love and the death he has shown together; here is part of it:

> Behold
> the Wedded God,
> so marked by rod,
> by spear, by scourge.
> The Rood [*cross*] His marriage bed
> on which He doth enfold
> His spouse nakéd.
> O Bride
> in God's embrace,
> Face to Face
> Body to Body!
> O surge
> of Love in agony.
> O passionate Breath,
> God spending
> His seed of Life in Death.
>
> That consummated Act
> of Union—Bride and Groom
> In fierce and sweet contact,
> Death finding doom.

Eric Gill knew exactly what he was doing in *The Nuptials of God*. From our sexual appetites and pleasure the churches have long since distilled the pure essence of spiritual love, to be consummated at the end of this world's coarse, corrupted order. Gill distrusted such abstraction. He expressed his lifelong agenda in a letter of 1934. To avoid offence, I use asterisks where Gill of course did not:

I wish I could get you to see the point about Christianity—e.g., when we "Marry" we don't say to a girl: Madam you realize that we are the embodiment of an idea (or do you?). We say: darling, we two persons are now one flesh—or words to that effect. It's a love affair first and last. . . . It's like getting married and, speaking analogically, we are f***ed by Christ, and bear children to him—or we don't. The Church is the whole body of Christians—the bride.[4]

Gill himself had feet of clay. He was a Roman Catholic and received major commissions from the Roman Church in England. But his diaries have brought to light a deeply unsettling side of his life; they list not just his adulteries, but his (sustained) experiments with incest and bestiality. It may take a strangely devout libertine to create such an image as *The Nuptials of God*, but when our admiration for an artist dissolves, we can find our admiration for his art dissolving too. Bear with me, nonetheless, for letting Gill's image stand in this book; here, in a few simple lines of an engraving, is the Mary Magdalene of our times.

Jesus and Mary Magdalene:
What Should *We* Make of the Gospel of John?

Gill has evoked the classic twofold drama of Christian belief: the drama of Jesus and the drama of the believer in relation to Jesus. The result of this double focus has always been strange. Particular events in the Middle East two thousand years ago are (in ways that may defy definition) "re-lived" in the lives of the believers who let themselves and their lives be defined by those events. The sets of events—one long past and far distant, the other here and now—are distinct, but in classic Christian belief inseparable. Our own survey of the gospels, however, has shown how much in the gospels' stories was formulated with the readers in mind; in this light it seems hard to trust the stories as an undistorted record of Jesus's life. Now that we have seen some of the avenues of thought and imagination that the gospels opened (and some of the strange destinations to which they took their explorers), let's briefly address this challenge. We will keep John's gospel in focus; this gospel has the most striking ambitions for its readers, and in it Mary Magdalene plays her greatest role.

John's gospel is a tour de force, keeping the past and present dramas in focus; part of the thrill is the content and character of the readers' growing self-understanding. John set out to bring his readers through *new birth from above* during their reading of his gospel. To do so, he made of his whole story a teasing, riddling, cajoling, inspiring text. And at its end he brought his readers, in their imagination, into the Eden of a re-created world; the reader as Mary Magdalene was united with Jesus as Eve had been at one with Adam. God himself had walked in paradise;

the Holy of Holies in Jerusalem, God's throne room on earth and the site of his self-disclosure, was decorated with the trees of paradise. Now the readers themselves, as Mary Magdalene, join in paradise the Jesus who himself is the Holy of Holies and the site of God's total self-disclosure on earth.

This is all very well, but we may well wonder how much of this story relays the actual facts of Jesus's life. We seem to be offered, at every move, only the inspiration and (inspiring) aims of the evangelist himself. All of us, whether believers or not, want to pin down the simple, historical truth about Jesus and Mary Magdalene. Did Jesus and Mary Magdalene really meet as John said they did? John himself, I think, would say that the only people who can give a proper answer to that are those who have been *reborn from above,* and their answer will be a resounding *yes.* (And as John would have it, only the reborn have even an inkling of what they are really claiming when they say so.) And what about those outside—and inside!—the churches who assess and judge John's story of Easter morning as a straightforward record of an event just as accessible to normal understanding as this morning's sunrise or the arrival of my latest e-mails? John would (I think) reckon their assessment quite valueless. Perhaps we can go farther still. We nowadays want to believe a story before we assess the significance of the event it describes; John might well have thought it absurd to believe such a strange story without first seeing the significance of the event it describes.

We think of John's text as there to be read and studied, but it was really written to be *undergone.* John's plan was dangerous. Told in Johannine style, the story of Jesus on earth could become just the possible and longed-for story of all believers; the historical drama of Jesus could collapse, and the real and only drama would lie *in the believer.* The external world we live in seems to be slipping from view; we are left, it seems, with just the work of the imagination and intellect. (John's Jesus exacerbates the danger; he himself is always in control of events, authoring and directing the drama, but by that token is hardly part of the drama himself.) John saw the danger and resisted it. He insists on the value of the material realm in which we live. His Jesus, the Word of God, *took flesh and dwelt among us;* he told his followers that in order to have life they must *eat* [even *munch at*] *his flesh and drink his blood*[5]—a command as frightening then as it is or should be now. John had to counter suggestions within his churches that the Christians at their sacred meal were given a part only in Jesus's spiritual life, freed from all taint of our fleshly existence.

Among the Gnostics the backdrop of the believers' drama was painted in as the cosmic drama of the Forefather and his progeny, Wisdom's fall and her rescue by the Saviour, and the creation of this crass world. The Gnostics had been placed in this world from which the Saviour was rescuing their spirit, back to the world of Wisdom and beyond to the Forefather. And the events of Jesus's life on earth? They were part of the backdrop too, revealing the outward movements and returns of the Spirit that undergird and shape all creation. Now Mary Magdalene—and so the reader—is playing the major part in a theatre of the mind; *here* is the action, in the transformative effect of the story upon the reader. Mary—and so the reader—is the protagonist, whose particular life is set against the backdrop of that eternal, universal drama.

Classic Christian doctrine claims at one vital point a move by God beyond all description—the move from Christ's eternity lived as God to a human life on earth begun in a mother's womb and ended by an execution. Jesus does not just reveal what had always been the case, nor does he change things on earth just by human response to such revelation; his death and rising also change the relationship—in God's application of his own criminal and family law—between humanity, the powers of evil, and the just judge of us all, and they launch the restoration of the whole created order. Within the Gnostic schemes, the emphases have moved. Here the role of Christ is an unchanging role through all created time; his years as a physical human (if such he really was) *revealed* the saving role of his eternal life and is significant precisely and only as an icon of that life. The Jesus of the Gnostic gospels is always stated or—as far as we can tell—presumed to be the *risen* Jesus, and the Valentinians disagreed among themselves about whether Jesus had really assumed a body quite like ours at all. We think of history as the story of this world, but that is the topic of least interest to the Gnostics, important only as the setting into which they had been born and from which they need to be rescued. The history that *matters* is the history of the spiritual world and of the Gnostic there; and here the Gnostics had, as both icon and inspiration, John's Mary Magdalene.

The Gnostics were children of their time. Sallustius, a Neoplatonic thinker of the fourth century, analyzed the myths of the pagan gods: there were theological myths, enjoyed by philosophers; physical and psychological myths, enjoyed by poets; and the myths blended from the two, suitable for solemn religious rituals, "since every rite seeks to give us union with the universe and the gods." Sallustius recalls the stories behind the greatest of the ancient mystery religions: the Mother of the Gods loved the young man Attis and kept him by her until he fell in love with a nymph; the Mother in her anger castrated him; he left his genitals with the nymph and returned to the Mother. Sallustius interprets: the Mother represents the eternal and life-giving realm, Attis is the creator of things that come into being and pass away, the nymphs preside over this mutable world, Attis leaves with them his own power to generate what comes to be and passes away, and he himself is reunited with the eternal, immutable gods. "These things," concludes Sallustius, "happened at no one time but are always true. The mind sees the whole process at once; words tell of one part first, then another. Since the myth is so intimately related to the universe we imitate the ordering of the universe in the order of the myth (for in what way could we more fittingly order ourselves?)."[6]

A historian will respect such a reading of myth and its power, but mainstream Christian thinkers, over against Gnostic Neoplatonists, have always insisted that the story of Jesus is irremovably anchored in the particular events of two thousand years ago. It is all the more startling that people outside the churches are now hearing the churches' claim quite differently—and quite wrongly. At the start of this book I mentioned *The Da Vinci Code;* you may be surprised to see the novel reappear here at the end. I introduce the novel as a vivid witness to the *sort* of Jesus many people of our generation are prepared to credit and to admire and the sort of Jesus whom (by contrast) they think the mainstream churches proclaim. The novel has spread the startling conviction that the Gnostic Jesus was fully human while the biblical Jesus is mere God. This is almost as far from the truth as it is possible to go. The biblical Jesus here in this world eats, drinks, weeps, and—in agony—*dies*, and so the biblical Jesus rescues the world. The Gnostic Jesus reveals to the Gnostic the realms of the spirit where Jesus himself belongs and leads the Gnostic there, and so rescues the Gnostic *from* the world.

Were Jesus and Mary Magdalene Married? A Retrospect

The biblical Jesus lives and dies; whatever else he is, he is human. But we have, for our own purposes, an additional question: was he married to Mary Magdalene? We have all the evidence before us now: our opening assessment in Chapter 1, John's Easter story in Chapter 3, the Gnostic texts in Chapters 7–9. Most vital here is John, who has given her, in his story of Easter morning, such a sensuous, intimate scene with Jesus. What inspired John to tell this story the way he did?

We can acknowledge and admire all John's allusions to the creation stories in Genesis and to the lovers of the Song of Songs and all his mystical purposes in doing so; but we can still ask, nonetheless, how he could have built these into his story if he did not know of some profound intimacy between Jesus and Mary Magdalene. And if we imagine such intimacy, we will likely think of marriage. Perhaps, when John's gospel was being compiled and edited, the memory was still alive of Mary's marriage to Jesus. Perhaps, indeed, more than just memories were still alive. By the second century the gospel was being ascribed to the Beloved Disciple, who lived in Ephesus until the 90s; modern scholars tend to agree that the gospel did indeed reach its present form in the 80s or 90s. If Mary Magdalene and Jesus had been married, the Beloved Disciple would certainly have known and would have been able to justify his gospel's portrayal of their extraordinary intimacy. (According to later stories, Mary Magdalene herself joined the Beloved Disciple in Ephesus.)

So far, so plausible. But John elaborated, with an air of similar intimacy, the stories of *all* Jesus's encounters with women to do justice to a capacity that John linked with women. The Samaritan woman met Jesus and saw more deeply into the truth of Jesus than Jesus's own disciples saw. Martha and Mary at Bethany secured the new life of their own brother, Lazarus. Mary at Bethany anointed Jesus's feet and dried them with her hair. (The two scenes with Jesus's mother, framing the story of Jesus's life on earth, reveal once more a woman's awareness, but with a different tone.) It *may* be, of course, that the John who knew of Mary's marriage to Jesus prepared for their climactic meeting on Easter Day by building a frisson of intimacy into his earlier stories of the Samaritan woman and Mary of Bethany. I admit, though, that I doubt it.

The Gnostics were devoted to John, valued Matthew and Luke, and showed almost no interest in (or even knowledge of) Mark. What more did such Gnostics know about Mary from sources now lost to us? I suspect the answer is stark: nothing. This leaves us little or no direct evidence on which to decide whether Jesus was ever (before or during his ministry) married. We are still where we were in Chapter 1. As historians, free from the constraints of the churches' doctrine, we simply do not know.

Is this uncertainty, after our long inquiry, frustrating? No, on the contrary. We can accept the historians' uncertainty and move on. The additional questions we need to face can no longer be closed down by appeal to the established fact or example of Jesus; some fresh air and daylight can reinvigorate old inquiries, long grown stale, about human nature and human life. Let's walk into this room with its newly opened windows and sharper light and see what might be found there.

The Marriage of Jesus: Why Does It Matter?

The question of whether Jesus and Mary Magdalene were married will not go away. But there is a more interesting question: why does it matter to so many people that they were or might have been? Perhaps our generation is just obsessed with sex; perhaps we will take any opportunity to undermine old certainties and the hierarchies that vouch for them. But there is, I think, rather more to it than that.

Christians believe themselves to be made in the image and likeness of God. This image has been sullied by the Fall; in and through Christ, who in his humanity was the perfect and unsullied image of God, we are called to recover that image in ourselves. This is an awe-inspiring claim. The immortal, eternal, limitless God has revealed himself utterly in the person and life of a mortal, limited, palpable human who (like us) was born, ate, drank, and died. And the claim has a dazzling implication: as and if we become more Christlike, so we become more perfectly human *and* we bear more perfectly the image of God.

Now this is still a largely formal, structural claim; we want to know in more detail, what is it in Jesus's nature and life that we are summoned to recover in our own. We have heard, in outline, one answer familiar in the churches' early centuries: a nature and life free from the turbulence of human passions. We undergo or suffer our passions (Lat. *passio*, "suffering"); under their invasion we lose all the proper dignity of self-control, and however high our ideals might be of selfless generosity and service to others, in our passions we generally look to our own advantage and our private satisfaction. Such passions are typified in our sexual urges. It became a commonplace that Jesus had been (as a matter of fact) sexually continent, but that did not yet clarify the character of that continence—a character that, in the early fifth century, was angrily contested. And the question that underlay the arguments then is the question fueling the present interest in Jesus's marriage: was Jesus really human?

Julian of Eclanum (386–454) had been married as a young man, but lived chastely for much of his life; his wife might have died or might have entered a nunnery when he took deacon's orders. (It was not unusual for aristocratic, philosophically minded Christians to renounce sexual activity once they had an heir.) Julian believed in the complete humanity of Christ; he also believed (with his hero, the theologian Pelagius) that God had given all of us the will with which to resist evil. Had Jesus, then, known "natural lust"? Yes, and had resisted it in the perfection and strength of his will.

Julian was combating the theology of the great Augustine (354–430), whose thought dominated western Europe for centuries. Augustine, an old man by the time of his dispute with Julian, had come a long way. For nine years in his youth he had been a "Manichee," a follower of the teachings of Mani, who was himself an heir of the Gnostics and proclaimed two gods, one good (the lord of spirit) and one evil (the lord of the material world and of our flesh). Augustine had long since renounced Manicheism, but his past would come back to haunt him.

The old Augustine was as committed as Julian, of course, to the scriptural view that Jesus had *taken the likeness of sinful flesh.*[7] But Augustine did not have the Pelagians' confidence in the power of the human will, for human life is marked by the gap between our desires and our will—and by the incapacity of our will to control those desires. Our desires dis-

Paradise Regained

It was easy for an author to condemn an enemy—in lurid terms—of all the crimes most repellent to the author's public. How startling it is, therefore, to hear a heresy hunter treat a strange group with reluctant respect. Here is Epiphanius in the fourth century inserting some sly comments where he can, but clearly with more evidence for than against the purity of the sect he is describing. He cannot resist a final swipe: "Their nakedness is not due to their feeling no shame, even if that is what they think, but because of their insatiable lust." But he knows, despite himself, that the groups he described are more honorable than he would have thought possible. Here, it seems, was a group whose daily and ritual lives conformed to the life (as they imagined it) of Eden:

> They say that these people construct their churches in caves, and build a fire underneath [the ground] to warm with vapors those gathered inside the building. There are wardrobe attendants, like bath attendants, at the doors, and each person on entering, whether man or woman, undresses outside and goes in as completely naked as at birth. All belonging to their sect are supposedly continent (such at least is their boast) and virgins (or so they deceive themselves). They do their readings and everything else naked. But if they consider that a "transgression" occurs (as they put it), they no longer receive the one who committed it into their gathering. They say he is Adam who ate from the tree, and they sentence him to be put out of their church as from paradise. For they consider their church to be paradise, and themselves to be of the company of Adam and Eve.

> *From Epiphanius,* Panarion 52.2.1–3.1[8]

tort our will itself, and so a terrible gap has been opened up by the Fall between God's will and our will. There is a seismic dislocation at the heart of human life, which mere human will cannot overcome; only God's forgiving and fortifying grace can rescue us. (Augustine's theology is often regarded as unattractively dark, but it is in many ways more humane than Pelagius's assessment that any wrongdoing is simply the failure of a feeble will.)

Nothing typified that hiatus between our desires and our will more vividly than our sexual urges. Here Augustine found the consequence of the crime of Adam and Eve. They had, in Eden, enjoyed perfect self-control in perfect conformity to God's will. (Did they have bodies capable of sexual intercourse? At first Augustine thought no, then yes. In that case, did they have sexual intercourse before the Fall? Again Augustine's thought evolved from no, to possibly, for the sake of procreation only and in subjection to the will.)[9] But a turbulent, uncontrollable, appetitive desire had overtaken their will to conform to the will of God. They ate the forbidden fruit, and in the instant after the Fall they felt not the reasoning will of God-directed love, but the visible movement of uncontrolled desire (Augustine has Adam in mind here) and so shame at their nakedness. And they were doomed to relay to every one of their descendants, born of sexual union, the turbulent, uncontrollable, appetitive urgencies of their new lust. Who could ever escape this punishment, passed (in a consequence that fitted the crime!) via sexual reproduction from generation to generation? Only a person not born through the postlapsarian urgencies of sexual desire, that is, only *Jesus,* born of the Virgin Mary. For Augustine, Julian's talk of Jesus and "natural lust" was a sleight of hand. Sexual desire is sexual desire and is experienced (in a man) as an erection; surely, then, Julian's position entailed the claim that Jesus had erections and nocturnal emissions. (Both Augustine and Julian acknowledged that it was abhorrent to speculate on and write about such things, but both did so.)[10]

Julian and Augustine were writing at cross-purposes. Both took it for granted that Jesus was continent, in perfect conformity to God's will: Julian, because of Jesus's perfect will; Augustine, because Jesus was freed from the lust that distorts all humans born since the Fall through sexual reproduction. For Julian, it was a matter of Jesus's moral perfection within the flesh, which was just as subject to (resistible) desires as ours is; for Augustine, a matter of Jesus's taking the likeness of sinful flesh—but not the (sexually generated) sinful flesh that is subject to (irresistible) desires. And Julian insisted that Augustine's Jesus had not been really human at all and that Augustine as an old man was still, deep down, a Manichee who believed that this physical world—and our physical bodies—are the irredeemable creation of a lesser god. Augustine, as portrayed by Julian, was an heir of the Gnostics and their darkest heresies.

Why does this matter to us, all these centuries later? Because it was an attempt on both sides to confirm that Jesus really was human, and for this both Julian and Augustine needed to clarify what conditions had to be satisfied in order for someone—anyone—to be declared "human."[11] The churches may nowadays dismiss the popular portrayals of Jesus that give him a wife and child, but these portrayals are a modern attempt to ensure the same. The churches' Jesus is a perfect human—perfectly human and the perfection of humanity. No one would claim that such a Jesus must have been married and a father. But a good many people, inside and outside the churches, would reckon that there must not have been any obstacle in principle (physical, moral, or theological) to his having been sexually active. On this view, it may in fact be true (in Jesus's particular case), but it is no longer self-evident (as intrinsic to humanity's highest calling), that Jesus's perfect conformity to God's will entailed his celibacy.

A lot has had to change for us to get this far. We do not diagnose ourselves or our passions as our forebears did; we have (rightly or wrongly) grown into a more romantic sensibility. Most of us would accept, I think, that our sexual nature reveals a lot about our frailties. Most of us feel we need a partner and, lacking one, will go to extraordinary lengths to secure one. We will let reason go and follow our animal desires; by sexual intercourse we are momentarily sated but then desire again; we are unstable in our loves and appetites. Sexual activity can be cruelly exploitative and violent or it can be a basic satisfaction of natural appetites; and, even at its best, informed by the most generous love for our partner, we are in sexual intercourse fulfilling (or hoping to fulfill) our own desires.

But a fulfilling sexual relationship is not for that reason merely selfish. Such a relationship can clearly engender a hopeful, purposeful, confident commitment to a partner, and, in many cases, it may well be that this hope, purpose, confidence, and commitment would all be diminished if the relationship were starved of its sexual fulfilment. That is, sex can be about far more than sex; and in our modern, romantic, view of marriage we will claim that husband and wife find in their sexual relations the most intense and purposeful satisfaction, for themselves and each other, of their shared need to give and receive love.

Such a relationship (and for the moment we keep our eyes on such relationships at their best) involves mutual need. So do our other most vital relationships, with our children, for instance. We need, for our own sake, not only those who love us; we need those whom we love. We invest ourselves in those we love; only by entrusting a large part of ourselves to others do we become completely ourselves. Such need is at the heart of human life, and so it should be. It makes us particular in our love; we can become overdefensive, overproud, overworried. Yes, but this is no reason to belittle such love, for through such particular, focused interdependence most of us become, in the deepest fulfilment accessible to human beings, who we really are. We do not aspire to the ancient ideal—however Christianized—of a life informed by magnanimous but dispassionate friendships that leave us dependant on no one and nothing except God.

(I am the first to admit that I have offered a—naively—romantic riff on twenty-first-century love within the Western world. Few relationships are quite like this even at their best, and a great many are nothing like it at all. Both physical and emotional yearning can be satisfied by causing immense harm.)

Let's draw some threads together. We do not inhabit the largely pagan world of the second century, and few of us share its presuppositions or its ascetic ideals. We may respect Julian and revere Augustine from the fifth century, but few of us, I think, would on this topic call ourselves Augustinian now. We *may,* in the romantic outlook of the modern West, have started to do justice at last to the part that sexual love can play in human life; sex is looking better, and (many thoughtful people would claim) so it should. Then the historians step up to the plate. It is quite possible that Jesus was married and sexually active; it is also quite possible that he was celibate (living as a lifelong warrior or a priest on permanent service or a self-consciously angelic figure); the possibilities are open.

No wonder, in this setting, that people are asking about Jesus and Mary Magdalene. Almost every week for eighteen months I gave a lecture here at the Temple Church in London about *The Da Vinci Code.* (A scene in the book is set in the church.) Every lecture was followed by questions, and every week I was asked the same question: why should Jesus not have been married? It was not in general asked aggressively. The questioners did not claim to be sure that Jesus *was* married; they just wanted to know why the churches are not gladly and openly celebrating the possibility. The churches often assume, with a patronizing sigh, that the question—most recently framed in the plot of this popular, scandal-mongering novel!—is shallow, meretricious, or both. (And no doubt some people do ask the question in the hope of embarrassing the churches.) But in general the question is part of an attempt by honest people to make sense in modern terms of the churches' own claim that Jesus was at once wholly God and wholly human. No one denies that a celibate can live a deeply fulfilled life, but if the historic reasons are fading that led the churches to see Jesus as celibate, why (it is asked) should the churches still *assume* that he was? There may of course be far more important things to ask about Jesus. Fine, but why (it is asked) do the churches not just enjoy the open possibilities about Jesus's marriage and then move on?

Masculine and Feminine: Christianity and Jung

Jesus was human, and Jesus was a *man*. There are many who resent any assumption that all humanity should or could be represented by a man. Once we dwell on the intimacy between Jesus and Mary Magdalene, we may find in Mary more than just a wife. Jesus becomes an icon of men, and Mary Magdalene of women; Jesus embodies God, and Mary Magdalene embodies God's Wisdom.

Jesus Had No Favourites

Faced with a widespread inclination, inside and outside the churches, to believe that Jesus might have been married, some theologians have mounted a fresh counterargument as follows. Could Jesus have favourites? Answer: of course not. His love is extended equally to all humanity. So he could not have been married, for he would have given to his wife—and would have treasured from his wife—all the particular tenderness and care that husband and wife owe exclusively to each other. *A married man,* writes Paul, *gives his mind to the affairs of this world and to how he can please his wife.*[12] This claim may take a more theological form. In the human person of Jesus God entrusted himself in total, freely given love to the world, and the world (in the persons of those around Jesus who variously resented, betrayed, abandoned, defamed, and killed him) rebuffed that love. *That* is the exchange to which the New Testament and churches direct our attention. And it involved a freely undertaken sacrifice on Jesus's part, not just at his death but throughout his adult life, lived without wife or children.

In its first form, this argument is not, I think, successful; and its second, more sophisticated, form it sidesteps the question. When Jesus was alive on earth, his love and concern were actually shown (only) to those whom he met, and he took sustained care of those closest to him. There was one particular disciple in

The Gnostics of the ancient world had a deep influence on the twentieth century's grandest attempt, by the psychologist Carl Gustav Jung (1875–1961), to define the relation between masculine and feminine principles in humanity. (In recognition of Jung's interest in the Gnostics, one of the Nag Hammadi codices was bought for the Jung Institute in Zürich and has been named the Jung Codex in the psychologist's honor.)

According to Jung, the feminine principle is Eros, or psychic relatedness, the masculine is Logos, or objective interest. The feminine, according to Jung, opens up areas in which the spirit makes us holy by making us whole. In contrast to the masculine style of consciousness—and its goals of intellectual perfection, clear focus, and specialization—the feminine style of consciousness moves towards completeness. It does not exclude in order to purify, as does the masculine, but instead embraces all elements

Jesus's entourage who was still remembered, when John's gospel was finished, as *the disciple whom Jesus loved,* and one particular family—Lazarus, Martha, and Mary in Bethany—that was known to be dear to him. Such close friendships do not lead us to charge him with favoritism when he was on earth. Marriage, of course, makes demands of a different order, but if Peter could travel the Mediterranean as a married man and apostle, so (we might think) could Jesus himself, the apostles' leader, have travelled Galilee as a married man. On this view, the following two claims, whether or not both are true, are not incompatible: first, that in Jesus God loved his whole creation; and, second, that Jesus loved his wife.

But what about now? If Jesus was married, then surely his wife, with him in heaven, will still attract his special love and will distort the emanation of the even, universal love the churches believe he pours out upon his whole world. No. *"In the resurrection,"* says Jesus himself, *"men will not marry nor women be given in marriage."*[13] A Jesus married on earth is not a married Jesus in heaven.

There are of course Christians all over the world who believe that the saints intercede for us at the throne of Christ, and Mary Magdalene is among those saints. But it is the prayers of Jesus's own mother, the Blessed Virgin Mary, the Queen of Heaven, whose prayers are most often invoked. In popular imagination, here is the surest way to Jesus's heart: "Hail, Mary, full of grace. . . . Pray for us sinners now and at the hour of our death."

in order to redeem. "The woman," he wrote, "is increasingly aware that love alone can give her full stature, just as man begins to discern that spirit alone can endow life with its highest meaning." We must bring to consciousness these preconscious archetypes, universal and independent of the cultures that have built on them, of male and female.[14]

Each of us, Jung argued, has both masculine and feminine elements in our personality; women have a masculine *animus,* and men have a feminine *anima.* Maleness and femaleness are defined not by an absolute, but by a relative predominance of one set of characteristics over the other, and we (urgently) need to recognize this contrasexuality within ourselves. Wholeness in the individual is an enlarged state in which there is not just the masculine or the feminine but both, in which there is vitality and enrichment because the two become one.

Jung saw that for the rediscovery of ourselves and the principles and polarities within us, we need to be offered stories we can (not analyze but) inhabit as stories about ourselves. Jung saw—as we ourselves have seen— that talk of heaven and earth could be intended as talk of the inner and outer world. As Jung interpreted the biblical and Gnostic texts, "divinity" is our unconscious, and "matter" is our consciousness. The great symbols of John's gospel enter our consciousness from the unconscious; they are manifested in the world below but they come from the world above. On the one hand, Jesus himself is the Self, breaking from the unconscious into our consciousness; and, on the other, the feminine style of spirit is to make progress downward into the dark, into the roots of earth, into an earthier unconscious. The Christian Trinity itself, wholly male, suffers from "the missing fourth," the feminine element embodied (outside the Trinity) in the Blessed Virgin Mary.

You will probably recognize these Jungian distinctions; they have themselves become the terms in which we tell the story of ourselves. But we should beware. It is unsettling to find Jung adopting a view of women that we have seen prevail in the ancient world; that is, the "missing fourth" to be added to the Trinity is material/"mater" (or "mother"), the dark substance of the flesh and the devil, the feminine as flesh, matter, dark and earthy. Jung effectively endorsed the old division between the man of heavenly, eternal, rational spirit, on the one side, and, on the other, the woman of the earthy, particular, relational powers of human generation. Jung was indeed an heir of the ancient Gnostics he so admired.[15]

Fifty years on, Jung's account has been popularized in an adapted form. Mary and Jesus become together an unsurpassable symbol of male and female as a pair in proper and fulfilled relation, and so a sign of the universal order—way beyond our control or analytical understanding—that engenders, shapes, and nurtures all life on earth. This can take Mary far beyond her Gnostic role; she is now an equal with Jesus. As he is human, so is she; as he is divine, so is she. Within our world, still so heavily influenced by androcentric Christianity, it can seem *rightly* countercultural to elevate Mary Magdalene to the standing enjoyed by Jesus himself. We can describe Jesus as the masculine, Mary Magdalene as the feminine, then combine them as a pair to represent together the wholeness possible within one person or between two people; and so they become an icon for our age.

We have moved a long way, here, from history and from any claims that could be properly assessed by historians and the methods of historiography. Our generation is looking for venerable terms and stories in which to do justice to what we are coming to believe about ourselves; and in this we doing no more than the Gnostics themselves did when they took over and remoulded whatever attracted them in the pagan and Christian thought of their time. There are those in our own generation who, to find the Jesus they need, are (unwittingly) striding ever farther down the path that more careful historians of Jesus had already (unwittingly) followed for over a hundred years when Albert Schweitzer surveyed their work at the start of the twentieth century. Here again are his perceptive words, with which we set out on our search for Mary Magdalene.

> The historical investigation of the life of Jesus did not take its rise from a purely historical interest; it turned to the Jesus of history as an ally in the struggle against the tyranny of dogma. . . . Each successive epoch of theology found its own thoughts in Jesus; that was, indeed, the only way in which they could make him live.

* * *

It is time to take our leave of Mary Magdalene. This has been a book of more questions than answers, and so it should be. But we have, at the book's end, questions far more important to address than those with which we started.

Historians of the early churches are confronted with a Jesus who was believed by those who first wrote about him to confound all human understanding. Mark and John devise a whole new form of literature, an upside-down apocalypse of heavenly truths revealed—with an awesome clash of categories—in a human life and death on earth. Mary Magdalene turns Mark's reader back to "Galilee," the start of the gospel, and to the revelation that the text has to offer. And in John's gospel Mary stands for John's reader in the paradise regained on Easter Day. This is a challenge to any historians who assess the gospels simply as either (fantastical or poetical or inaccurate or reliable or inspired) "history" or "biography."

What difference will these rediscovered contours make to modern believers and theologians? Such readers are invited by the Bible itself to discover for themselves what *new birth from above* this strange Jesus might bring to their understanding of themselves and the world. Here too lies a challenge. First, visionary journeys to heaven are strange to us now; so, therefore, is their upside-down inversion into a heavenly being's life on earth. Second, it would be hard work even to try to reimagine ourselves into the mind-sets of the first century CE; we would be deluding ourselves to think that we could really succeed, and we cannot see in advance what gain (if any) we would have from a partial, uncertain, success. To take just one vital example of the images central to John's project and alien to ourselves, we are hard pushed to imagine—without indulging in mere fantasy—that we have been readmitted to life in paradise.

Should Christians, then, just abandon Mark and John to the historians and continue to graze from the surface of the texts what familiar nutrition they can? No. Mark and John attempted to open their readers' eyes to the world as those readers had never seen it before—as a place of disclosure, where God's victory can (despite all appearances) be seen, and where believers live at once within and beyond the obvious condition of the world. We may be ready, in our generation, to reengage our imagination, stretched and prized open by Mark's and John's stories as Mark and John intended, and so to recognize such imagination as a vital faculty of faith.

And now let's move out beyond the historians, believers, and theologians. We *all* of us have good reason to be interested in the Mary Magdalene of past and present. We all wonder how different loves—physical and spiritual love, erotic and selfless love—might be related. In doing so we are the heirs to all the Christian thought that has defined Mary Magdalene through the ages. The achievement and hopes of our own generation have redefined her, and the decades to come will reassess and redeploy her yet again.

Mary Magdalene has generally been defined as a symbol of two forms of love, which—in the life that men have imagined for her—she lived out one after the other: the first, rampantly sexual, self-indulgent, dangerous to men, and catastrophic for herself; the second, spiritual, selfless, obedient. During the Middle Ages we found a different momentum among women who could imagine themselves without embarrassment to be as close to Jesus as Mary Magdalene had been, and a strange halfway house among monks who had been self-consciously feminized by their calling to womanly peacefulness and domesticity.

Mary Magdalene has for decades been an icon of women as victims. But she is changing. She now represents the women who are escaping from victimhood in the twenty-first century as Mary herself has escaped from calumny; she is no longer the prostitute (used by men), but the woman falsely charged (by men) with prostitution. So she is becoming an example and an inspiration, a symbol of women's growing self-affirmation. Modern women can see as their own struggle Mary's struggle to be heard against the protests of Peter's patriarchal arrogance and fear.

There are now some churches within which she is a welcome icon of women's leadership. Churches have classically ordained functionaries to mediate (in ways not always easy to define) between God and his people, to represent God to the people and the people to God, speaking for each to the other. Christian tradition has generally invested men (and only men) with this "priestly" task; it was only in the twentieth century that some Western churches began to ordain women as priests. No modern church would invoke the (heretical) Gnostics as a precedent, but their Mary Magdalene does invite us to think again about the *character* of ministry. First, Mary represents the Gnostic (in Valentinian terms, a woman's role) as the Beloved Disciple who rises to the purity of Spirit; so (and only so) she can come to represent the Saviour. From this viewpoint she represents the progress to which the Gnostic is called and the end to which that progress leads. And second, being Jesus's companion on earth, she can represent as well the creative Wisdom of heaven and the Spirit of the Fullness; the ultimate revelation accessible on earth is of a still irreducible *pair* of male and female, each with its own embodiment, each incomplete without the other. Mary, then, has representative roles of her own, sometimes progressive, sometimes revelatory, and in these roles Jesus loves her more dearly than he loves any of the other disciples. She will, according to most Gnostic texts, be ultimately absorbed into the male, but she has *as herself* a vital role in the Gnostic understanding of the Gnostic's own fulfilment that is both now and not yet.

Beyond the churches, Mary's roles are growing. Readers of *The Da Vinci Code* will know that she has in our own age been reinvented as the mother of Jesus's child Sarah. She is being made to carry a lot of freight, in good measure because the New Testament offers so few and such limited models for women (let alone, for family life); there is so little on which to rest so much that we value. Jesus is, in the imagination of our age, evolving too; he is becoming a husband and a father. So Mary Magdalene is invoked now not just in a confrontation of the sexes, but in a search for harmony between them. She is becoming a symbol of love at an elusive intersection, the meeting point on which both men and women may "converge" to engender and share a single human sensibility that incorporates, without fear, the characteristics linked for millennia with women or with men, but not with both.

Another generation will come and go before it is clear whether and how Christian doctrine can accommodate such convergence. But we have good reason meanwhile to be grateful for John and the communities that sponsored and used his gospel and left it right at the heart of biblical, orthodox tradition. In this book I have tried to open our eyes to the claims embedded in the Bible itself that women might have a capacity for knowing Jesus distinct from—and more intimate than—the knowledge generally granted to men. In John's gospel it is Mary Magdalene who stands for all of us in the re-created paradise where humanity can meet its God and be at peace.

The Easter Garden

We began this chapter with Mary Magdalene and Jesus on Good Friday, depicted by an artist with utter simplicity. Let's end with them as well, two days later, as the sun rises on the garden that inspired John, Thomas, and the Gnostics. It has inspired the artists of Europe for centuries, none of them greater than the Venetian Titian (active 1506–1576).

> *Mary turns round and sees Jesus standing there, and does not know that it is Jesus. "Woman," says Jesus, "why are you weeping? Who are you looking for?" She thinks he is the gardener and says, "Sir, if you have taken him away, tell me where you have put him and I will take him away."*
>
> *Jesus says to her, "Mary." She turns and says to him, in Hebrew, "Rabbouni" (which means "Teacher").*
>
> *Jesus says to her, "Do not go on touching me, for I am not yet ascended to the Father. But go to my brothers and tell them: I am going to my Father and your Father, to my God and your God."*
>
> *John 20.14–18*

As the Renaissance took hold of Europe in the fifteenth century, more changed than just the priorities, skills, and aims of artists. The thought of Plato, the greatest of all Greek philosophers, reentered the bloodstream of Europe. It brought with it a new aesthetic. Greek thought knew nothing of Adam and Eve and their Fall. The human body could be admired for

Noli Me Tangere (oil on canvas, ca. 1514), by Titian.
Photo: © The National Gallery, London.

its beauty without any guilty fear of its sexual allure. Beauty attracts the beholder. The beauty of the human—and in particular the male—nude naturally stirred the love of the beholder, just as the beauty of intellectual and moral truth could and should stir the love of those who discerned it. Plato—and his readers in the Renaissance—spoke of love for divine beauty as a tumultuous passion stirring the soul, for nothing in human experience was more like such love than the erotic longing fired in one person by the physical beauty of another.

Titian's *Noli Me Tangere* ("Do not touch me," painted in Venice, Italy, around 1514, now in London) is among the most famous of all paintings to show Jesus and Mary Magdalene on Easter morning. Behind Jesus is flock of sheep, the care of Jesus the Good Shepherd; under his feet the grasses spring to life. Jesus at his resurrection was often shown holding a flagstaff, the banner showing the cross on which he had died and so defeated death; but here he carries a mattock, sign of the gardener that Mary took him to be. Mary kneels before him; her left hand rests on the jar of ointment she has brought with her, and her right hand reaches out towards his loincloth. Jesus draws back, holding his shroud to him. But even as he avoids her touch, he leans over her in the gentlest gesture of protection and love. He looks down at her tenderly.

Jesus is almost bare, a classical figure representing the perfection of human beauty; Mary is richly clothed in scarlet and white. Jesus stands higher than she, but is off balance and leans on his staff. She is crouching and earthbound, but therefore able to stretch out to him. Earthly beauty is reaching out for the beauty of the divine. Between Jesus and Mary is the shaft of the mattock he holds. It divides their figures. But her arm reaches across it, longing to touch and uncover her beloved. Between them too is Jesus's white shroud, for they are separated by his death. Her hand ventures past this too, but to no avail; the divine cannot be grasped or unveiled by such a touch as this. So near and yet so far; so far and yet so poignantly near.

As Jesus stands above Mary's figure, so the tree rises above the shrub behind Mary. Jesus stands higher than Mary, but Mary is at the centre of the painting. The tree, which crowns Jesus's figure and mirrors the angle of his mattock, reinforces too the figure of Mary. It extends the line of her body and head upward to the top of the painting; Jesus's head intersects with the tree trunk, his arm crosses it. On the picture's plane, where visual links are the links that matter, she is part of his space and he is part of hers.

Watch the curve starting at the hem of Mary's dress, running almost flat along her body and then turning steeply upward through the tree to heaven; and watch the second curve, starting at Jesus's feet and rising almost vertically up his flank, turning with the lean of his body and flattening out to follow the line of the hill beyond to the town. The earthly Mary is at the base of a curve that soars to heaven; the heavenly Jesus bends the curve of his figure towards earth and the people that live here (not least to that tiny figure with his dog, coming down the hill).

Titian has painted a profoundly sensuous scene. We may find here—and are right to find—a palpably erotic charge. This Mary Magdalene can so easily be seen as the former prostitute; she who had been the object of men's desire now longs, herself, for a physical touch, for an earthly love and an earthly lover. But we diminish the glory of this painting, if we fail to see—as Titian saw—in Jesus's classical figure the divine beauty that Mary is right to long for.

Human and divine love, erotic and spiritual love—the churches have tried for two thousand years to define and distinguish them. But Titian will have no such distinction; his Mary, by her sensuous longing for Jesus, rises to heaven; Jesus, avoiding her touch, leans over Mary herself with utter tenderness and extends his love towards that sleepy town beyond. Mary must not cling to the Jesus who has not yet ascended to heaven; but it is Mary who rises to heaven here, while her Jesus gives himself to earth. This is Easter, when heaven is wedded to earth and all creation is made new.[16]

Appendices

APPENDIX A

Jesus and the Sinful Woman (Luke 7.36–50)

What are we to make of the story of the sinful woman who wept over Jesus's feet and dried them with her hair, once we accept there is no evidence that she was Mary Magdalene at all? The sensuous, apparently erotic, actions in this story are the woman's, not Jesus's, but he does not rebuff her. On the contrary, he accepts this tribute of her love without embarrassment.

> *One of the Pharisees used to ask Jesus to eat with him, and coming into the Pharisee's house he reclined for dinner. And look, there was a woman who was a sinner in the city; learning that Jesus was a guest in the house of the Pharisee, buying an alabaster jar of perfume and standing behind Jesus by his feet in tears, she began to wet his feet and there she was, wiping them with the hair of her head and kissing his feet and anointing* [that is, rubbing and massaging, not just wetting][1] *them with the perfume.*

Luke imagines a formal dinner party in Middle Eastern and Greco-Roman style, at which the host and guests reclined on couches along three sides of a square table. The diners had their heads towards the table and their feet pointing outward, sometimes supported by a footrest. The food was served to the central table. The diners propped themselves up on their left arm. In Greek style, the dinner would likely be attended by male host and male guests only; in Roman style, the host's wife would have been reclining or (with less dignity) sitting next to her husband, perhaps with other women as guests. In a grand household, slaves (not least the guests' own slaves) might sit at the guests' feet. Additional women might well be present later in the party as entertainers, and it was customary for uninvited persons to stand around the walls to watch a party.[2]

The woman dries Jesus's feet with her hair, which must then have been loose. In Greco-Roman culture, at least some unmarried women wore their hair unbound; married women wore it bound. Only in extreme circumstances might a married woman loosen her hair in public: in supplication to a god, when disaster loomed; or when a god had answered her prayer and she went to the god's shrine to give thanks; or in public mourning or bereavement. (Prayer at a shrine could involve holding the feet of the god's statue in obeisance.) Jewish custom, also androcentric, sensed an erotic charge in a woman's unbound hair. A Jewish man could divorce his wife without payment for her support if she broke "Jewish custom"; that is, "if she goes out with her hair unbound or she spins in the street or she speaks with any man."[3]

Long, loosened hair could be seductive, and so could the woman's actions at Jesus's feet. (A philanderer in one comic plays relishes being "at ease in a bedroom, where luxurious, voluptuous young women will rub my feet with perfume"; another, in a second play, "enjoys having my feet rubbed with fair soft hands—isn't it magnificent!")[4] Readers have assumed for generations that this woman's sin had been sexual; she was a prostitute who had serviced her clients with the same sensuous care with which, at Jesus's feet, she now laments and renounces her profession. No other woman, after all, would be at a dinner party by herself and fondling a man's feet. This may be right, but the host's response is then surprising:

> *The Pharisee who had invited Jesus said to himself, "This man,*
> *if he were a prophet, would know who is touching him and what*
> *sort of woman she is, that she is a sinner."*

That is, it would take a *prophet* to realize that the woman is a sinner; her sinfulness is not obvious just from her appearance and behavior. The word for sinner here (*hamartōlos*) is quite general; Luke does not use the word for prostitute (*pornē*). The woman had been, by the standards of the time, immoral, and her immorality may have been sexual. But that is not what Luke actually tells us; perhaps his own interest in this story lies elsewhere.

We need to watch the story unfold in its place within Luke's carefully constructed narrative. A prophet was already on the scene: John the Baptist, the cousin of Jesus who had predicted Jesus's coming and baptized him. The Baptist had, with fierce warnings of God's impending punishment, summoned the people to repentance. And Luke has been presenting Jesus too as a prophet, after the model of the Old Testament prophets Elijah and Elisha. Jesus has raised a dead child to life, as both Elijah and Elisha had. *"A great prophet,"* exclaims the crowd about Jesus, *"has arisen among us!"*[5]

Now John's disciples come to quiz Jesus, and Jesus then instructs the crowd about John: John is a prophet, *"and more than a prophet, but the least in the kingdom of God is greater than he."*[6] Luke himself adds a note here that the people and tax collectors had been baptized by John when he called for repentance, and so they had vindicated God; but the Pharisees rejected the purposes of God for themselves, refusing John's baptism. Jesus contrasts the ascetic John with himself. John had mourned the wrath to come, but the people had not wept with him; Jesus himself had come eating and drinking, and his opponents complained, *"Look, a glutton and drinker, friend of tax-farmers and wrongdoers."* And throughout, concludes Jesus, *"Wisdom has been vindicated in all her children."*[7]

And so we reach the story of the sinful woman. At Jesus's feet, the woman takes the position and role of a slave; she is humiliating herself. Her hair is loose—in supplication, thanksgiving, or mourning Luke does not specify. She is also wildly extravagant; alabaster was among the most expensive materials for a perfume jar, and it was famously luxurious to apply perfume (perhaps in powdered form) to the feet. This weeping woman *may* be seductive, but she is primarily just unsettled and unsettling. Luke now gives us a short dialogue that will define this story as a story of the woman's forgiveness.

> *Jesus spoke up and said to him, "Simon, I have something to say to you." "Teacher," said Simon, "tell me." "There were two debtors in debt to one creditor: one owed him as much as a workman might earn in fifty days, the other as much as a workman might make in five hundred." Neither of them could pay; and he let them both off. Which of them will love him more?" "I suppose," said Simon, "the one who was let off more." "You are right," said Jesus.*
>
> *And turning to the woman he said to Simon, "You see this woman? I came into your house, you gave me no water for my feet; but she has wet my feet with her tears and has wiped them with her hair. You gave me no kiss; but since I came in she has not stopped kissing my feet. You did not anoint my head with oil; but she has anointed my feet with perfume. This is the reason I tell you her sins—her many sins—have been forgiven: she has loved deeply. But the person to whom little is being forgiven, loves little."*

"This is the reason I tell you her sins—her many sins—have been forgiven: she has loved deeply." I admit this is a clumsy translation, designed to do some justice to an oddly clumsy sentence. The little parable of the debtors, which Luke has probably introduced into this scene from some other source, would suggest that Jesus should now say, (A) "She has been forgiven many sins, and therefore she loves deeply," and the Greek sentence can (just) be read that way. But the more natural sense of the

Greek is (B) "She has loved deeply, and therefore she has been forgiven her many sins"; and this, if the story of the debtors were not there, is what we would expect Jesus to say. So perhaps Luke had in front of him a simple story of love winning forgiveness (B), which he has muddled by introducing the debtors, so that it is now a story of forgiveness winning love (A). And this makes a real confusion: the woman cannot have known on her entry that she had been forgiven (Jesus, after all, has not yet told her), so how can she feel the love that will follow from that forgiveness?

This is odd; Luke is not often so clumsy. I suspect we are being misled by reading the story in isolation from its context. Luke still has in mind the story and influence of John the Baptist, who appeared before Jesus and called for repentance for the forgiveness of sins. Luke does not mention any encounter of the Baptist and the woman. He does not need to; he just expects that his readers will be reading the gospel as a sequential whole *and will themselves encounter the Baptist before reaching the story of the woman.* Luke wrote his own account of the Baptist, at the gospel's start, to stir his readers to repentance and has just reminded those readers of the Baptist's stern demands and tone. First the Baptist, and now—with a quite different tone!—the Jesus of whom the Baptist spoke. The woman is vindicating God by the repentance the Baptist called for; Simon, one among the Pharisees who dismissed the Baptist, is flouting God's own plan.

Luke invites his readers to hear the Baptist's preaching, to repent, and so (as the Baptist promised) to win forgiveness of their sins. They will then come to Jesus with tears of grateful love and will hear Jesus declare the forgiveness they have, by their repentance, already secured. The stark contrast between John's preaching and Jesus's, one after the other, is seen in action upon the reader in the reception of Luke's story.

> *Jesus said to the woman, "Your sins are forgiven." And those who were at dinner with him began to say among themselves, "Who is this who even forgives sins?" But he said to the woman, "Your faith has saved you; go in peace."*

The scene ends. Wisdom was always represented as a woman in Jewish tradition and was contrasted with the seductive, adulterous women who will tempt young men away from Wisdom's path. Now Wisdom has been vindicated by this most unlikely of all her children, a sinful woman who has repented and come to the source of all wisdom. And in the very next verses Luke tells of the other women who had been healed of evil spirits and illnesses and valued Jesus as they should: Mary Magdalene, Joanna, and Susanna. Luke will round off this section of his gospel with a double story he inherits from Mark, the story of a woman who comes up to Jesus covertly for healing from her haemorrhage intertwined with the story of the daughter of Jairus, the ruler of the synagogue. The woman is told, *"Your faith has saved you; go in peace"* and Jairus is told, *"Just have faith, and your daughter will be saved."*[8] Faith and its consequences are spreading.

APPENDIX B

The Gnostics and the Female Powers of Creation

We have watched the Gnostics think through the logic of androgynous
and of male and of female powers; the female is generally the last to
emerge and the first to be reabsorbed. Here is a summary of three texts.
The first, the *Secret Book of John,* is often (and misleadingly) read as
defining the first specifically female power as utterly primordial. For
effective validation of the female powers in creation, we must look elsewhere, to the subtle exegesis of biblical tradition in two other texts: in the
fragments of the Valentinian thinker Theodotus, preserved by Clement,
and in the Nag Hammadi treatise *On the Origin of the World.*

First, then, the rhapsodic account of the primal One in the *Secret Book
of John* (a foundational text for many Gnostics). He is the father of everything, pure light into which no eye can gaze, invisible spirit, more than a
god, total perfection, beyond limit, beyond measuring, beyond naming,
neither corporeal nor incorporeal, beyond time; he is pure mind, life that
gives life, the blessed one that gives blessing, the knowledge that gives
knowledge. His Forethought emerges, his image; she is "prior to everything, the Mother-Father, the first man, the holy spirit, the thrice-male, the
thrice-powerful, the thrice-named androgynous one." The Father looks
at her and she conceives a spark of light; this is Christ, the only-begotten
child of the Father-Mother. This Christ descends from heaven to speak to
John; his single figure seems to be first a youth, then an old man, then a
servant. He speaks to John: "John, why are you afraid? I am the one who
is always with you. I am the Father, I am the Mother, I am the Son."

This has become, for many modern readers, a famous declaration of
God the Trinity as Father, Mother, and Son. But we should beware. The
Forethought who acts as Mother-Father, emerging from the invisible
Spirit-Father as his image, is thrice-male and thrice-androgynous; and
the trinitarian figure appears to John in three male forms. We can see
why. The authors of the *Secret Book* must do justice to the mysterious
emergence of male and female from the utterly transcendent spirit who
is thought of, by default, as Father. In this story the emergence of the
unambiguously female is repeatedly deferred; when she does emerge as
Wisdom she will act improperly and alone, which will lead to the cosmic
Fall, and so the powers of ignorance will spread their dark dominion.

But we should not stop just here. Some Gnostics did make some subtle claims for a creation enlivened throughout by a female power. The Valentinians worked on the premise of spirit, soul, and dense matter, three layers of cosmic and of human creation. Here is one such Valentinian account, from Theodotus. It takes the biblical story as its starting point. God said, *"Let us make a Human in our image and a likeness."*. . . *So God made the Human, in the image of God he made him, male and female he made them.* . . . *God moulded the human as dust from the earth, and breathed into his face the breath of life, and the human became a living soul.* Imagine, first, the middle realms, beneath the realm of spirit, but still far above coarse earth. Here the Demiurge made an earthy soul, like that of animals; this is the human *in an image.* And the Demiurge breathed into this human a soul like his own soul; this made the human *a living soul, in the likeness* of the Demiurge himself. The earthy soul functions as clothing for the demiurgic soul within; as Adam will say of Eve, who had been hidden within him, *"Here is bone from my bones, flesh from my flesh."*[1]

Now imagine the equivalent but prior sequence in the higher spiritual realm. Here the demiurgic soul is the clothing for the spirit, which is hidden within it and will emerge as bone from the demiurgic bone. And finally, imagine the equivalent and final sequence on our lower earth. Here Eve or Life is hidden within Adam and emerges as bone from his bones. At each stage, the clothing is the lower form, wrapped around the higher. The demiurgic soul is wrapped around spirit, the earthy soul is wrapped around the demiurgic—and Adam is wrapped around Eve. It is in each case the female power that promises a higher life.

And finally, here is a simplified summary of the last layer of creation, as expounded in the Gnostic text *On the Origin of the World.* Throughout, the emphasis is on the creative, life-giving female powers, Faith, her daughter Wisdom, and Wisdom's daughter Eve-of-Life. They are forever at work against the arrogance and delusion of the lesser gods. *"I am the Lord God,"* said the chief of these gods, the god of the Jewish Scriptures, *"and there is no other god beside me"*; how wrong he was. On Day One God said, *"Let there be light."* Interpreted by the Gnostic group of the *Origin*: on Day One the chief of the lesser gods throws out a challenge: "If anything existed before me, let it appear, so that we may see its light." *And there was phōs* [i.e., *light* or *man*]. Interpreted: immediately light came out of the heaven above and passed through all of the heavens of the earth. And as that light appeared, a human likeness appeared within it, very wonderful; this was the Adam of Light. On Day Four *God said, "Let there be lights in the vault of heaven, to divide the day from the night."* Interpreted: the Adam of Light stayed for about two days, and on his departure Wisdom got permission to make the light-giving bodies of heaven.[2]

On Day Six God said, *"Let us make a Human in our image and a likeness."* Interpreted: the lesser god says to his associates, "Let us create a man out of earth, according to the image of our body and according to the likeness of this being [the Adam of Light] to serve us." *For male and female he made them.* But in a countervailing move, Wisdom-Life, knowing the powers' plan, creates through her daughter, Eve-of-Life, a hermaphrodite who shall become the instructor, the wisest of all beings—that is, the serpent of Eden. So Eve-of-Life is creating the serpent of knowledge while the lesser gods are moulding the Adam of Day Six. This Adam, made solely by male powers, is an inanimate abortion; he has no soul or life, for these are endowed by female powers. This is a dramatic turnabout; in other Gnostic systems, creatures are abortive who are made only and wholly by female powers.

And on Day Seven *God rested from all the work he had made.* This is the lesser god's day of rest, the Sabbath. So we reach Day Eight. *God moulded the human as dust from the earth, and breathed into his face the breath of life, and the human became a living soul. . . . And Adam called his wife Eve, because she was the mother of all living things.*[3] Interpreted: after the day of rest Wisdom sent her daughter Life, called Eve, as an instructor so that she might make Adam, who had no soul, arise, so that his descendants might become containers of light. When Eve saw her male counterpart prostrate, she had pity on him and said, "Adam, Become alive! Arise upon the earth!" Adam arose and opened his eyes. When he saw her he said, "You shall be called Mother of the Living. For it is you who have given me life."

So, in summary: the first Adam, of Light, is of spirit and appeared on Day One; the second Adam is of soul and appeared on Day Six; the third Adam is a creature of the earth and appeared on Day Eight. And the real Eve, the instructor and giver of life, leaves just her likeness with Adam and goes on to occupy the Tree of Knowledge.[4]

NOTES

PREFACE: Mary Magdalene

1. From the Coptic. In the Greek, "For certainly he, knowing her—without faltering—loved her."

2. Interview with the newspaper *Il Giornale,* March 2005, reported at www.theage.com.au/articles/2005/03/16/1110913654115.html?oneclick=true.

3. Quoted by L. Knight-Jadczyk (from a writing of 1982) in an article posted at www.cassiopaea.org/cass/grail_5g.htm.

4. Encyclical *Sacerdotalis Caelibatus* (Paul VI), 1967, 1; Vatican II, 53.II.13.

5. Albert Schweitzer, *The Quest of the Historical Jesus,* trans. W. Montgomery (London: Black, 1910), 4–5.

6. Schweitzer, *The Quest of the Historical Jesus,* 396–97.

ONE: With Jesus in Galilee

1. Luke 24.9; Rom. 16.7. For Joanna, see R. Bauckham, *Gospel Women: Studies of the Named Women in the Gospels* (London, New York: Clark, 2002), 109–202. For an additional link with the Herodian court, see Menaem in Acts 13.1, who is described as *syntrophos* (Gk, "brought up with" [Herod Antipas]), a term of honor as well as a description.

2. Luke 10.38–42 (with their brother Lazarus, John 12.1–8); Acts 9.36–40; 12.12; 16.14–15; 18.2.

3. Mark 15.40; Matt. 27.56; John 19.25. In the days immediately after the ascension of Jesus, the eleven disciples (now without the traitor Judas Iscariot) sustained fervent and unified prayer *together with the women and Mary the mother of Jesus and his brothers* (Acts 1.14).

4. Matt. 13.55; Mark 1.29–31.

5. Luke 14.26; 1 Cor. 9.5.

6. Mark 6.7–13; Matt. 10.5–42, esp. 10.5–6, 23; 11.1; Luke 10.1–6; John 21.1–3. I acknowledge a counterargument. There were, Josephus tells us, 204 towns and villages in Galilee (*Life* 235). If Jesus spent three days in each, with half a day's walk from each to the next, he will have been travelling around Galilee itself for two years.

7. Luke 23.49. Tatian is dependent only on Luke here.

8. Luke 7.36–50.

9. Gen. 1.28.

10. For Jesus's possible marriage as a "low status" Jew suspected of being illegitimate, see B. Chilton, *Rabbi Jesus: An Intimate Biography* (New York: Doubleday, 2000), e.g., 3–23. D. B. Martin, in *Sex and the Single Savior* (Louisville, KY: Westminster John Knox, 2006), sketches the history of arguments and assumptions about Jesus's sexuality (91–102).

11. There had, it seems, been a Ben Stada who advocated the worship of foreign gods and had, in Lydda, been condemned to death by a rabbinic court and stoned. His name was an appropriate code for the Jesus who had apparently introduced the worship of himself. See M. Smith, *Jesus the Magician* (London: Victor Gollancz, 1978), 47, 178; Babylonian Talmud *Shabbat* 104b; cf. 67a; also Tosefta *Shabbat* 11.15; Palestinian Talmud *Shabbat* 12.4.

12. L. Ginzberg, *The Legends of the Jews* (Baltimore: Johns Hopkins University Press, 1998), 3: 255–58.

13. On Qumran and the Essenes, most recently, see C. H. T. Fletcher-Louis, *All the Glory of Adam: Liturgical Anthropology in the Dead Sea Scrolls* (Leiden: Brill, 2002), 131–34.

14. We nowadays use—in various and contested ways—the distinction between sex and gender. The ancient world did not understand the physiological relation between the sexes in the way we do; the view commonly held then, that women were imperfectly formed men, was both a product and a vindication of social expectations and inequalities. A famous account of sex and gender in the ancient world is T. Laqueur, *Making Sex: Body and Gender from the Greeks to Freud* (Cambridge, MA: Harvard University Press, 1990). On obstetrics, see G. E. R. Lloyd, *Science, Folklore and Ideology: Studies in the Life Sciences in Ancient Greece* (Cambridge: Cambridge University Press, 1983), 58–111. Chastity made as telling a point then as it might now.

15. Matt. 22.30. Luke 20.34–38 is more startling. *"Those who have been made worthy to attain that* [ultimate] *aeon and the resurrection from the dead neither marry nor are given in marriage, for they cannot even die any more, for they are equal to angels."* They are already children of the resurrection before the final rising.

16. 1 Cor. 7.1–40; 9.5; Mark 3.20–21; Matt. 11.19.

TWO: At Jesus's Death and Resurrection

1. Luke 23.49. This is more poignant than it seems. The Psalms include a prayerful lament, as from a person drawing near to death: *You have distanced my acquaintances from me, I have been handed over and have not escaped. Will you really do wonders among the dead? Or will doctors raise them up, will they acknowledge you? You have distanced from me my friend and neighbor, and my acquaintances from my misery* (Ps. 87.9, 11, 19, Gk).

2. Luke 23.55.

3. For a lively survey of the reasons given for and against the view that the gospel once had a fuller conclusion, see N. C. Croy, *The Mutilation of Mark's Gospel* (Nashville, TN: Abingdon, 2003).

4. John 20.31 is usually translated, "Jesus is the Christ, the Son of God." The grammar of the Greek suggests that it *should* be translated, "the Christ, the Son of God, is Jesus."

5. Dan. 7:13, 18.

6. Mark 4.11–12; Isa. 6.9–10; also Mark 6.52; 7.18; 8.14–21; 9.32.

7. Mark 4.35–41 (Ps. 89.9); 5.1–20; 5.35–43; 6.45–52 (Job 9.8; Exod. 33–34, 1 Kings 19.11; God's name, Exod. 3.13); 9.6; 9.15; 10.32.

8. Mark 14.8–9. For the parody of a rich man's feast in Cumae, southern Italy, Petronius writes in *Satyricon* that Trimalchio has a winding sheet brought in and some of the unguent that will be used to wash his bones. He opens a flask of spikenard, anoints all the guests, and says, "I hope I shall like this as much in the grave as I do on earth. . . . Now you must imagine you have been asked to a festival in honour of my past life" (78).

9. Mark 14.27–29; 14.50–52; 14.61–62.

10. Ps. 22.1; Mark 15.33, 38.

11. Mark 15:46–47.

12. Mark may be combining, from two sources, a burial story (featuring *Mary Magdalene and Mary of Joses*, and a large stone) and an Easter story (featuring *Mary Magdalene, Mary of James, and Salome*, ointment, and just a tomb sufficiently protected for the corpse to be safe from scavenging animals); the second Mary was likely the same person, best known in different circles for different sons. The women in Mark's combination of these two stories have a jar of ointment, but no apparent access to the tomb.

13. Mark 16.2; Ps. 24.heading, 7, 9, Gk.

14. Mark 16.5; 14.62, Rev. 4.1.

15. Mark 16.6. In Peter's proclamation we hear, in similarly stately terms, of *Jesus of Nazareth, a man shown forth by God, whom God has raised* (Acts 2.22–24).

16. Mark 14.28; 16.7.

17. We may tend, as modern readers with a dedication to accuracy, to take Mark's emphatic expressions too literally. The women *said nothing to anyone* (16.8). Does this mean utter

and sustained silence about what they had seen? Not necessarily. When Jesus had healed a leper, he commanded, *"See you say nothing to anyone, but go and show yourself to the priest"* (1.44); the healed man, then, *was* supposed to pass on the news of his healing, even if not the identity of the healer.

18. 1 Cor. 12.4. On Paul and transformative journeys to heaven, central to his thought, see R. Griffith-Jones, *The Gospel According to Paul* (San Francisco: HarperSanFrancisco, 2004).

19. Zeph. 1.7; Zech. 2.13. The Greek texts have, in each case, not a call to be silent, but—just as fittingly—to *beware,* to *take care.* Cf. Hab. 2.20. In the next section of Zechariah (3.1–10) the high priest Jesus/Joshua appears before the tribunal of God's angel. The angel orders that he be changed out of his dirty clothes into clean clothes and declares that his guilt has been taken away.

20. Mark 14.17 has Jesus coming to the supper "with the Twelve." They *may* be joining a larger group (cf. 14.12–14) within which they can be distinguished as special (cf. 14.20).

21. Mark 4.41.

22. Mark 8.31–33; 9.33–37; 10.35–40.

23. Robin Griffith-Jones, *The Four Witnesses* (San Francisco: HarperSanFrancisco, 2000).

24. Gen. 32.30.

25. The readers may have trusted the narrator, but would still have wondered if the narration, at this crucial moment, was wholly dependent on the testimony of mere women. We may object that the only friendly witnesses to the crucifixion had been women, who must have provided the details, but that was at least a public event. There are occasions in Jewish history when women are given a glimpse of the divine, and their testimony is, predictably, distrusted (R. Bauckham, *Gospel Women: Studies of the Named Women in the Gospels* [London, New York: Clark, 2002], 270–77).

26. Mark 10.45; 1.31; 16.6; 5.33; 5.41–42. Readings that recognize Mark's gospel as a verbal and thematic echo chamber have as their most notorious opportunity and challenge the *young man* in a *linen cloth* who leaves the cloth and runs away naked at Jesus's arrest (14.51–52). Jesus will be buried in a linen cloth, and the women at the tomb will see there a *young man* in a white robe (15.46; 16.5). Interpretations abound. In particular, hints of baptism have been found here. The young man who ran away was, by his nakedness, prepared for baptism into the death of Jesus and for burial with him (Rom. 6.3–4) and is seen, reborn to life, in the white robe of the initiate. But we remember that the second young man, in the tomb, represents Jesus, so the first would be a symbol of Jesus too, and his running away would surely be a symbol of the fear to which Jesus himself did not succumb. Now, the young man who ran away left behind his cloth, and Jesus, who, despite his fear, stays to die, will be wrapped in such a cloth. The second young man, who represents Jesus in the tomb, wears the garment of glory, not of death. Such shimmering hints should warn us that we are not dealing with cut-and-dried personifications and allegories, but with a story that was written to be mysterious.

27. Matt. 27.62–65; Dan. 6.17. See R. C. Carrier, "The Plausibility of Theft," in R. M. Price and J. J. Lowder, eds., *The Empty Tomb* (New York: Prometheus, 2005), 360.

28. Matt. 2.11.

29. Matt. 28.15.

30. Matt. 27.61.

31. Those who suspect that Mark's gospel originally had a fuller ending speculate (reasonably enough) that Matt. 28.8–10, 16–20 may be based on that ending.

32. Luke 23.55; 6.17; 10.1; 19.37; 24.9; 24.33; Acts 1.15.

33. Luke 24.3.

34. Luke 24.9; 8.1–3; 24.10.

35. Paired parables: Luke 13.18–21; 15.4–10. Peter 5.8–10; 9.22 (cf. Mark 8. 31–33); 22.32.

36. Luke 2.49–50; 23.46; 24.5.

37. Luke 9.44–45; 18.34.

38. Luke has a fine sense of narrative; his deferral of the women's names may be for emphasis. Cf. his treatment of Peter's denials: he adds the most poignant detail, at the third denial, that Jesus looked at Peter (22.61); Luke has spared Peter only to make his fall all the more dramatic.

39. Luke 24.12.

40. Luke 24.25–26, 34; it is striking that Luke relays in this way the news of Peter's encounter with Jesus, 24.32, 35.

41. It is not such a stupid idea; "spirit" could describe an angel, for instance, or an ethereal element of Jesus that had been immune to death. Jesus invites them to touch him, to show he is not immaterial, and eats in front of them, to show he is not an angel (Luke 24.36–43). On angels not eating, see Tob. 12.19.

42. Luke 24.44–49.

THREE: In Paradise

1. For more on this reading of John, see R. Griffith-Jones, *The Four Witnesses* (San Francisco: HarperSanFrancisco, 2000), 342–77; and with full references and discussion of the similar texts to reach us from the ancient world, see R. Griffith-Jones, "John: Transformation by a Text," *Experientia*, vol. 1 (Atlanta: Society of Biblical Literature, forthcoming).

2. W. Meeks, "The Stranger from Heaven in Johannine Sectarianism," a classic article reprinted in J. Ashton, ed., *The Interpretation of John* (Edinburgh: Clark, 1986), 141–73 (162). Meeks sees the gospel and its Jesus as defining and defending a community. Their real role is far more personal: to bring readers to new birth from above, and so to paradise.

3. Gen. 1.1, 3.

4. John 1.14; 1.12; 1.14; 3.11.

5. John 1.38–39; also 6.56; 14.10–11; 14.23; 15.1–9.

6. John 1.41, 45, 49.

7. John 2.13–23.

8. R. Patai, *The Hebrew Goddess* (Detroit: Wayne State University Press), 1990, 111–36, argued from rabbinic evidence that the ancient cherubim were replaced in the second century BCE by two new and more obviously sexed figures (male and female), which survived until 70 CE; Philo and Josephus were *embarrassed* by these figures and the sexual license that accompanied their annual display.

9. John 2.18–20.

10. John 1.51; chaps. 7–9; 4.23. See Griffith-Jones, *The Four Witnesses*, 317–41.

11. John 3.1–21.

12. John 4.1–42, esp. 4.19; 4.29; 4.42.

13. John 5.1–29, esp. 5.1–8, 25, 28.

14. Jesus has recently and grandly juxtaposed the figure with the name of God, *"When you lift up the Son of the Human One, then you will know that It Is I"* (8.28).

15. John 9.1–41, esp. 9.17, 33, 35–38, 39.

16. John 10.1–5.

17. John 11.1–44.

18. Raymond E. Brown, *The Gospel According to John*, Anchor Bible 29, 29A (Garden City, NY: Doubleday, 1966–70), vol. 1, 175.

19. Gen. 24.1–21; 29.1–14; Exod. 2.16–20;

20. Song 4.12–15.

21. For the sinful Samaritan woman, see too the magisterial commentaries by the Lutheran Rudolf Bultmann, *The Gospel of John*, trans. G. R. Beasley-Murray, R. W. M. Hoare, and J. K. Riches (Philadelphia: Westminster Press, 1971), and the Roman Catholic Rudolf Schnackenburg, *The Gospel According to St. John*, trans. K. Smyth, et al. (New York:

Crossroads, 1968–82). On her many marriages: Sarah was married seven times and lost each husband to the demon Asmodeus, Tob. 3.7; the woman in the Sadducees' fable had seven husbands, Mark 12.18–23. The Gnostic commentator Heracleon saw how perceptive the woman was, in Origen, *Commentary on John,* 13.10.57–11.74; 13.10–35; 15.91–19.118; 25.147–50; 31.187–92; 32.200–202. Cf. E. H. Pagels, *The Johannine Gospel in Gnostic Exegesis* (Atlanta: Scholars Press, 1989), 86–93. The Reformer Martin Luther was recorded as saying in an informal conversation: "Christ was an adulterer for the first time with the woman at the well, for it was said, 'Nobody knows what he is doing with her' (John 4.27). Again with Magdalene, and still again with the adulterous woman (John 8.1–11), whom he let off so easily" (*Table-Talk* entry 1472 [from 1532]). Luther sensed the sensuous intimacy of the stories; he was not, of course, claiming that Jesus was a serial lover.

22. John 11.25–27, 31, 45.

23. S. van Tilborg, *Reading John in Ephesus* (Leiden: Brill, 1996), 155–64.

24. John 1.18.

25. John 13.3–8; 12.1–8; 14.9; chap. 17, esp. 17.11–13, 15, 24.

26. John 19.5; Gen. 2.1–2; John 19.30.

27. The details of the baptismal ritual and symbolism deployed at Dura-Europos are unclear. Candidates may have entered through the western door from the assembly hall and have been anointed with oil on entrance; such oil, in Syriac ritual, granted not exorcism, but perfection. The emphasis may not, then, have been on Paul's promise—familiar in the West—that in baptism Christians are *baptized into Christ's death and buried with him by baptism into death, so that as Christ was raised from the dead by the glory of the Father, even so we also should walk in newness of life* (Rom. 6.3–4). See *The Excavations at Dura-Europos* 8.2: C. H. Kraeling, *The Christian Building* (New Haven, CT: Dura-Europos Publications, 1967), 71–88, 190–97. More recent research has suggested that the frescoes may show not the women at the tomb but a bridal procession; we shall hear more, in chapter 7, of baptism and bridal imagery.

28. John 20.8.

FOUR: Making Mary Male

1. *God the only son,* the best attested of the three readings found in early manuscripts. *Who belongs at the Father's breast,* literally, *the one who is into the lap/bosom of the Father,* apparently with a sense of movement or focused attention, as in to take up the position. *He has shown the way:* emphatic "he"; the verb *exēgēsato* could be expected to mean *he has led,* but in the New Testament this verb is used to mean "to explain" or "to reveal" divine secrets.

2. Luke 23.43.

3. These ideas are beautifully expounded by April D. De Conick in *Voices of the Mystics: Early Christian Discourse in the Gospels of John and Thomas* (Sheffield: Academic Press, 2001) and now *Recovering the Original Gospel of Thomas* (New York, London: Clark, 2005). The debate between Johannine and Thomasine churches had been diagnosed (rather differently) by G. Riley in *Resurrection Reconsidered: Thomas and John in Controversy* (Minneapolis: Fortress, 1995). See also April D. De Conick, *Seek to See Him: Ascent and Vision Mysticism in the Gospel of Thomas* (Leiden: Brill, 1996). For *Thomas,* I have gratefully used the translations and studies of A. Guillaumont et al., *The Gospel According to Thomas* (Leiden: Brill, 1959); T. O. Lambdin in James M. Robinson, ed., *The Nag Hammadi Library in English* (Leiden: Brill, 1977); A. Marjanen, *The Woman Jesus Loved* (Leiden: Brill, 1996); and April D. De Conick in her various monographs and articles.

4. *Gospel of Thomas* 5; 77.

5. Jesus spoke in Aramaic, the New Testament is in Greek, and the *Gospel of Thomas* is written in Coptic, but is the translation of a Greek text that was likely translated itself from Syriac.

6. I incline to the arguments of J. P. Meier in *A Marginal Jew: Rethinking the Historical Jesus,* vol. 1 (New York: Doubleday, 1991), 124–39, 153–66; Thomas's versions are, in every case, derived from the biblical versions. Among more recent treatments of Thomas's gestation is N. Perrin, *Thomas and Tatian: The Relationship Between the Gospel of Thomas and the Diatesseron* (Atlanta: Society of Biblical Literature, 2002). De Conick's conclusion:

"This places the complete *Gospel of Thomas* at a date no later than 120 CE, making the accretions contemporary to the composition of the Johannine literature and the Pastoral Epistles. It also grounds Thomas's theology *inside* early orthodoxy rather than outside. . . . The *Gospel of Thomas* is quite [congruent] with early Syrian Christianity" (*Recovering the Original Gospel of Thomas*, 240). The literature on Thomas is vast; for a recent collection of essays (two of which are on women disciples and Gnosticism), see R. Uro, ed., *Thomas at the Crossroads* (Edinburgh: Clark, 1998).

7. *Gospel of Thomas* 17. Thomas relays several parables of Jesus that are familiar from the biblical gospels, and some of these, in the Bible, have explanations attached. It has long been suspected that the explanations were not provided by Jesus, but were added by Jesus's followers to help the audience or readers. In Thomas these explanations are missing. Does this help show that Thomas wrote before the explanations were composed and added to the parables? In itself, no. To explain such a parable was to devalue it; readers would be spared the very effort the parable was there to stimulate.

8. I have elsewhere argued at length that Mark and John were both acutely alert to this cryptic character of Jesus's self-revelation (see R. Griffith-Jones, *The Four Witnesses* [San Francisco: HarperSanFrancisco, 2000]) and that Paul knew it would take a quasi-mystical transformation of the reader's understanding to grasp the gospel (see R. Griffith-Jones, *The Gospel According to Paul* [San Francisco: HarperSanFrancisco, 2004]). For explanations within Thomas: Saying 28, structured A-B-A, almost has in B an explanation to A; Saying 64 makes businessmen and merchants the obvious and apparently noncryptic target (although cf. the new merchant's wisdom, 109); Saying 78 makes (quite clearly) a point alien to the New Testament versions (Matt. 11.7–8: Luke 7.24–5).

9. On Thomas's supposed dullness: (1) In John 11.16 Thomas is misguided but brave: *"Let's go too, ourselves, so that we may die with him."* Grammatically, *him* should refer not to Jesus but to Lazarus, and perhaps in a canny ambiguity it does, to speak of the death necessary for rebirth from above. (2) In 13.36–14.11 Peter asks a question and Jesus replies; then Thomas asks a corollary and Jesus replies; then Philip asks a corollary to Thomas's question and Jesus replies. All three are missing the point of Jesus's promises, but it is Philip (not Thomas) who gets the most brusque response from Jesus. (3) In 14.22–24 (referring just to *Judas, not Iscariot*) John may be drawing on a vision-and-ascent tradition that had developed in proto-Thomasine circles before their leader Judas was given his nickname Thomas (Aram., "Twin") or Didymus (Gk, "Twin").

10. *Gospel of Thomas* 18; 20.

11. Gen. 2.25; 3.7.

12. "Clothes" could be read in many ways. In the *Dialogue of the Savior* (see Chapter 8), Matthew wants to understand the clothes the disciples will be given when they depart the decay of the flesh. Jesus, interjecting, assures him that the malign "governors" of this world have garments that will perish, unlike the garments to be given to the children of truth when they strip themselves (143.11–23).

13. The motif was familiar in the mysteries and so entered pagan philosophy, e.g., Plotinus, *Enneads* 4.4 [28]5 (11–31). Souls do not need to fall to the uttermost depths, for even if their movement has proceeded quite far, it is possible for it to halt; and nothing prevents them, before they reach the outermost regions of being, from beginning to shed their garments again.

14. Mark 10.10–13. According to J. J. Buckley in *Female Fault and Fulfillment in Gnosticism* (Chapel Hill: University of North Carolina Press, 1986), 84–104, Saying 114 (see below) demands that women become male, a stage prior to becoming a living spirit (114; 22).

15. Mark 15.40; 16.1.

16. Gen. 2.16–17.

17. *Gospel of Thomas* 18; Matt. 21.21; *Gospel of Thomas* 106.

18. On Saying 37, see A. D. De Conick and J. Fossum, "Stripped Before God: A New Interpretation of Logion 37 in the *Gospel of Thomas*," *Vigiliae Christianae* 45 (1991): 123–50; De Conick, *Seek to See Him*, 143–47. On Gnostic visions, see D. Merkur, *Gnosis* (Albany: State University of New York Press, 1993): the key to Gnosis is the Gnostics'

distinctive type of visions, neither objective nor allegorical, but paradoxically according the same reality to the world as to the visions themselves.

19. *Gospel of Thomas* 108.

20. *Gospel of Thomas* 75. On *monachos* (Gk, "bachelor"; cf. Coptic *oua ouōt,* "single one"), see De Conick, *Recovering the Original Gospel of Thomas,* 190–91.

21. It is Mary who asks a similar question at the climax of the Nag Hammadi tractate the *Wisdom of Jesus Christ:* "Holy Lord, where did your disciples come from and where are they going and what should they do here?" (114.9–12). "Who are you?" is also asked in the *Gospel of Thomas* by the disciples (43) and by "them" (91).

22. Luke 17.34.

23. Song 1.16; 3.1; 3.7.

24. John 5.18; Phil. 2.6; John 18.9; 17.12.

25. Saying 61 is hard to interpret; various translations have been offered, each as part of an overall view of the gospel and influenced by it. "Who are you, you human one, [speaking] as though [you came] from whom? [*or* from someone special? *or* from the One? *or* from a single one? *or* from a stranger?]. You took your place on my couch and ate from my table." Salome knows this Jesus as a human being, but he speaks as though he is of some strange and nonhuman origin. Who, then, is he claiming to be? She speaks of a closeness, perhaps as near to union as is possible in this world. Jesus said, "I am he who is from the Same [*or* from the Equal One, *or* from the Undivided]. To me was given from the things of my Father." We can fill a small gap in the manuscript with the conjectures in round brackets: (Salome said,) "I am your disciple." (Jesus said to her,) "Therefore I say, If he is the Same [*or* he is equal, *or* he is destroyed], he will be filled with light; but if he is divided, he will be filled with darkness." Further on "equality," Clement, in *Excerpts from Theodotus* (56.2), records the claim that if Adam had maintained the three elements of his being (spirit, soul, and flesh) in proper harmony, his progeny would have been "equal and righteous, and the teaching would have been in all"; that is, on the human level there is need for a particular balance between these three elements just as there is also in the cosmos (under God's direction).

26. Those last two paragraphs from Jesus hint at editorial development. They contain two successive sayings of Jesus without an intervening question from the disciples; and the first may be a saying borrowed from elsewhere and prefaced, "Therefore I say . . .".

27. Cf. Luke 17.20–21.

28. *Gospel of Thomas* 5, 77.

29. John 1.18.

30. John 20.19–23; 20.22; Gen. 2.7; John 20.23; 20.29. According to J. Ashton, "The fourth evangelist conceives his own work as an apocalypse—in reverse, upside down, inside out" (*Understanding the Fourth Gospel* [Oxford: Oxford University Press, 1991], 405; part 3, passim).

31. Perrin (in *Thomas and Tatian*) does not find rich links specific to Syriac (and so to the gospel's early life) between Sayings 113 and 114; he suggests *parisā* ("spread out," 113.4) might have suggested *pārsā* ("to be separating," the idea—but not a term—of 114.1).

32. Marjanen, *The Woman Jesus Loved,* 48–49. This Mariamne is introduced as a sister of Philip. There is also Thecla, who, dedicating herself to chastity and refusing to marry her fiancé, offered to cut off her hair to accompany Paul on his mission to Antioch, but perhaps did not do so (in the next scene she wins a man's heart). After her second rescue, she yearned for Paul, "took young men and maidservants and girded herself and sewed her mantle into a cloak after the manner of men"; she was protected by her entourage. Paul commissioned her to go and preach; for her mission she was given money and clothes by a well-wisher, a woman (*Acts of Paul and Thecla* 25, 40, 41, in Wilhelm Schneemelcher, ed., *New Testament Apocrypha,* trans. R. McL. Wilson, 2 vols. [Louisville, KY: Westminster John Knox, 1991–92], 2: 243, 246). Mygdonia, who told her husband she would not sleep with him again, cut her hair, but as part of mourning (*Acts of Thomas* 114, in Schneemelcher, ed., *New Testament Apocrypha,* 2: 385).

33. Philo *Questions and Answers on Exodus* 1.8.

34. Nicole Loraux, *The Experiences of Tiresias,* trans. P. Wissing (Princeton, NJ: Princeton University Press, 1995), 227ff.

35. John 15.1.

36. For the androgynous Jesus, see *Secret Book of John* NHC II, 2, 10–14 and Appendix B of this book. For the statue, see J. Wilpert, "Early Christian Sculpture," *Art Bulletin* 9 (1926–7), 105. For the statue and the theme, see T. Mathews, *The Clash of Gods: A Reinterpretation of Early Christian Art* (Princeton, NJ: Princeton University Press, 1993), 115–41; R. Jensen, "The Femininity of Christ in Early Christian Iconography," *Studia Patristica* 29 (1996): 269–82. For hermaphrodite gods, see M. Delcourt, *Hermaphrodite: Myths and Roles of the Bisexual Figure in Classical Antiquity,* trans. J. Nicholson (London: Studio, 1961).

FIVE: Not a Christian, but a Christ

1. The chapter's title is from the *Gospel of Philip* 67.26–27. Cf. 61.30–31: "You saw Christ and became Christ; you saw the Father and will become Father." The clause I have translated "Where we were inserted" can be rendered "Where we have been thrown"; the twentieth-century philosopher Martin Heidegger explored our "thrownness" as a fundamental condition of human existence.

2. Cf. 5.8.29; Epiphanius, *Panarion* 26.2.6.

3. A straightforward answer would be, all and only those who (as far as we know) were known to themselves and to their contemporaries as such "Knowers of Knowledge." But this creates more problems than it solves. To see why, we might imagine various loosely linked groups of clever people, in our own time, calling themselves "Intellectuals" devoted to the "Intellect." There will be other clever people who do not join any of these self-styled groups, but may nonetheless call themselves intellectuals; and that is certainly what we would call them. There may be yet other groups of clever people, similar in aspiration and organization to the Intellectuals, who simply name themselves differently, after an inspirational founder or teacher, perhaps. (In politics, after all, we have had the Free-Marketeers and the Communists, named for their ideas, and the Thatcherites, Reaganites, and Marxists, named after their heroes.) The Intellectuals may also attract followers who are not, by normal standards, intellectuals at all. To get a grip on these Intellectuals and their own view of the Intellect, we would need to know more about them than their self-designation.

4. 1 Cor. 8.1; 1 Tim. 1.4; 6.20.

5. John 17.3.

6. On the orthodox reception of John, see R. E. Brown, *The Gospel of John,* vol. 1, Anchor Bible (New York: Doubleday, 1966), lxxxi–lxxxiii. On the letters of John, see R. E. Brown, *The Epistles of John,* Anchor Bible (New York: Doubleday, 1982), 47–68, 104–6, 762–63. On the Gnostics, see Hippolytus, *Refutation of All Heresies* 5.6.3ff; 5.12.1ff; Irenaeus, *Against Heresies* 1.8.5 (Ptolemy). On Gaius and Cerinthus, from Dionysius Bar Salibi's twelfth-century commentary on Revelation, which drew on Hippolytus, see Brown, *Epistles,* 766–71. On John against Cerinthus, see Irenaeus, *Against Heresies* 3.11.1. Irenaeus has an additional story, that one day John the disciple saw Cerinthus in the public baths at Ephesus and ran out shouting, "Let us save ourselves; the bathhouse may fall down, for Cerinthus is in there, the enemy of truth" (3.3.4).

7. The collection discovered at Nag Hammadi is generally described as a "library." Did it in fact, before its burial, constitute a "library" of books owned and valued over time by a single community? We cannot be sure. See A. H. B. Logan, *The Gnostics* (London: Clark, 2006), chap. 1.

8. I will be using "Gnostic" to encompass both the Valentinians, to whom we shall be giving the most attention, and the more radical sectarian groups such as the Sethians. Some scholars now follow Origen's lead (in the next quotation) and distinguish Valentinians from Gnostics.

9. Irenaeus, *Against Heresies* 1.25.6 (Marcellina); 1.25.1–5 (Carpocratians).

10. Rev. 2.12–29.

11. Irenaeus, *Against Heresies* 1.13.3 (Marcus and the Marcosians). Tertullian, *Indictment* 6, 30; Eusebius, *History* 5.13 (Philoumena); Tertullian, *Baptism* 1.2 (Cainites). Cf. Julia of Antioch, Manichaean propagandist, in Mark the Deacon, *Life of Porphyry* 85–91; and Bassa the Lydian, who travelled as an *electa* and spread the Manichaean creed. For more details, see M. Scopello, *Femme, Gnose et Manichéisme* (Leiden: Brill, 2005).

12. 1 Cor. 14.34–35.

13. Acts 21.8–9.

14. On the Montanists, see Eusebius (at length), *History* 5.16–18; see also C. Trevett, *Montanism* (Cambridge: Cambridge University Press, 1996), 33–35 (on the succession).

15. Or "our race" of self-consciously distinct Gnostics within, on, or beyond the margins of certain churches that appealed to Peter's authority? Less likely, for Jesus in *Faith-Wisdom* has already confirmed Peter's authority in the terms of Matthew's Jesus.

16. M. D. Goulder, *Paul and the Competing Mission in Corinth* (Peabody, MA: Hendrickson, 2001).

17. *Apocalypse of Peter* 78.22–30. For Peter in Gnosticism, see P. Perkins, *The Gnostic Dialogue* (New York: Paulist Press, 1980), 113–56; and E. H. Pagels, "Visions, Appearances and Apostolic Authority: Gnostic and Orthodox Traditions," in U. Bianchi et al., eds., *Gnosis* (Göttingen: Vandenhoeck & Ruprecht, 1987), 415–30.

18. John 13.23; 1.18.

19. For an account of such a school, as revealed by the *Ascension of Isaiah,* see R. Griffith-Jones, *The Gospel According to Paul* (San Francisco: HarperSanFrancisco, 2004), 94–97.

20. C. Markschies, *Gnosis,* trans. J. Bowden (London, New York: Clark, 2003), 16–17. For our purposes, the distinctions between gnosis and Gnosticism (13–16) are not relevant.

21. See Philo, *Who Is the Heir* 11.55; *On the Special Laws* 4.123; *On the Creation* 46.135–50.144. Classically, see Plato, *Laws* 716C; Philo, *On Rewards and Punishments* 7.45. Eloquently summarized by G. Filoramo, *A History of Gnosticism* (Oxford: Blackwell, 1990), 38–46. Recently, on discerning the influence of Aristotle's followers on the Gnostics, see G. P. Luttikhuizen, *Gnostic Revisions of Genesis Stories and Early Jesus Traditions* (Leiden: Brill, 2006), 39–42. Cf. self-knowledge. In a growing knowledge about yourself, you are both the subject (the knower) and the object (the thing known) of the knowledge; there is no clear distinction between the knower and the known. And coming to know this knowledge will change you, the person who comes to know it; arguably, as you acquire this knowledge about yourself, *you will become yourself as you have not been before.*

22. We will be looking at the Greek and Jewish influences on Gnosticism, but not at those from farther east.

23. Within rabbinic Judaism, "The temple corresponds to the whole world and to the creation of man who is a small world" (Midrash Tanhuma, Pequde 3), quoted by C. A. Moray-Jones, in "The Temple Within" (*Paradise Now* [Atlanta: Society of Biblical Literature, 2006], 173), in his discussion of visionaries' "descent" to their sight of the divine chariot as the descent into their own being (170–77). In general, see G. P. Conger, *Theories of Macrocosms and Microcosms in the History of Philosophy* (New York: Columbia University Press, 1922).

24. *On the Creation* 29.69–71; on mind being able to reach upward towards the great mind, see *Who Is the Heir?* 48.230–36; 53.263–4; 31.154-5; *On the Migration of Abraham* 39.220.

25. *Pistis Sophia* 2.87 [199.2–4; 200.1–3].

SIX: Wisdom, Eve, and Mary Magdalene

1. See also *Against Marcion* 1.2; cf. Eusebius, *History* 5.27; Epiphanius, *Panarion* 24.6.1 (on Basilides).

2. Acts 8.9–24.

3. On Simon and Helen, see Robert M. Grant, *Gnosticism and Early Christianity* (New York: Columbia University Press, 1966), 70–96.

4. For a survey of passages in the Gnostics and Philo, see M. Meyer, "Making Mary Male: The Categories 'Male' and 'Female' in the Gospel of Thomas," *New Testament Studies*

31 (1985): 554–70; and S. Petersen, *"Zerstört die Werke der Weiblichkeit!" Maria Magdalena, Salome und andere Jüngerinnen* (Leiden: Brill, 1999).

5. *Timaeus* 27D–30C; 30A; 69B; 68E; 69C; 40E; 42B–D.

6. *Republic* 514A–517A.

7. *Phaedrus* 246A–252C. NHC VI,5 is a translation (so divergent from the original as to be almost a paraphrase) of a passage in Plato's *Republic* (588A–589B) that describes the human as a hybrid of a many-headed beast (the passions), lion (courage), and man (reason).

8. *Republic* 10.613B and *Thaeatetus* 176A, B, Christianized in Clement, *Strōmateis* 7.3.10, 13, with emphasis on the passionless state, which the true Gnostic attains. (Passionless, but not cold: "The standards of this Gnostic assimilation to the Lord are gentleness, kindness and a noble devoutness.")

9. *Symposium* 189D–193E.

10. Gen. 1.31–2.3.

11. Gen. 2.17; 3.5.

12. For a recent treatment of Genesis, dating Genesis 1 and 2–3 in the last centuries BCE, see C. Amos, *Genesis* (Peterborough: Epworth, 2004).

13. Mark 1.13; 10.6–9; Gen. 2.9; Rev. 22.2.

14. Sir. 6.27–28; Prov. 4.6; Wis. 8.2.

15. This character is, of course, already at odds with those Gnostics who put no value on Jesus.

16. *Sēma* means "sign" (cf. *sēmainein*, "to point out"), so it comes to mean specifically the sign of a burial, a grave barrow or tomb. So the body (*sōma*) is a tomb (*sēma; Gorgias* 493A; *Cratylus* 400C). Plato multiplies the puns: the *sōma* can also be seen as a "safe" in which the soul is kept locked (playing on *sōzein*, "to save") or a "sign," since it is through the body that the soul gives any signs.

17. For four errors of detail in the biblical account of creation, see the *Secret Book of John,* NHC II,1, 13.19–25 (movement was not above the waters); 15.1ff. (the creation of Adam, using Gen. 1.26); 22.22–28 (the Fall); 23.1–4 (Eve).

18. W. A. Meeks, "The Image of the Androgyne," in *In Search of the Early Christians* (New Haven, CT: Yale University Press, 2001), 14, n. 88.

19. Thus far, the Gnostics shared ground with some of the greatest Jewish thinkers of the early centuries CE. Philo, under the influence of Plato, was sure that the physical world (apparently described in Gen. 1) was the material version of the world that had already been perfectly designed in God's thought. As architects perfect their designs and only then start on the building itself, so God *thought* the physical world before he created it. Within this thought was God's thought of the Human, and this thought was itself the image of God. The physical Human was then made *according to the image of God;* that is, he was the image of the image. And so in turn the whole of our creation was the image of an image that preexisted in the mind of God (*On the Creation* 4.15–8.29).

20. Gen. 3.5, 22.

21. Hippolytus, *Refutation of All Heresies* 6.29.

22. The Gnostic myths may seem strange—and rather *pointless*—now. We have forgotten the questions the Gnostics asked and so fail to understand their answers. Just two examples. First, Spirit is surely single and undifferentiated. If the Gnostics, saved and ascending, are becoming pure spirit, will they just merge into the vast spirit, losing all their individuality? Plato (dwelling on intellect rather than spirit) had posed such a question centuries before; it had vexed philosophers ever since. The Valentinian angels offered an answer. The realm of the spirit was undivided but differentiated; each individual Gnostic, united with her or his spiritual counterpart, would be absorbed but not dissolved into the realm of the spirit. Second, the Father is pure thought. But what can pure thought think except pure thought? Such thought must think itself, and that sounds oddly empty of content. Once more Plato had formulated the problem. The Gnostic myths offered (if only in theatrical form) an answer: Forefather (or Depth) thought Forethought. Thinker and Thought then together engender thoughts.

SEVEN: United in the Bridal Bedroom

1. The text reads: "Mary his mother, and *her* sister, and the Magdalene." I have adopted the generally accepted emendation; the scribe had in mind the Mary who was, it seems, the sister(-in-law?) of Jesus's mother (John 19.25). Epiphanius mentions Salome and Mary as sisters of Jesus (*Panarion* 78.8.1; 78.9.6).

2. For the spring festival of Dionysus, see W. Burkert, *Homo Necans: The Anthropology of Ancient Greek Sacrificial Ritual and Myth* (Berkeley: University of California, 1983), 232–38; for Eleusis, see 283–86. For Decius Mundus, see Josephus, *Jewish Antiquities* 18.72. Eleusis is parodied by Lucian, in *Alexander* 38–39: on the last day of Alexander's new festival, Rutilia (a very pretty woman with whom Alexander was in love) was lowered from the roof as the Moon, to join Alexander who was lying down, pretending to be asleep; they then embraced each other, in public, with even Rutilia's husband looking on.

3. For discussion, see M. L. Turner, "On the Coherence of the *Gospel According to Philip*," in J. D. Turner and A. McGuire, eds., *The Nag Hammadi Library After Fifty Years* (Leiden: Brill, 1997), 223–50. For *Philip,* I have gratefully used the translations and studies of R. McL. Wilson, *The Gospel of Philip* (London: Mowbray, 1962); W. W. Isenberg in James M. Robinson, ed., *The Nag Hammadi Library in English* (Leiden: Brill, 1977); and A. Marjanen, *The Woman Jesus Loved* (Leiden: Brill, 1996).

4. In Wilhelm Schneemelcher, ed., *New Testament Apocrypha,* trans. R. McL. Wilson, 2 vols. (Louisville, KY: Westminster John Knox, 1991–92), 2: 340. For the Syriac, most conveniently, see R. Murray, *Symbols of Church and Kingdom,* rev. ed. (London, New York: Clark, 2006), 133.

5. *Gospel of Philip* 53.24–54.5; 67. 27–30. See R. M. Grant, "The Mystery of Marriage in the *Gospel of Philip*," *Vigiliae Christianae* 15 (1961): 129–40; J. J. Buckley, "A Cult-Mystery in the *Gospel of Philip*," *Journal of Biblical Literature* 99 (1980): 569–81; E. H. Pagels, "The Mystery of Marriage in the *Gospel of Philip*," in B. A. Pearson, ed., *The Future of Early Christianity: Essays in Honor of Helmut Koester* (Minneapolis: Fortress, 1991), 442–52; "Ritual in the *Gospel of Philip*," in J. D. Turner and A. McGuire, eds., *The Nag Hammadi Library After Fifty Years* (Leiden: Brill, 1997), 280–94; Turner, "On the Coherence of the *Gospel According to Philip*," 223–50; E. Thomassen, "How Valentinian Is the *Gospel of Philip*?" in Turner and McGuire, eds., *The Nag Hammadi Library After Fifty Years,* 251–79; A. D. De Conick, "The True Mysteries: Sacramentalism in the *Gospel of Philip*," *Vigiliae Christianae* 54 (2001): 225–61; "The Great Mystery of Marriage: Sex and Conception in Ancient Valentinian Traditions," *Vigiliae Christianae* 57 (2003): 307–42. On heavenly journeys, see A. D. De Conick, "Heavenly Temple Traditions and Valentinian Worship: A Case for First-Century Christology in the Second Century," in C. C. Newman et al., eds., *The Jewish Roots of Christological Monotheism* (Leiden: Brill, 1999), 308–41. In what follows, Clement, *Excerpts from Theodotus,* commentary in R. P. Casey, ed., *The Excerpta of Clement of Alexandria* (London: Christophers, 1934); F. Sagnard, ed., *Clément d'Alexandre, Extraits de Théodote* (Paris: CERF, 1970).

6. Cf. Hippolytus, *Refutation of All Heresies* 6.36.4.

7. *Gospel of Philip* 67.9–11.

8. In another version, Jesus was already attended by angels when she met him, and her children are the spiritual seeds that will become the spiritual humans, made partly after her own image and partly after the angels' (Irenaeus, *Against Heresies* 1.4.5).

9. Matt. 18.10.

10. Clement, *Excerpts from Theodotus* 68.

11. *Gospel of Philip* 69.8; Song 3.4; Irenaeus, *Against Heresies* 3.7.1; Clement, *Excerpts from Theodotus* 79–80; 21.3.

12. An image borrowed from Paul (Gal. 4.27), and by Paul from Isaiah (54.1).

13. *Gospel of Philip* 59.6.

14. *Gospel of Philip* 58.26–59.6; 70.23–29.

15. *Gospel of Philip* 53.6–9.

16. *Gospel of Philip* 64.10–12; cf. 67.2–5; 69.4–8.

17. *Gospel of Philip* 59.6–10.

18. My translations are circumspect. Neither of the Coptic words is the straightforward term for "wife," *s'hime,* which Philip uses frequently and unambiguously (65.20; 70.19; 76.7; 82.1), but not of Mary in relation to Jesus. Greek *koinōnos* is used of a marriage partner in Mal. 2.14; 3 Macc. 4.6. In Philip's Coptic, the *koinōn-* word group is used of sexual partnership in 61.10–12; 65.3–5; 78.18; 82.1; *hōtre* of Mary Magdalene in 59.10; and the *hōtr* word group of sexual partnership in 76.6–9; 78.25–26. Philip uses the noun (*hōtr,* masculine form) to speak of the partner with which the male Adam was united, the Spirit that was both his mother and his "spiritual partner" together (70.22–29).

19. Irenaeus *Against Heresies* 1.21.3; *Gospel of Philip* 65.27–66.19; 86.6–7. Cf. *Gospel of Philip* 74.18–22: "He who has been anointed possesses everything. He possesses the resurrection, the light, the cross, the holy spirit. The Father gave him this in the bridal chamber." On unity at the Eucharist, see 58.11–17; on the bridal bedroom on the Lord's Day, see Clement *Excerpts from Theodotus* 63.1.

20. M. A. Williams, *Rethinking "Gnosticism": An Argument for Dismantling a Dubious Category* (Princeton, NJ: Princeton University Press, 1996), 116–17.

21. 1 Cor. 16.20; Rom. 16.16.

22. *Gospel of Thomas* 108; *Second Apocalypse of James* 56.14–16 (50.5–23); *Discourse on the Eighth and Ninth* 57.26–7; *Odes of Solomon* 28.6–7.

23. *Gospel of Philip* 59.6; 58.24–6.

24. Cf. *Tripartite Tractate* 128.19ff. For the inscription, see E. Thomassen, *The Spiritual Seed* (Leiden: Brill, 2006), 350–51; it is discussed at length in P. Lampe, "An Early Christian Inscription in the Musei Capitolini," in D. Hellholm, H. Moxnes, and T. K. Seim, eds., *Mighty Minorities: Essays in Honor of Jacob Jervell* (Oslo: Scandinavian University Press, 1995), 79–92.

25. Irenaeus, *Against Heresies* 1.21.5.

26. *Gospel of Philip* 65.27–66.4; 70.5–9; cf. 76.23–30.

27. Song 3.6–7. R. Patai, *Man and Temple,* rev. ed. (New York: Ktav, 1967), 90.

28. *Gospel of Philip* 69.14–25; 67.30–68.17; cf. *Gospel of Thomas* 22. For separation of animals "outside or below," on the one hand, from "those who belong above and those who belong within," on the other, see *Gospel of Philip* 79.11–13.

29. *Gospel of Philip* 61.29–35.

30. *Gospel of Philip* 68.24–25; 70.9–17.

31. A. Boeckh, ed., *Corpus Inscriptionum Graecarum,* 4 vols. (Berlin: 1828–77), 9595a; Thomassen, *The Spiritual Seed,* 351–53.

32. For the Gnostic reading, see J. Wilpert, *I Sarcofagi cristiani antichi* (Rome: Pontificio Istituto di Archeologia, 1929–36), pl. 25.4; for the pagan-Christian reading, *Museo nazionale romano: Le Sculture* 1/8 (c. 1995), cat. III, 12 (158–60).

33. John 17.11–16; Irenaeus, *Against Heresies* 1.6.4.

34. Clement, *Strōmateis* 3.27–29; *Excerpts from Theodotus* 67.

35. *Gospel of Philip* 64.31; 65.1; cf. 82.1; 78.20–21; Clement, *Strōmateis* 3.59.

36. Philip's imagery of the bridal bedroom is ill-equipped to help him here. He needs to present men and women as united with female and with male angels, respectively, and so must move away from the Valentinian premise that all Gnostics—men and women—should, in the setting of the bridal bedroom, be seen as the bride in union with an angelic bridegroom.

37. Epiphanius, *Panarion* 26.8.1–9.5.

38. John 6:53.

39. *Pistis Sophia* 4, 381.6–10; discussed in Marjanen, *The Woman Jesus Loved,* 189–202.

40. *Gospel of Philip* 67.9–27.

41. The *Secret Book of John* was a foundational text for various Gnostic groups; two other copies were found at Nag Hammadi and a fourth elsewhere. See also Appendix B. On Codex II, see Williams, *Rethinking "Gnosticism,"* 253–5. *The Reality of the Realms* is launched as an account of Col. 1.13 and Eph. 6.12.

42. From *Exegesis on the Soul* 127.19–32; 132.7–133.10; *Second Treatise of the Great Seth* 57.7–18; 65.18–30. For the soul's prostitution, see also *Authoritative Teaching;* here the soul strips off this world while her true garment clothes her within, and her bridal clothing is placed on her in beauty of mind, not in pride of flesh (32.2–8). The bridegroom has been linked from the start with food (22.24–6), and at the end the rational soul "came to rest in him who is at rest. She reclined in the bridal chamber. She ate of the banquet for which she had hungered" (34.9–13).

43. *Book of Thomas the Contender* 144.8–12.

EIGHT: The *Gospel of Mary*

1. From the Coptic. In the Greek, "For certainly he, knowing her—without faltering—loved her."

2. For the *Gospel of Mary,* I have gratefully used the translations and studies of G. W. MacRae and R. McL. Wilson in James M. Robinson, ed., *The Nag Hammadi Library in English* (Leiden: Brill, 1977); A. Pasquier, *L'Évangile selon Marie* (Québec: Université Laval, 1983); A. Marjanen, *The Woman Jesus Loved* (Leiden: Brill, 1996); and E. A. de Boer, *The Gospel of Mary,* Society for New Testament Studies Supplement 260 (New York, London: Clark, 2004). On Mary, see K. L. King, "Prophetic Power and Women's Authority: The Case of the Gospel of Mary Magdalene," in B. M. Kienzle and P. J. Walker, eds., *Women Preachers and Prophets Through Two Millennia of Christianity* (Berkeley: University of California Press, 1998), 21–41. Just under half of the *Gospel of Mary* survives, in a Coptic translation of a text originally written in Greek. We have as well two small fragments from a Greek text of the gospel from two different third-century manuscripts and likely from a different recension of the text (the corresponding sentences in our Coptic text are not an accurate translation of the Greek fragments). For the Greek text, see D. Lührmann, "Die griechischen Fragmente des Mariaevangeliums P Oxy 3525 und P Ryl 463," *Novum Testamentum* 30 (1988): 321–338. In its present form the gospel is slightly baffling. Why does Peter first ask Mary to relay the secrets Jesus entrusted to her and then deny that Jesus had done so? It is possible that two discordant texts have been joined together to make our gospel, with some insertions by editors to link them; the editors would have inherited at least one of Peter's contrasting sayings. We still have to ask, of course, why *this* was the final form in which the editors wanted to leave their text and why they did not iron out the anomaly. The change in Peter's attitude leads Pasquier (*L'Évangile selon Marie,* 7–10, 96–101) to view Mary's account of her vision and instruction from Jesus as an originally independent text, inserted here; Peter's objection had once been to Mary's claim that the Saviour had made "us" human, so including herself, a woman. Other divisions have been suggested.

3. De Boer argues against this familiar interpretation and identifies the "opposite nature" as the culprit (*Gospel of Mary,* 44ff.).

4. But note "My peace bring her [peace] forth to you" (de Boer), *"Que ma paix s'engendre en vous"* (Pasquier): *jpo,* "to beget/give birth to" or "to obtain."

5. John 20.19, 21, 26; Luke 17.20–23; Matt. 7.7; 16.24; 4.23.

6. *Anthrōpos* is Greek for "human being"; *anēr,* for "man," specifically male. *Rōme* is Coptic for "human being"; *hoout,* for a male, such as Mary Magdalene must become at the end of the *Gospel of Thomas.*

7. Jesus himself departs, but only as he departs at the end of another Gnostic text in the same codex: "He became invisible to their external sight" (*Wisdom of Jesus Christ* 126.18–127.1). And this physical sight, we shall soon discover, is not the faculty that will give the disciples understanding.

8. Perhaps read, following Greek of P Oxy 3525, "When I once saw the Lord in a vision," suggesting more than one vision. The connection between the vision and the explanation is disputed; see de Boer, *The Gospel of Mary,* 73–74.

9. Mark 9.2–8.

10. Luke 12.34. The version in the *Gospel of Mary* is familiar from Justin, Macarius, and Clement of Alexandria (Pasquier, *L'Évangile selon Marie,* 101–3).

11. Numenius, according to Macrobius, *On the Dream of Scipio* 1.12.4; Proclus, *On the Timaeus* 1.148.1–6; 3.355.12–15; Servius, *On the Aeneid* 6.127; Poimandres (*Corpus Hermeticum* 1) 25.

12. *Gospel of Mary* 17.4–9.

13. Cf. *Gospel of Peter* 14.58–60 (Peter, Andrew, and Levi); *Didascalia,* ed. P. de Lagarde (Göttingen: Dieterich, 1911), 88–89; see also Pasquier, *L'Evangile selon Marie,* 22, n.14. At Mark 2.14 Jesus calls Levi, "sitting at the toll-booth," to follow him; but Levi is not named among the twelve apostles (Mark 3.16–19). Matthew (9.9) has *Matthew* sitting at the toll-booth and called, and specifies Matthew in the list of apostles as "the toll-collector" (10.3).

14. From *First Apocalypse of James* 40.22–26; 41.15–19.

15. The Coptic uses a word derived from Greek *gumnazein* twice. The disciples had, at Mary's instigation, been "discussing as an exercise" the words of the Saviour (9.23). Then Peter discusses Mary's claims in the same spirit—too aggressively, yes, but still in the style of the Greek gymnasium. Here are philosophers discussing the questions to which their master had given rise.

16. John 14.27; 4.27.

17. For the *Dialogue of the Savior* I have gratefully used the translation of S. Emmel in Robinson, ed., *The Nag Hammadi Library in English.* We are used, by now, to sets of sayings compiled into dialogues between Jesus and his followers; the *Dialogue of the Savior* is typical of the genre. Various editors had been at work on the material in this dialogue before it reached its present form. It now starts with (part of) a set of instructions for a heavenly journey and includes one account of the world's beginning and another of human fall and rescue; each of these may well have circulated independently before incorporation into the present dialogue. In this dialogue Mary Magdalene is mentioned ten times, questioning and commenting. She is one of three followers who are named; the others, who also take an active part in the conversation, are Matthew and Judas (the Judas Thomas of the *Gospel of Thomas,* not Judas Iscariot). The twelve disciples are once mentioned as a group.

18. *Dialogue of the Savior* 132.5–9; 141.3–4; 127.19–21; 131.16–18; 131.20–22; 135.4–16; 138.11–22; 143.11–23.

19. *Dialogue of the Savior* 131.19–132.5; Luke 2.51.

20. Matt. 6.34; 10.l0; 10.24.

21. *Dialogue of the Savior* 141.12–13; 142.11–13.

22. For the *Pseudo-Clementines,* see Schneemelcher, ed., *New Testament Apocrypha,* 2: 483–541, following there the reconstruction of the confused text tradition by J. Irmscher and G. Strecker, 484–89. For Peter's enemy, see *Letter of Peter to James* 2.3–7; for the attack on Paul (picking up on Gal. 2.11), *Proclamations,* at *Homilies* II.16–17; XVII.13–19. A comparable analysis, among our Gnostic texts, might run as follows. In *Pistis Sophia* John is described as a virgin and kisses the breast of Jesus; John (the Beloved Disciple) leans on the breast of Jesus on the last evening Jesus spent with his disciples before his death (John 13.23). So far, so good. But James, arguably the brother of John, also kisses Jesus's breast in *Pistis Sophia,* and Jesus twice addresses him as "You beloved one." Our author knows of the action and epithet in relation to one of the supposed brothers and ascribes them to the other too; he is, then, not fantastical, just unreliable.

23. *Dialogue of the Savior* 144.5–146.4.

NINE: Faith-Wisdom

1. On references in the notes to passages in *Pistis Sophia:* numbering is to the classic edition by C. Schmidt, *Pistis Sophia* (Copenhagen: Gyldendalske Boghandel-Nordisk Forlag, 1925); e.g., 1.17 [26, 10–20] refers to Book 1, Chapter 17, printed on p. 26, lines 10–20. These page and line numbers are tracked in C. Schmidt and V. MacDermot, *Pistis Sophia,* Nag

Hammadi Studies IX (Leiden: Brill, 1978); I use MacDermot's translation with gratitude. *Pistis Sophia* is likely related to another Coptic text preserved in a second manuscript, the Bruce Codex; this appears to be the text to which *Pistis Sophia* refers twice as the *Two Books of Jeu* (2.99 [246, 21; 247, 4–5]). We appear, then, to have in these two manuscripts a batch of documents that may well have been thought of, by the time of their completion, as a loosely ordered set: first *The Books of Jeu;* then *Pistis Sophia,* Book 4; and finally the text to which we shall be giving most attention, *Pistis Sophia,* Books 1–3. D. Good's article in E. Schüssler Fiorenza, ed., *Searching the Scriptures,* 2 vols. (London: SCM, 1994), 2:678–707, is particularly helpful; she and I have rather different viewpoints.

2. On the identity of Mary, especially in *Pistis Sophia,* see F. Stanley Jones, ed., *Which Mary? The Marys of Early Christian Tradition* (Atlanta: Society of Biblical Literature, 2002). A Mary is mentioned 197 times in *Pistis Sophia,* Books 1–3. Eleven times she is specified as Mary the mother of Jesus; twelve times, as Mary Magdalene. But what of all the other occasions? It is usually reckoned that the Mary being referred to is Mary Magdalene. But this consensus has recently been challenged. The argument is as follows.

   "Mariham" is the first of the followers to intervene in the dialogue. Jesus gives her permission to interpret part of his opening exposition, "Mariham, you blessed one . . . speak openly." She does so. Jesus praises her: "Excellent, Maria. . . . You are blessed beyond all women upon earth." Surely this is an allusion to the welcome of Elizabeth, the cousin of the Blessed Virgin Mary, when the pregnant Mary visits her: *"Blessed are you among women"* (Luke 1.42). Aren't the authors of *Pistis Sophia,* Books 1–3, indicating to readers that this Mary, the first to speak with Jesus, is Jesus's mother? Similar praise is lavished on Mary at all her later interventions. Surely, then, we should recognize this Mary, Jesus's mother, in all the many speeches made by a "Mary" with no mention of "the Magdalene."

   The argument is flawed. Jesus has already exclaimed to his disciples as a group, "Rejoice and be glad, because you are blessed beyond all men upon earth." Our authors actually distinguish, more than once, the two Marys. Maria the mother of Jesus and "the other Mariham, the blessed one" have both received a particular form and likeness; and "Mariham, you blessed one" and Maria the mother of Jesus each give two interpretations of a speech of Jesus. For the praise of the "blessed" Mariham, our authors are likely drawing on a second story from Luke's gospel, in which a woman from the crowd said to Jesus, *"Blessed is the womb that gave you birth, and the breasts that nursed you."* Jesus replied, *"Blessed rather are those who hear the word of God and keep it"* (Luke 11.27–28). And such people are precisely represented in *Pistis Sophia* by the blessed Mary Magdalene.

   But what about the two versions of the name Mary that we have seen in use here, Maria and Mariham? Whenever a Mary is actually specified as the mother of Jesus, the name is spelled "Maria," but this spelling is also used for "Maria the Magdalene." (We have already encountered a single episode in which one Mary is referred to both as Mariham and Maria; the same happens in at least three more scenes.)

   What, then, of the *characters* of the two Marys on the occasions when one or other is specified? The mother of Jesus is specified only in Book 1; her two long speeches are both about the earthly Jesus, her son. She is praised for her comments in just the phrase used to praise most of the other disciples: "Excellent, well done." And Mary, specified as Magdalene? She is given far higher, more specific praise. Jesus extols her as the pure spiritual one, even as pure spirit. In Book 3 we hear occasionally from "Maria Magdalene," frequently from "Maria" without any further detail; this unspecified "Maria" is repeatedly praised, e.g., "Excellent, you all blessed Maria, you spiritual one"; "Excellent, you spiritual one of pure light." These are the terms in which Jesus has previously praised the Magdalene; she is surely the recipient of such praise here.

   For "Excellent, Maria," see *Pistis Sophia* 1.17; 1.19 [26, 17; 28, 20–24]; "Rejoice,"1.8 [15, 15–17]; particular likeness, 1.59 [117, 1–2]; and the Marys' interpretations, 1.60–62 [119–125].

3. Over a hundred pages into the text, a scribe has inserted a heading, "The Second Book of the Pistis Sophia" (2.63 [127, 1]); hence the name by which the whole treatise is known.

4. *Pistis Sophia,* Book 4, was once clearly a separate but related text. It is far more starkly esoteric than Books 1–3 and was probably written before them. Mary is the first to ask Jesus a question, and she asks the second question too. Jesus gives lengthy accounts of

the realms of punishment. The disciples plead with him to have mercy on themselves and on humankind, and he undertakes a ritual for the forgiveness of their sins. The disciples quiz him further, asking Jesus what punishment awaits those guilty of particular sins. Mary asks about slanderers, then Salome asks about an otherwise sinless murderer. Now Peter interjects: "My Lord, let the women cease to question, that we also may question." Jesus says to Mary and the women, "Give way to the men, your brothers, that they may question also." Peter answers and says, "My Lord, a robber, . . . what is his punishment?" (4.146 [377.14ff.]) And with this brisk exchange, the series of questions is back on course. What a strange text this is. Peter's complaint is upheld by Jesus. (Perhaps other women too had spoken; Jesus addresses "Mary and the women"—more, that is, than just Mary and Salome.) But the interruption is forgotten, and Mary reemerges with John at the end.

5. Faith-Wisdom brought back up to the Twelfth Realm, see *Pistis Sophia* 2.75 [167] and returned by Jesus to the Thirteenth, 2.77, 2.81 [171, 178]. The upward route is described from 2.83 [184] and is undertaken from 2.94 [218].

6. For Jesus and the Barbēlo, "which is the body which I wore in the height," and Mary his mother, see *Pistis Sophia* 1.8 [13, 20–23]; for the Barbēlo as parent to Jesus and Faith-Wisdom herself, 4.137 [356, 24–25]. On the Saviour and Faith-Wisdom, see *Wisdom of Jesus Christ* 106.14–24; for the two Marys, 1.59 [116, 25–117, 22–23]. The character Faith-Wisdom appears elsewhere, with differing roles; for *On the Origin of the World,* see Appendix B.

7. *Pistis Sophia* 1.31 [45.14–46.2].

8. Authades is the Jaldabaoth of the *Secret Book of John.* For Authades, see *Pistis Sophia* 1.30–31 [44, 4–46, 22]; 1.55 [104–7].

9. Martha, *Pistis Sophia* 1.38 [61.20–25]; John, 1.40 [65.23–25] and 1.41 [68.5–6]; Andrew, 1.45 [77.5–15]; Thomas, 1.46 [81.14–18] and 1.46 [83.20–84.1]; James, 1.51 [94.19–21] and 1.52 [97.19–26]; Philip 1.42 [71.4–17].

10. *Pistis Sophia* 1.36 [58, 9–21]; cf. Jesus's insistence that anyone may speak who is filled with the spirit of light, 2.72 [162, 19–21]; 1.37 [60, 5–20].

11. The change to Jesus as "First Mystery." *Pistis Sophia* 2.63 [129.7]. Peter hating Mary's race (perhaps of women, perhaps of Gnostics), 2,72 [162.14–18]; see Ch. 5, note 15, above.

12. *Pistis Sophia* 2.84 [187.6–20].

13. *Pistis Sophia* 2.87 [199.2–4; 200.1–3].

14. *Pistis Sophia* 2.95 [219.8–18].

15. Irenaeus, *Against Heresies* 1.13.3; *Gospel of Thomas* 108; *Papyri Graeci Magici* 8.36–37; Epiphanius, *Panarion* 26.3.1.

16. *Pistis Sophia* 2.96 [233, 1].

17. *Pistis Sophia* 3.111 [281ff.]; then 2.97 [from pp. 230–33].

18. *Pistis Sophia* 2.100 [247–253], 3.132 [338.1–339.8].

19. *Pistis Sophia* 2.88 [201, 8–25]. Regarding J. Schaberg's other passages (*The Resurrection of Mary Magdalene* [New York, London: Continuum, 2002], 184): 3.105 [266, 16] is spoken by John, not Mary. 4.138 [357–59]: Mary does not know better than her brothers before she asks how Jesus's own followers ("we") can avoid punishment; her obeisance is more extreme (she kisses his hands and weeps) and wins his compassion.

20. Leaving parents: Exod. 21.17; Matt. 15.4. Salome: *Pistis Sophia* 3.132 [338, 1–339, 8].

21. Readers may expect me to invoke the more familiar contraries, charismatic and routinized authority. But the pair should be invoked with caution. It was developed by the protestant theologian Rudolf Sohm in relation to the early churches as part of a late nineteenth-century argument over the "routinization"—and, in some Protestant eyes, decline—of the charismatic churches into so-called Early Catholicism. Sohm's paradigm was adopted (with due acknowledgment) by the great sociologist Max Weber and has since been reimported to New Testament studies (with acknowledgment to Weber, but generally not to Sohm) as a paradigm tried and tested elsewhere that would bring fresh light to New Testament questions.

22. 1 Cor. 1.14–16; 16.15–16.

23. John 21.22.

24. Matt. 16:15–19; *Gospel of Thomas* 13.

25. Rev. 2.12–29.

26. Cf. D. K. Shuger, *The Renaissance Bible* (Berkeley: University of California Press, 1994), 191.

TEN: From the Magdalene to La Madeleine

1. Jesus's words in John 12.7 are notoriously hard to interpret in detail.

2. Hippolytus, *Commentary on the Song of Songs* 6.1–7.2 (Song 1.7); 24.2 (the women and the synagogue at the grave). There survives only Hippolytus's commentary on chaps. 1–3 of the Song. He would have treated the later chapters as a dialogue exclusively between Christ and the gentile churches; see G. N. Bonwetsch, *Studien zu den Kommentaren Hippolyts zum Buche Daniel und hohen Liede* (Leipzig: Hinrichs, 1897), 89.

3. Hippolytus, *Commentary on the Song of Songs* 2.9. Do not, urges Hippolytus, be like Judas, but pour the ointment over the head of Christ (with reference to John 12.4, Mark 14.30). In 2.29, *And the scent of your oils is above all fragrances, and your name is oil poured out* (Song 1.2–3). Interpreted: the ointment is the Holy Ghost; "with longing, Martha brought this ointment, with which she wet Jesus. Judas began to hate this ointment and betrayed Jesus for thirty pieces of silver. He complained about the ointment, 'Why has this ointment been wasted?' It cost three hundred pieces of silver to buy. What a sure significance this [*coincidence of numbers*] has! And then, what was this ointment if not Christ himself?" We can only speculate if Hippolytus would, in handling chaps. 4–8 of the Song, have invoked the biblical contrasts between Mary and Martha.

4. Evagrius (346–99), *Sententiae ad Virginem* 55, quoted in P. Brown, *The Body and Society* (New York: Columbia University Press, 1988), 276. This motif is already in Tertullian: "How many men and women in the ranks of the Church have appealed to continence and preferred to be wedded to God' (*On the Exhortation to Chastity* 13). Athanasius (296–373), in *Apologia ad Constantinum* 33.49, quoted in Brown, says: "We possess upon earth, in the state of virginity, a picture of the holiness of angels. Accordingly, such as have attained this virtue, the Catholic Church has been accustomed to call the brides of Christ" (*Body and Society,* 259). The New Testament itself was responding too to the dark warnings of the Old Testament's prophets, who had seen in Israel's syncretism an adulterous betrayal of her husband, her God; see, e.g., Hos. 1.2; 3.1; Jer. 2.20; 3.1; Ezek. 16.

5. Origen, *Commentary on the Song of Songs,* prologue 1.1ff.

6. Origen, *Commentary on the Song of Songs,* prologue 2.36. Origen's famous (mis)reading of Ignatius, *Letter to the Romans* 7.2: "I write this alive, but in love with death. My passionate love [i.e., all my earthly desire] has been crucified, there is in me no more fire of affection for material things."

7. Song 1.12; Origen, *Commentary on the Song of Songs* 2.9.11, on Song 1.2.

8. Origen, *Commentary on Matthew,* on Matt. 26.6–13.

9. The long (later) ending of Mark added the details of Mary Magdalene from Luke to the Easter appearance accorded her by John: *"Risen early on the first day of the week, he appeared first to Mary Magdalene, from whom he had cast seven devils"* (Mark 16.9).

10. Luke 7.36–50; 8.2; Mark 16.9; Luke 8.3; Luke 10.38–42.

11. John 11; John 12.1–8; Mark 14.3–9, merging the stories of Mark and John into one.

12. Matt. 28.9; John 20.11–16; Mark 16.1–8; John 20.17–18. Further details would be added: Mary Magdalene as the bride of the Beloved Disciple at the wedding of Cana in Galilee (whose bride and groom John does not name at all, 2.1–12) or as the woman taken in adultery (John 7.53–8.11). See Haskins, *Mary Magdalene* 155–58. The story that John and Mary were the groom and bride at Cana is first clearly acknowledged in the *Golden Legend* (which rejects the story).

13. Luke 10.42.

14. D. Mycoff, trans., with notes, *The Life of Saint Mary Magdalene and of Her Sister Saint Martha* (Kalamazoo, MI: Institute of Cistercian Studies, 1989), 1736–48. "That best part" alludes to Mary in Luke 10.42.

15. D. Cavalca, *The Life of Saint Mary Magdalene,* trans. V. Hawtrey (London: Bodley Head, 1904), as by unknown author 136–37, and for a qualification, 284.

16. Classically, see R. Krautheimer, "Introduction to an 'Iconography of Medieval Architecture,'" *Journal of the Warburg and Courtauld Institutes* 5 (1942): 1–33.

17. The closing lines of the play took on a life of their own as a sequence in the Easter liturgies of France. These verses are headed, in some traditions of the Song's Latin translations, "The Voice of Mary Magdalene speaking to the Church."

18. Petrus Vallium Sarnaii Monachus, *Historia Albigensis,* ed. P. Guébin and E. Lyon (Paris: Société de l' Histoire de France, 1926–39), 1.10–11; Rainerius Sacconi, "Summa de Catharis," ed. A. Dondaine, *Un Traité Néo-Manichéen du XIIIe Siècle* (Rome: 1939), 75.

19. Song 1.12; 6.2; 5.6.

20. From P. Dronke, *Nine Medieval Latin Plays* (Cambridge: Cambridge University Press, 1994), 100–101.

21. E.g., Acts 3.1–10; 9.32–43.

22. For this suspicion that some historical memory (from the "Burgundy Cycle" associated with Count Girart) does underlie this account, see V. Saxer, "Le culte de la Madeleine à Vézelay et de Lazare à Autun: un Problème d'Antériorité et d'Origine," *Bulletin de la Société des Fouilles archéologiques et des Monuments historiques de l' Yonne* (1986): 3 (refining his own earlier position).

23. For Mary of Egypt within the Eastern church, see Cyril of Scythopolis (sixth century), *The Life of St. Kyriacus,* and at length Sophronius, Bishop of Jerusalem (560–638), *The Life of Mary of Egypt;* in the West, the translation of Sophronius by Paul the Deacon (*Patrologia Latina* 73[1], cols. 671–90). For translations and a full discussion, see B. Ward, *Harlots of the Desert* (Kalamazoo. MI: Institute of Cistercian Studies, 1987), 26–56.

24. By 1119 the Count of Nevers complained that Vézelay was profaning relics of Lazarus and Martha; they were clearly not of the same importance to the monks as Mary's. Her fame was spreading; in 1084 we have the first recorded use of Madeleine as a first name, with a second around 1093–96 at Mans.

25. There are various claimants to the body of Mary and to smaller relics: Vézelay and St. Maximin, of course; Rome (where one body seems to be divided between the two churches of St. John Lateran and St. Maria-del-Popolo); and churches in Montserrat and Naples. Her hair is also at Chartres, in Rome, and elsewhere. Imagine for a moment that Jesus touched her on her forehead on Easter morning; then the skin he touched would be immensely sacred. Both St. Maximin and, in Paris, St. Denis claim to have this patch of skin.

26. Mary the hermit: *Vita eremetica,* catalogued BHL (*Bibliotheca Hagiographica Latina*), nos. 5453–56: versions printed in *Speculum* 18 (1943): 335–9 and 53 (1978): 16–25; interpolated version, *MEFRM* (*Melanges de l'École Française de Rome. Moyen Age*) 104/1 (1992): 177–80. Mary the sister of Martha: *Vita evangelica,* sermon formerly attributed to Odo of Cluny, fusing all the gospel passages, BHL 5439, discussed in *MEFRM* 104/1 (1992): 37–70. Rescue from Provence: *Translatio posterior, MEFRM* 104/1 (1992): 169–77. Mary and her companions to France: *Vita apostolica, BHL* 5443–49, version printed in *MEFRM* 104/1 (1992): 164–9. The *Life* ascribed to Rabanus, late twelfth century: translated by D. Mycoff, *The Life of Saint Mary Magdalene and of her Sister Saint Martha* (Kalamazoo, MI: Cistercian Publications, 1989). The version of Mary's story that pervaded Europe is in Jacob of Voragine's *Golden Legend* (compiled 1255–66).

27. E.-M. Faillon, *Monuments inédits sur l'apostolat de sainte Marie-Madeleine en Provence* (Paris: Migne, 1848), vol. 1, cols. 455–476: the tomb of Mary, with engraving, cols. 461–62. Faillon insisted that the scenes from the life of Christ (which survive) were *distinct* from the sculptures, seen by hagiographers (including "Rabanus'), which showed the life of Mary. For Faillon's defense against the skeptics, see vol. 1, cols. 337ff., 1341ff.

28. Adam of Eynsham, *Life of St. Hugh of Lincoln,* ed. D. L. Douie and H. Fraser (London: 1962), 2: 169–70, cited in S. Haskins, *Mary Magdalen: Myth and Metaphor* (New York: Riverhead, 1993), 413, n. 23.

29. J. Sclafer, "Iohannes Gobo Senior OSB, 'Liber Miraculorum b. Mariae Magdalenae,'" *Archivum Fratrum Praedicatorum* 63 (1993), no. 84, 201–3, cited in K. L. Jansen, *The Making of the Magdalen: Preaching and Popular Devotion in the Later Middle Ages* (Princeton, NJ: Princeton University Press, 2000), 330; Gobo was the Dominican prior of the royal convent of St. Maximin, 1304–28 (Jansen, 247).

30. The words of Bernard's sermon have not survived. For the occasion see, most fully, Odo of Deuil, *De Profectione Ludovici VII in Orientem,* ed. and trans. V. G. Berry (New York: Columbia University Press, 1948), 8–10. For Bernard's preaching and letters on the Crusade, see e.g., his letters 363, 457, 458, 510. For the details that can be reconstructed, see P. J. Cole, *The Preaching of the Crusades to the Holy Land, 1095–1270* (Cambridge, MA: Medieval Academy of America, 1991); J. R. Sommerfeldt, *Bernard of Clairvaux on the Spirituality of Relationship* (New York: Newman, 2004), 70–73; and now J. Phillips, *The Second Crusade* (New Haven, CT: Yale University Press, 2007), 61–79.

31. Matt. 10.37; 16.24.

32. R. Rosenstein, "New Perspectives on Distant Love: Jaufre Rudel, Uc Bru, and Sarrazina," *Modern Philology* 87.1 (1990): 225–38; M. Switten, "Singing the Second Crusade," in M. Gervers, ed., *The Second Crusade and the Cistercians* (New York: St. Martin's, 1992), 71.

33. Bernard, *Sermons on the Song of Songs* 11.

34. Bernard, *Sermons on the Song of Songs* 10, 12.

35. John 19.25–27.

36. John 2.1–12.

37. For the history of John and Mary Magdalene, see note 12 above. For the Virgin Mary and Mary Magdalene in the later Middle Ages, see Jansen, *The Making of the Magdalen,* chap. 10.

38. Bernard, *Sermons on the Song of Songs* 85.12–13.

39. H. Belting, *The Image and Its Public* (New Rochelle, NY: Caratzas, 1989), 241 (n. 21), 75. The hymn is *Planctus ante nescia,* often printed, for example, in K. Young, *The Drama of the Medieval Church* (Oxford: Oxford University Press, 1933), vol. 1, 496–98. For Mary's cry to the cross, D. Cavalca, *The Life of Saint Mary Magdalene,* trans. V. Hawtrey (London: Bodley Head, 1904), as by unknown author, 236–37.

40. St. Anselm, *Prayer to St. Mary Magdalene* (Oratio 74), 51–69. I have gratefully used the translation of B. Ward, *Anselm: Prayers and Meditations* (London: Penguin, 1980), 201–6 (202).

41. *An Homilie of Marye Magdalene* (London, 1565).

42. The forms of this affective devotion were vividly illustrated in the London exhibition *Seeing Salvation;* catalogue, G. Finaldi, ed., *The Image of Christ* (London: National Gallery, 2000). For a review of the exhibition, see R. Griffith-Jones, *Apollo* (August 2000): 50–52.

43. Quoted in Haskins, *Mary Magdalen,* 200 (my translation).

44. On unitive and bridal mysticism in the Middle Ages, see J. Leclercq, F. Vandenbroecke, and L. Bouyer, *The Spirituality of the Middle Ages* (London: Burns and Oates, 1968), 358–64, 374–78. The passage from Mechtilde is excerpted from *The Flowing Light of the Godhead* and *Letter XVIII,* 1.73–78 (Leclercq et al., *Spirituality of the Middle Ages,* 375–76, 362).
   Gregory the Great, *Homiliae in Evangelia* 33.2, *Corpus Christianorum,* SL 141 (Turnhout: Brepols, 1999), 289 (PL 76, 1238–46): a warning to the clergy not to be proud or unforgiving in the face of others' sins. Cf. *Homily 25* (PL 76, 1189–94): "Lo, the guilt of the human race is cut off whence it proceeded. For in paradise a woman gave death to man, now from the tomb a woman announces life to men; and she tells the words of the Life-Giver just as a woman told the words of the death-bearing serpent."

45. Quoted in M. Warner, *Monuments and Maidens* (London: Vintage, 1996), 195–96 (Vision 7.64).

46. Margery Kempe, *Book of Margery Kempe,* ed. S. B. Meech and H. E. Allen, Early English Texts Society 212 (London: Oxford University Press, 1940), chaps. 29, 80, 36, modernized.

47. St. Bernard, *Sermons on the Song of Songs,* from 12.8–9.

48. For the likely links with Antoninus's movement of reform, see S. Wilk, "The Cult of Mary Magdalen in Fifteenth-Century Florence," *Studi medievali* 26 (1985): II, 685–93.

49. See the classic books by C. W. Bynum, *Jesus as Mother* (Berkeley: University of California Press, 1982); *Holy Feast and Holy Fast* (Berkeley: University of California Press, 1987).

50. A. Hufstader, "Lefèvre d'Étaples and the Magdalen," *Studies in the Renaissance* 16 (1969): 31–60, at 44

ELEVEN: The Nuptials of God

1. Published as the frontispiece to Gill's occasional magazine, *The Game,* vol. 6, no. 34 (January 1923), small octavo, 8 pages (Christmas issue). *The Game* was devotional and committed to social reform.

2. On the restoration of Mary Magdalene's moral—and, perhaps in popular speculation, her physical—virginity, see Jansen, *The Making of the Magdalen,* 240–44, 286–94. In the Roman litany of the late Middle Ages, Mary Magdalene headed the choir of virgins.

3. Rev. 21.1–2.

4. Letter from Eric Gill to Reyner Heppenstall, 12 September 1934, in F. MacCarthy, *Eric Gill* (London: Faber, 1989), 162.

5. John 1.14; 6.53–56.

6. A. D. Nock, *Sallustius: Concerning the Gods and the Universe* (Cambridge: Cambridge University Press, 1926), para. 4 (Nock 9).

7. Rom. 8.3.

8. Quoted in A. D. De Conick, *Recovering the Original Gospel of Thomas* (London and New York: Clark, 2005), 192.

9. R. Sorabji, *Emotion and Peace of Mind* (Oxford: Oxford University Press, 2000), 406–8.

10. Augustine, *Unfinished Work in Answer to Julian* 4.47–67, most conveniently in J. E. Rotell, ed., *The Works of Saint Augustine* I/25 ("Answer to the Pelagians" III, trans. R. J. Teske) (New York: New City Press, 1990).

11. This question of definition was more complicated than most, since Jesus could be thought to define humanness, not to be subject to any definition formulated without reference to himself. And alongside Jesus stood the primordial, pre-Fall Adam, another figure who helped define humanness. The argument matters too because, in the thought of the church, Augustine won; the effect has been incalculable.

12. 1 Cor. 7.33.

13. Matt. 22.20.

14. A. B. Ulanov, *The Feminine in Jungian Psychology and in Christian Theology* (Evanston: NW University, 1971), 164, 166. I have drawn through Ulanov on C. G. Jung, *Mysterium Coniunctionis* (*Collected Works,* ed. Sir Herbert Read, etc., 14; London: Routledge, 1963), 179–80; "Answer to Job," *Psychology and Religion: West and East* (CW 11, 1958), 395; "Woman in Europe," *Civilization in Transition* (CW 10, 1964), 185; *Psychology and Alchemy* (CW 12, 1953), 144–180, 148, 150, 160, 167, 180; "A Psychological Approach to the Trinity," *Psychology and Religion: West and East* (CW 11, 1958), 172.

15. It is unsettling too to see women still being defined (as in the ancient world and ever since) *by reference* to those more spiritual men and (as throughout the last two centuries) by exclusive reference to love.

16. In my commentary on Titian's painting I am gratefully indebted to the sermon preached in the 1990s at Lincoln College, Oxford, by Neil MacGregor, then Director of the National Gallery, London. J. Drury, *Painting the Word* (New Haven, CT; London: Yale University Press and National Gallery, 1999), 117–20, also draws on the sermon.

APPENDIX A: Jesus and the Sinful Woman

1. *Aleiphō* means "I anoint," and the term was used as well of, e.g., plastering or daubing (a wall), polishing (a table), and oiling (a harness); this is rubbing, not just pouring. (Liquid or semiliquid perfume could be poured, according to Athenaeus, *Deipnosophistae* 15.689c; Athenaeus seems unsure whether perfume for the feet was an unguent or powder, 15.690a; cf. *staktē,* or coming-out-in-drips, used of oil of myrrh.)

2. For the cost of alabaster, see Athenaeus, *Deipnosophistae* 15.686c, 691e: slaves passed round myrrhs in alabasters and other golden vessels; the ultimate extravagance was to abandon alabaster vessels and instead to dip doves in perfume that they sprinkled from their wings as they flew around the room. Perfume applied to head (for moisture), or to chest or under the nostrils (for the scent to rise to the nose), 15.687d, 690a. In Petronius's *Satyricon*: slaves sitting at feet, 64, and paring nails of diners, 31 (bare feet at dinner, 72). Entertainers come in at the appropriate moment: 52 (host's wife!), 23, 53, 59, 78. Ointment running down forehead into eyes, 65. "I am ashamed to tell you what followed: in defiance of all convention, some long-haired boys brought ointment in a silver basin, and anointed our feet as we lay, after winding little garlands round our feet and ankles," 70. For Jewish reports of washing feet in oil as sign of extraordinary prosperity, see Deut. 33.24. Asher's territory (just to the west of Galilee) was particularly suited to the olive. The story in Sifre Deut. 33.24 para 355 (148a) plays on this: the merchant cannot believe the quantity of oil borne by an olive tree in Galilee; his slave even washed his feet in oil (Strack-Billerbeck 1.427f; cf. A. Legault, "An Application of the Form-Critique Method to the Anointings in Galilee and Bethany," *Catholic Biblical Quarterly* 16 (1954): 131–41).

    Within an overall similarity, there were differences between Roman, Greek, and Jewish customs and, within each of these, between the customs of different classes. Luke—writing about a Jewish Pharisee's dinner for a largely non-Jewish readership—may have left clues that would have identified for his readers a particular type of party; but they are clues we can no longer spot.

3. For Greco-Roman customs, see C. H. Cosgrove, "A Woman's Unbound Hair in the Graeco-Roman World, with Special Reference to the Story of the 'Sinful Woman' in Luke 7.36–50," *Journal of Biblical Literature* 124/4 (2005): 675–92; and add Tibullus 1.3.23–32 on thanksgiving. Jewish: Mishnah, *Ketuboth* 7.6. Early Christian: Hermas *Similitudes* 9.9.5; 9.13.8, for the seductive dangers of women's bare shoulders and unbound hair.

4. For the philanderers, fragments quoted in Athenaeus, *Deipnosophistae* 12.553c.

5. Luke 3.7–9; 1 Kings 17.17–24; 2 Kings 4.32–37; Luke 7.16.

6. Luke 7.28.

7. Luke 7.33–35.

8. Luke 8.50.

APPENDIX B: The Gnostics and the Female Powers of Creation

1. Gen. 1.26–7; 2.7; 2.23.

2. Isa. 45.5, Gk; Gen. 1.3, 14.

3. Gen. 2.2; 2.7, 3.20.

4. *Secret Book of John*, version in NHL II,1, from 2.1–14; 2.26–4.10; 5.5–10; 6.10–19; 9.7–11; 14.19–24. Theodotus in Clement, *Excerpts from Theodotus* 50–54. *On the Origin of the World*: the creation of chaos (the stated point of the text being to show that chaos was not eternal, 97.24–29) will be paralleled by the creation of the Adams. The immortal man of light: 103.19; 107.26; 108.1–21; 111.29–33; 112.10. The Adam of Day Six: 112.34–113.1; 115.3–15. The Adam of Day Eight, 116.1–8. Summary, 117.29–35.

SUGGESTIONS FOR
FURTHER READING

On Mary Magdalene in general, S. Haskins, *Mary Magdalen: Myth and Metaphor* (New York: Riverhead, 1993) is encyclopedic and indispensable. M. Malvern, *Venus in Sackcloth: The Magdalen's Origins and Metamorphoses* (Carbondale: Southern Illinois University Press, 1975) is poetic and attractive. For a focus on the New Testament and the Gnostics, see A. Marjanen, *The Woman Jesus Loved* (Leiden: Brill, 1996); J. Schaberg, *The Resurrection of Mary Magdalene* (New York and London: Continuum, 2002); A. G. Brock, *Mary Magdalene, the First Apostle: The Struggle for Authority* (Cambridge, MA: Harvard Theological Studies, 2003); B. Chilton, *Mary Magdalene: A Biography* (New York: Doubleday, 2005); E. A. de Boer, *The Gospel of Mary* (London, New York: Clark, 2004).

On ascetics in the early churches, the classic work is P. Brown, *The Body and Society* (New York: Columbia University Press, 1988).

For the reading of John explored here, more detail is available in R. Griffith-Jones, *The Four Witnesses* (San Francisco: HarperSanFrancisco, 2000), 342–77. For Paul, visions of heaven, and the conditions of an angelic life, see R. Griffith-Jones, *The Gospel According to Paul* (San Francisco: HarperSanFrancisco, 2004). For Mary Magdalene in *The Da Vinci Code,* see Robin Griffith-Jones, *The Da Vinci Code and the Secret of the Temple* (Grand Rapids, MI: Eerdmans; Norwich: Canterbury, 2006).

For the Nag Hammadi library and other texts, the definitive edition will now be M. Meyer, ed., *The Nag Hammadi Scriptures* (San Francisco: HarperOne, 2007). See also J. M. Robinson, ed., *The Nag Hammadi Library in English* (Leiden: Brill, 1977); B. Layton, *The Gnostic Scriptures* (London: SCM, 1987). For a selection of these and other texts, see W. Foerster, ed., *Gnosis,* trans. R. McL. Wilson et al., 2 vols. (Oxford: Clarendon, 1972–74).

For gospels, see R. J. Miller, ed., *The Complete Gospels* (Sonoma, CA: Polebridge, 1994). For other early Christian texts, see W. Schneemelcher, ed., *New Testament Apocrypha,* trans. R. McL. Wilson, 2 vols (Louisville, KY:

Westminster John Knox, 1991–92). For introductions and commentaries, see E. Schüssler Fiorenza, ed., *Searching the Scriptures,* vol. 1, *A Feminist Introduction,* vol. 2, *A Feminist Commentary* (London: SCM, 1994).

On the Gnostics, H. Jonas, *The Gnostic Religion* (Boston: Beacon, 1958), is old but a classic. E. H. Pagels, *The Gnostic Gospels* (New York: Random House, 1979) is seminal and has brought the texts to a very wide audience. See also P. Perkins, *The Gnostic Dialogue: The Early Church and the Crisis of Gnosticism* (New York: Paulist Press, 1980); B. Layton, ed., *The Rediscovery of Gnosticism,* 2 vols. (Leiden: Brill, 1980–81); M. A. Williams, *Rethinking "Gnosticism": An Argument for Dismantling a Dubious Category* (Princeton, NJ: Princeton University Press, 1996); J. D. Turner and A. McGuire, eds., *The Nag Hammadi Library After Fifty Years* (Leiden: Brill, 1997); C. Markschies, *Gnosis: An Introduction* (New York, London: Clark, 2003); A. N. B. Logan, *The Gnostics: Identifying an Early Christian Cult* (New York, London: Clark, 2006). On method, see K. L. King, *What Is Gnosticism?* (Cambridge, MA: Harvard University Press, Belknap Press, 2003). On the Valentinians, see E. Thomassen, *The Spiritual Seed* (Leiden: Brill, 2006).

On women in Gnosticism, see J. J. Buckley, *Female Fault and Fulfillment in Gnosticism* (Chapel Hill: North Carolina University Press, 1986); the valuable and wide-ranging essays in K. L. King, ed., *Images of the Feminine in Gnosticism* (Harrisburg, PA: Trinity, 1998); R. S. Kraemer and M. R. D'Angelo, eds., *Women and Christian Origins* (New York, Oxford: Oxford University Press, 1999), in particular the articles by A. McGuire, "Women, Gender and Gnosis" and M. R. D'Angelo, "Reconstructing 'Real' Women from Gospel Literature: The Case of Mary Magdalene."

Successive books and articles by A. D. DeConick are masterly, most recently *Recovering the Original Gospel of Thomas* (London, New York: Clark, 2005).

INDEX OF PASSAGES

INDEX OF SUBJECTS AND NAMES

Page references followed by *fig* indicate an illustrated figure or photograph.

ACKNOWLEDGEMENTS

I owe a great debt of gratitude to Felicity Bryan and Peter Ginsberg, to Eric Brandt, Lisa Zuniga, and their team at HarperOne in the United States, and to Christine Smith at SCM-Canterbury in the UK. Reginald Piggott has drawn the maps and charts with characteristic elegance.

The Temple Church in London was built in the Middle Ages to recall the Church of the Holy Sepulchre in Jerusalem, identified for seventeen hundred years as the site of Mary Magdalene's encounter with Jesus on Easter Day. It is (as our congregation and many visitors will testify) a beautiful and uplifting place to visit, and it is an inspiring place to work. I am grateful to my colleagues here for their friendship and patience.

This book is dedicated to two boys, Henry and Louis, of whom their mother, Tethys, is rightly proud.

The Temple Church
London

10 FEBRUARY 2008
The Anniversary of the Consecration of the Round Church
of the Temple by Heraclius, Patriarch of Jerusalem, 10 February 1185.